Mastering Machine Learning with Spark 2.x

Create scalable machine learning applications to power a
modern data-driven business using Spark

Alex Tellez
Max Pumperla
Michal Malohlava

BIRMINGHAM - MUMBAI

Mastering Machine Learning with Spark 2.x

First published: August 2017

Production reference: 1290817

Published by Packt Publishing Ltd.
Livery Place
35 Livery Street
Birmingham
B3 2PB, UK.
ISBN 978-1-78528-345-1

www.packtpub.com

Credits

Author
Alex Tellez
Max Pumperla
Michal Malohlava

Reviewer
Dipanjan Deb

Commissioning Editor
Veena Pagare

Acquisition Editor
Larissa Pinto

Content Development Editor
Nikhil Borkar

Technical Editor
Diwakar Shukla

Copy Editor
Muktikant Garimella

Project Coordinator
Ulhas Kambali

Proofreader
Safis Editing

Indexer
Rekha Nair

Graphics
Jason Monteiro

Production Coordinator
Melwyn Dsa

About the Authors

Alex Tellez is a life-long data hacker/enthusiast with a passion for data science and its application to business problems. He has a wealth of experience working across multiple industries, including banking, health care, online dating, human resources, and online gaming. Alex has also given multiple talks at various AI/machine learning conferences, in addition to lectures at universities about neural networks. When he's not neck-deep in a textbook, Alex enjoys spending time with family, riding bikes, and utilizing machine learning to feed his French wine curiosity!

First and foremost, I'd like to thank my co-author, Michal, for helping me write this book. As fellow ML enthusiasts, cyclists, runners, and fathers, we both developed a deeper understanding of each other through this endeavor, which has taken well over one year to create. Simply put, this book would not have been possible without Michal's support and encouragement.

Next, I'd like to thank my mom, dad, and elder brother, Andres, who have been there every step of the way from day 1 until now. Without question, my elder brother continues to be my hero and is someone that I will forever look up to as being a guiding light. Of course, no acknowledgements would be finished without giving thanks to my beautiful wife, Denise, and daughter, Miya, who have provided the love and support to continue the writing of this book during nights and weekends. I cannot emphasize enough how much you both mean to me and how you guys are the inspiration and motivation that keeps this engine running. To my daughter, Miya, my hope is that you can pick this book up and one day realize that your old man isn't quite as silly as I appear to let on.

Last but not least, I'd also like to give thanks to you, the reader, for your interest in this exciting field using this incredible technology. Whether you are a seasoned ML expert, or a newcomer to the field looking to gain a foothold, you have come to the right book and my hope is that you get as much out of this as Michal and I did in writing this work.

Max Pumperla is a data scientist and engineer specializing in deep learning and its applications. He currently works as a deep learning engineer at Skymind and is a co-founder of aetros.com. Max is the author and maintainer of several Python packages, including elephas, a distributed deep learning library using Spark. His open source footprint includes contributions to many popular machine learning libraries, such as keras, deeplearning4j, and hyperopt. He holds a PhD in algebraic geometry from the University of Hamburg.

Michal Malohlava, creator of Sparkling Water, is a geek and the developer; Java, Linux, programming languages enthusiast who has been developing software for over 10 years. He obtained his PhD from Charles University in Prague in 2012, and post doctorate from Purdue University.

During his studies, he was interested in the construction of not only distributed but also embedded and real-time, component-based systems, using model-driven methods and domain-specific languages. He participated in the design and development of various systems, including SOFA and Fractal component systems and the jPapabench control system.

Now, his main interest is big data computation. He participates in the development of the H2O platform for advanced big data math and computation, and its embedding into Spark engine, published as a project called Sparkling Water.

I would like to thank my wife, Claire, for her love and encouragement.

About the Reviewer

Dipanjan Deb is an experienced analytic professional with over 17 years of cumulative experience in machine/statistical learning, data mining and predictive analytics across finance, healthcare, automotive, CPG, automotive, energy, and human resource domains. He is highly proficient in developing cutting-edge analytic solutions using open source and commercial software to integrate multiple systems in order to provide massively parallelized and large-scale optimization.

www.PacktPub.com

For support files and downloads related to your book, please visit www.PacktPub.com. Did you know that Packt offers eBook versions of every book published, with PDF and ePub files available? You can upgrade to the eBook version at www.PacktPub.com and as a print book customer, you are entitled to a discount on the eBook copy. Get in touch with us at service@packtpub.com for more details. At www.PacktPub.com, you can also read a collection of free technical articles, sign up for a range of free newsletters and receive exclusive discounts and offers on Packt books and eBooks.

https:/ / www. packtpub. com/ mapt

Get the most in-demand software skills with Mapt. Mapt gives you full access to all Packt books and video courses, as well as industry-leading tools to help you plan your personal development and advance your career.

Why subscribe?

- Fully searchable across every book published by Packt
- Copy and paste, print, and bookmark content
- On demand and accessible via a web browser

Customer Feedback

Thanks for purchasing this Packt book. At Packt, quality is at the heart of our editorial process. To help us improve, please leave us an honest review on this book's Amazon page at `https:/ / www. amazon. com/ dp/ 1785283456`.

If you'd like to join our team of regular reviewers, you can e-mail us at `customerreviews@packtpub.com`. We award our regular reviewers with free eBooks and videos in exchange for their valuable feedback. Help us be relentless in improving our products!

Table of Contents

[ ]

Preface

Big data – that was our motivation to explore the world of machine learning with Spark a couple of years ago. We wanted to build machine learning applications that would leverag models trained on large amounts of data, but the beginning was not easy. Spark was still evolving, it did not contain a powerful machine learning library, and we were still trying to figure out what it means to build a machine learning application.

But, step by step, we started to explore different corners of the Spark ecosystem and followed Spark's evolution. For us, the crucial part was a powerful machine learning library, which would provide features such as R or Python libraries did. This was an easy task for us, since we are actively involved in the development of H2O's machine learning library and its branch called Sparkling Water, which enables the use of the H2O library from Spark applications. However, model training is just the tip of the machine learning iceberg. We still had to explore how to connect Sparkling Water to Spark RDDs, DataFrames, and DataSets, how to connect Spark to different data sources and read data, or how to export models and reuse them in different applications.

During our journey, Spark evolved as well. Originally, being a pure Scala project, it started to expose Python and, later, R interfaces. It also took its Spark API on a long journey from low-level RDDs to a high-level DataSet, exposing a SQL-like interface. Furthermore, Spark also introduced the concept of machine learning pipelines, adopted from the scikit-learn library known from Python. All these improvements made Spark a great tool for data transformation and data processing.

Based on this experience, we decided to share our knowledge with the rest of the world via this book. Its intention is simple: to demonstrate different aspects of building Spark machine learning applications on examples, and show how to use not only the latest Spark features, but also low-level Spark interfaces. On our journey, we also figure out many tricks and shortcuts not only connected to Spark, but also to the process of developing machine learning applications or source code organization. And all of them are shared in this book to help keep readers from making the mistakes we made.

The book adopted the Scala language as the main implementation language for our examples. It was a hard decision between using Python and Scala, but at the end Scala won. There were two main reasons to use Scala: it provides the most mature Spark interface and most applications deployed in production use Scala, mostly because of its performance benefits due to the JVM. Moreover, all source code shown in this book is also available online.

We hope you enjoy our book and it helps you navigate the Spark world and the development of machine learning applications.

What this book covers

Chapter 1, *Introduction to Large-Scale Machine Learning*, invites readers into the land of machine learning and big data, introduces historical paradigms, and describes contemporary tools, including Apache Spark and H2O.

Chapter 2, *Detecting Dark Matter: The Higgs-Boson Particle*, focuses on the training and evaluation of binomial models.

Chapter 3, *Ensemble Methods for Multi-Class Classification*, checks into a gym and tries to predict human activities based on data collected from body sensors.

Chapter 4, *Predicting Movie Reviews Using NLP*, introduces the problem of nature language processing with Spark and demonstrates its power on the sentiment analysis of movie reviews.

Chapter 5, *Online Learning with Word2Vec*, goes into detail about contemporary NLP techniques.

Chapter 6, *Extracting Patterns from Clickstream Data*, introduces the basics of frequent pattern mining and three algorithms available in Spark MLlib, before deploying one of these algorithms in a Spark Streaming application.

Chapter 7, *Graph Analytics with GraphX*, familiarizes the reader with the basic concepts of graphs and graph analytics, explains the core functionality of Spark GraphX, and introduces graph algorithms such as PageRank.

Chapter 8, *Lending Club Loan Prediction*, combines all the tricks introduced in the previous chapters into end-to-end examples, including data processing, model search and training, and model deployment as a Spark Streaming application.

What you need for this book

Code samples provided in this book use Apache Spark 2.1 and its Scala API. Furthermore, we utilize the Sparkling Water package to access the H2O machine learning library. In each chapter, we show how to start Spark using spark-shell, and also how to download the data necessary to run the code.

In summary, the basic requirements to run the code provided in this book include:

- Java 8
- Spark 2.1

Who this book is for

Are you a developer with a background in machine learning and statistics who is feeling limited by the current slow and small data machine learning tools? Then this is the book for you! In this book, you will create scalable machine learning applications to power a modern data-driven business using Spark. We assume that you already know about machine learning concepts and algorithms and have Spark up and running (whether on a cluster or locally), as well as having basic knowledge of the various libraries contained in Spark.

Conventions

In this book, you will find a number of text styles that distinguish between different kinds of information. Here are some examples of these styles and an explanation of their meaning. Code words in text, database table names, folder names, filenames, file extensions, pathnames, dummy URLs, user input, and Twitter handles are shown as follows: "We also appended the magic column row_id, which uniquely identifies each row in the dataset." A block of code is set as follows:

```
import org.apache.spark.ml.feature.StopWordsRemover
val stopWords= StopWordsRemover.loadDefaultStopWords("english") ++
Array("ax", "arent", "re")
```

When we wish to draw your attention to a particular part of a code block, the relevant lines or items are set in bold:

```
val MIN_TOKEN_LENGTH = 3
val toTokens= (minTokenLen: Int, stopWords: Array[String],
```

Any command-line input or output is written as follows:

```
tar -xvf spark-2.1.1-bin-hadoop2.6.tgz
export SPARK_HOME="$(pwd)/spark-2.1.1-bin-hadoop2.6
```

New terms and **important words** are shown in bold. Words that you see on the screen, for example, in menus or dialog boxes, appear in the text like this: "Download the **DECLINED LOAN DATA** as shown in the following screenshot"

 Warnings or important notes appear like this.

 Tips and tricks appear like this.

Reader feedback

Feedback from our readers is always welcome. Let us know what you think about this book-what you liked or disliked. Reader feedback is important for us as it helps us develop titles that you will really get the most out of. To send us general feedback, simply email feedback@packtpub.com, and mention the book's title in the subject of your message. If there is a topic that you have expertise in and you are interested in either writing or contributing to a book, see our author guide at www.packtpub.com/authors.

Customer support

Now that you are the proud owner of a Packt book, we have a number of things to help you to get the most from your purchase.

Downloading the example code

You can download the example code files for this book from your account at http://www.packtpub.com. If you purchased this book elsewhere, you can visit http://www.packtpub.com/support and register to have the files emailed directly to you. You can download the code files by following these steps:

1. Log in or register to our website using your email address and password.
2. Hover the mouse pointer on the **SUPPORT** tab at the top.
3. Click on **Code Downloads & Errata**.
4. Enter the name of the book in the **Search** box.
5. Select the book for which you're looking to download the code files.

6. Choose from the drop-down menu where you purchased this book from.
7. Click on **Code Download**.

Once the file is downloaded, please make sure that you unzip or extract the folder using the latest version of:

- WinRAR / 7-Zip for Windows
- Zipeg / iZip / UnRarX for Mac
- 7-Zip / PeaZip for Linux

The code bundle for the book is also hosted on GitHub at `https:/ / github. com/ PacktPublishing/ Mastering- Machine- Learning- with- Spark- 2. x.` We also have other code bundles from our rich catalog of books and videos available at `https:/ / github. com/ PacktPublishing/ .` Check them out!

Downloading the color images of this book

We also provide you with a PDF file that has color images of the screenshots/diagrams used in this book. The color images will help you better understand the changes in the output. You can download this file from `https:/ / www. packtpub. com/ sites/ default/ files/ downloads/ MasteringMachineLearningwithSpark2. x_ ColorImages. pdf.`

Errata

Although we have taken every care to ensure the accuracy of our content, mistakes do happen. If you find a mistake in one of our books-maybe a mistake in the text or the code- we would be grateful if you could report this to us. By doing so, you can save other readers from frustration and help us improve subsequent versions of this book. If you find any errata, please report them by visiting `http:/ / www. packtpub. com/ submit- errata,` selecting your book, clicking on the **Errata Submission Form** link, and entering the details of your errata. Once your errata are verified, your submission will be accepted and the errata will be uploaded to our website or added to any list of existing errata under the Errata section of that title. To view the previously submitted errata, go to `https:/ / www. packtpub. com/ books/ content/ support` and enter the name of the book in the search field. The required information will appear under the **Errata** section.

Piracy

Piracy of copyrighted material on the internet is an ongoing problem across all media. At Packt, we take the protection of our copyright and licenses very seriously. If you come across any illegal copies of our works in any form on the internet, please provide us with the location address or website name immediately so that we can pursue a remedy. Please contact us at copyright@packtpub.com with a link to the suspected pirated material. We appreciate your help in protecting our authors and our ability to bring you valuable content.

Questions

If you have a problem with any aspect of this book, you can contact us at questions@packtpub.com, and we will do our best to address the problem.

1

Introduction to Large-Scale Machine Learning and Spark

"Information is the oil of the 21st century, and analytics is the combustion engine."

--Peter Sondergaard, Gartner
Research

By 2018, it is estimated that companies will spend $114 billion on big data-related projects, an increase of roughly 300%, compared to 2013 (`https://www.capgemini-consulting.com/resource-file-access/resource/pdf/big_dat a_pov_03-02-15.pdf`). Much of this increase in expenditure is due to how much data is being created and how we are better able to store such data by leveraging distributed filesystems such as Hadoop.

However, collecting the data is only half the battle; the other half involves data extraction, transformation, and loading into a computation system, which leverage the power of modern computers to apply various mathematical methods in order to learn more about data and patterns, and extract useful information to make relevant decisions. The entire data workflow has been boosted in the last few years by not only increasing the computation power and providing easily accessible and scalable cloud services (for example, Amazon AWS, Microsoft Azure, and Heroku) but also by a number of tools and libraries that help to easily manage, control, and scale infrastructure and build applications. Such a growth in the computation power also helps to process larger amounts of data and to apply algorithms that were impossible to apply earlier. Finally, various computation-expensive statistical or machine learning algorithms have started to help extract nuggets of information from data.

One of the first well-adopted big data technologies was Hadoop, which allows for the MapReduce computation by saving intermediate results on a disk. However, it still lacks proper big data tools for information extraction. Nevertheless, Hadoop was just the beginning. With the growing size of machine memory, new in-memory computation frameworks appeared, and they also started to provide basic support for conducting data analysis and modeling—for example, SystemML or Spark ML for Spark and FlinkML for Flink. These frameworks represent only the tip of the iceberg—there is a lot more in the big data ecosystem, and it is permanently evolving, since the volume of data is constantly growing, demanding new big data algorithms and processing methods. For example, the **Internet of Things (IoT)** represents a new domain that produces huge amount of streaming data from various sources (for example, home security system, Alexa Echo, or vital sensors) and brings not only an unlimited potential to mind useful information from data, but also demands new kind of data processing and modeling methods.

Nevertheless, in this chapter, we will start from the beginning and explain the following topics:

- Basic working tasks of data scientists
- Aspect of big data computation in distributed environment
- The big data ecosystem
- Spark and its machine learning support

Data science

Finding a uniform definition of data science, however, is akin to tasting wine and comparing flavor profiles among friends—everyone has their own definition and no one description is *more accurate* than the other. At its core, however, data science is the art of asking intelligent questions about data and receiving intelligent answers that matter to key stakeholders. Unfortunately, the opposite also holds true—ask lousy questions of the data and get lousy answers! Therefore, careful formulation of the question is the key for extracting valuable insights from your data. For this reason, companies are now hiring *data scientists* to help formulate and ask these questions.

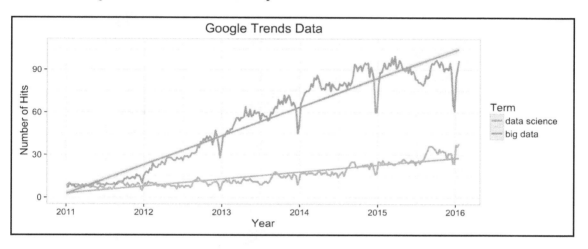

Figure 1 - Growing Google Trend of big data and data science

The sexiest role of the 21st century – data scientist?

At first, it's easy to paint a stereotypical picture of what a typical data scientist looks like: t-shirt, sweatpants, thick-rimmed glasses, and debugging a chunk of code in IntelliJ... you get the idea. Aesthetics aside, what are some of the traits of a data scientist? One of our favorite posters describing this role is shown here in the following diagram:

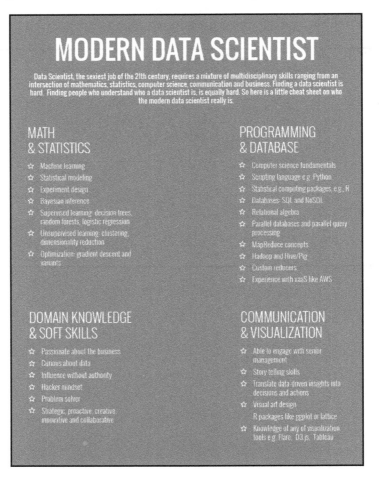

Figure 2 - What is a data scientist?

Math, statistics, and general knowledge of computer science is given, but one pitfall that we see among practitioners has to do with understanding the business problem, which goes back to asking intelligent questions of the data. It cannot be emphasized enough: asking more intelligent questions of the data is a function of the data scientist's understanding of the business problem and the limitations of the data; without this fundamental understanding, even the most intelligent algorithm would be unable to come to solid conclusions based on a wobbly foundation.

A day in the life of a data scientist

This will probably come as a shock to some of you—being a data scientist is more than reading academic papers, researching new tools, and model building until the wee hours of the morning, fueled on espresso; in fact, this is only a small percentage of the time that a data scientist gets to truly *play* (the espresso part however is 100% true for everyone)! Most part of the day, however, is spent in meetings, gaining a better understanding of the business problem(s), crunching the data to learn its limitations (take heart, this book will expose you to a ton of different feature engineering or feature extractions tasks), and how best to present the findings to non data-sciencey people. This is where the true *sausage making* process takes place, and the best data scientists are the ones who relish in this process because they are gaining more understanding of the requirements and benchmarks for success. In fact, we could literally write a whole new book describing this process from top-to-tail!

So, what (and who) is involved in asking questions about data? Sometimes, it is process of saving data into a relational database and running SQL queries to find insights into data: "for the millions of users that bought this particular product, what are the top 3 OTHER products also bought?" Other times, the question is more complex, such as, "Given the review of a movie, is this a positive or negative review?" This book is mainly focused on complex questions, like the latter. Answering these types of questions is where businesses really get the most impact from their big data projects and is also where we see a proliferation of emerging technologies that look to make this Q and A system easier, with more functionality.

Some of the most popular, open source frameworks that look to help answer data questions include R, Python, Julia, and Octave, all of which perform reasonably well with small (X < 100 GB) datasets. At this point, it's worth stopping and pointing out a clear distinction between big versus small data. Our general rule of thumb in the office goes as follows:

If you can open your dataset using Excel, you are working with small data.

Working with big data

What happens when the dataset in question is so vast that it cannot fit into the memory of a single computer and must be distributed across a number of nodes in a large computing cluster? Can't we just rewrite some R code, for example, and extend it to account for more than a single-node computation? If only things were that simple! There are many reasons why the scaling of algorithms to more machines is difficult. Imagine a simple example of a file containing a list of names:

```
B
D
X
A
D
A
```

We would like to compute the number of occurrences of individual words in the file. If the file fits into a single machine, you can easily compute the number of occurrences by using a combination of the Unix tools, sort and uniq:

```
bash> sort file | uniq -c
```

The output is as shown ahead:

```
2 A
1 B
1 D
1 X
```

However, if the file is huge and distributed over multiple machines, it is necessary to adopt a slightly different computation strategy. For example, compute the number of occurrences of individual words for every part of the file that fits into the memory and merge the results together. Hence, even simple tasks, such as counting the occurrences of names, in a distributed environment can become more complicated.

The machine learning algorithm using a distributed environment

Machine learning algorithms combine simple tasks into complex patterns, that are even more complicated in distributed environment. Let's take a simple decision tree algorithm (reference), for example. This particular algorithm creates a binary tree that tries to fit training data and minimize prediction errors. However, in order to do this, it has to decide about the branch of tree it has to send every data point to (don't worry, we'll cover the mechanics of how this algorithm works along with some very useful parameters that you can learn in later in the book). Let's demonstrate it with a simple example:

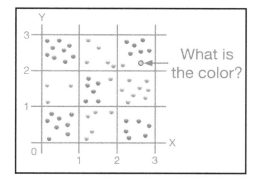

Figure 3 - Example of red and blue data points covering 2D space.

Consider the situation depicted in preceding figure. A two-dimensional board with many points colored in two colors: red and blue. The goal of the decision tree is to learn and generalize the shape of data and help decide about the color of a new point. In our example, we can easily see that the points almost follow a chessboard pattern. However, the algorithm has to figure out the structure by itself. It starts by finding the best position of a vertical or horizontal line, which would separate the red points from the blue points.

The found decision is stored in the tree root and the steps are recursively applied on both the partitions. The algorithm ends when there is a single point in the partition:

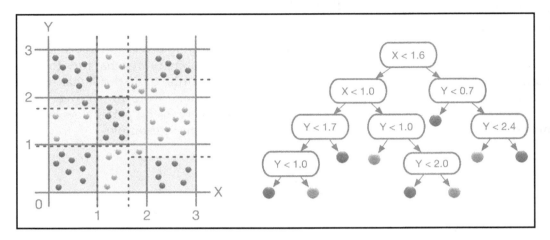

Figure 4 - The final decision tree and projection of its prediction to the original space of points.

Splitting of data into multiple machines

For now, let's assume that the number of points is huge and cannot fit into the memory of a single machine. Hence, we need multiple machines, and we have to partition data in such a way that each machine contains only a subset of data. This way, we solve the memory problem; however, it also means that we need to distribute the computation around a cluster of machines. This is the first difference from single-machine computing. If your data fits into a single machine memory, it is easy to make decisions about data, since the algorithm can access them all at once, but in the case of a distributed algorithm, this is not true anymore and the algorithm has to be "clever" about accessing the data. Since our goal is to build a decision tree that predicts the color of a new point in the board, we need to figure out how to make the tree that will be the same as a tree built on a single machine.

The naive solution is to build a trivial tree that separates the points based on machine boundaries. But this is obviously a bad solution, since data distribution does not reflect color points at all.

Another solution tries all the possible split decisions in the direction of the X and Y axes and tries to do the best in separating both colors, that is, divides the points into two groups and minimizes the number of points of another color. Imagine that the algorithm is testing the split via the line, $X = 1.6$. This means that the algorithm has to ask each machine in the cluster to report the result of splitting the machine's local data, merge the results, and decide whether it is the right splitting decision. If it finds an optimal split, it needs to inform all the machines about the decision in order to record which partition each point belongs to.

Compared with the single machine scenario, the distributed algorithm constructing decision tree is more complex and requires a way of distributing the computation among machines. Nowadays, with easy access to a cluster of machines and an increasing demand for the analysis of larger datasets, it becomes a standard requirement.

Even these two simple examples show that for a larger data, proper computation and distributed infrastructure is required, including the following:

- A distributed data storage, that is, if the data cannot fit into a single node, we need a way to distribute and process them on multiple machines
- A computation paradigm to process and transform the distributed data and to apply mathematical (and statistical) algorithms and workflows
- Support to persist and reuse defined workflows and models
- Support to deploy statistical models in production

In short, we need a framework that will support common data science tasks. It can be considered an unnecessary requirement, since data scientists prefer using existing tools, such as R, Weka, or Python's scikit. However, these tools are neither designed for large-scale distributed processing nor for the parallel processing of large data. Even though there are libraries for R or Python that support limited parallel or distributed programming, their main limitation is that the base platforms, that is R and Python, were not designed for this kind of data processing and computation.

From Hadoop MapReduce to Spark

With a growing amount of data, the single-machine tools were not able to satisfy the industry needs and thereby created a space for new data processing methods and tools, especially Hadoop MapReduce, which is based on an idea originally described in the Google paper, *MapReduce: Simplified Data Processing on Large Clusters* (`https://research.google.com/archive/mapreduce.html`). On the other hand, it is a generic framework without any explicit support or libraries to create machine learning workflows. Another limitation of classical MapReduce is that it performs many disk I/O operations during the computation instead of benefiting from machine memory.

As you have seen, there are several existing machine learning tools and distributed platforms, but none of them is an exact match for performing machine learning tasks with large data and distributed environment. All these claims open the doors for Apache Spark.

Enter the room, Apache Spark!

Created in 2010 at the UC Berkeley AMP Lab (Algorithms, Machines, People), the Apache Spark project was built with an eye for speed, ease of use, and advanced analytics. One key difference between Spark and other distributed frameworks such as Hadoop is that datasets can be cached in memory, which lends itself nicely to machine learning, given its iterative nature (more on this later!) and how data scientists are constantly accessing the same data many times over.

Spark can be run in a variety of ways, such as the following:

- **Local mode:** This entails a single **Java Virtual Machine** (**JVM**) executed on a single host
- **Standalone Spark cluster:** This entails multiple JVMs on multiple hosts
- **Via resource manager such as Yarn/Mesos:** This application deployment is driven by a resource manager, which controls the allocation of nodes, application, distribution, and deployment

What is Databricks?

If you know about the Spark project, then chances are high that you have also heard of a company called *Databricks*. However, you might not know how Databricks and the Spark project are related to one another. In short, Databricks was founded by the creators of the Apache Spark project and accounts for over 75% of the code base for the Spark project. Aside from being a huge force behind the Spark project with respect to development, Databricks also offers various certifications in Spark for developers, administrators, trainers, and analysts alike. However, Databricks is not the only main contributor to the code base; companies such as IBM, Cloudera, and Microsoft also actively participate in Apache Spark development.

As a side note, Databricks also organizes the Spark Summit (in both Europe and the US), which is the premier Spark conference and a great place to learn about the latest developments in the project and how others are using Spark within their ecosystem.

Throughout this book, we will give recommended links that we read daily that offer great insights and also important changes with respect to the new versions of Spark. One of the best resources here is the Databricks blog, which is constantly being updated with great content. Be sure to regularly check this out at `https://databricks.com/blog`.

Also, here is a link to see the past Spark Summit talks, which you may find helpful: `http://slideshare.net/databricks`.

Inside the box

So, you have downloaded the latest version of Spark (depending on how you plan on launching Spark) and you have run the standard *Hello, World!* example....what now?!

Spark comes equipped with five libraries, which can be used separately--or in unison--depending on the task we are trying to solve. Note that in this book, we plan on using a variety of different libraries, all within the same application so that you will have the maximum exposure to the Spark platform and better understand the benefits (and limitations) of each library. These five libraries are as follows:

- **Core**: This is the Spark core infrastructure, providing primitives to represent and store data called **Resilient Distributed Dataset** (**RDDs**) and manipulate data with tasks and jobs.
- **SQL** : This library provides user-friendly API over core RDDs by introducing DataFrames and SQL to manipulate with the data stored.
- **MLlib (Machine Learning Library)** : This is Spark's very own machine learning library of algorithms developed in-house that can be used within your Spark application.
- **Graphx** : This is used for graphs and graph-calculations; we will explore this particular library in depth in a later chapter.

- **Streaming** : This library allows real-time streaming of data from various sources, such as Kafka, Twitter, Flume, and TCP sockets, to name a few. Many of the applications we will build in this book will leverage the MLlib and Streaming libraries to build our applications.

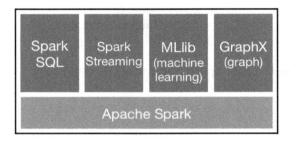

The Spark platform can also be extended by third-party packages. There are many of them, for example, support for reading CSV or Avro files, integration with Redshift, and Sparkling Water, which encapsulates the H2O machine learning library.

Introducing H2O.ai

H2O is an open source, machine learning platform that plays extremely well with Spark; in fact, it was one of the first third-party packages deemed "Certified on Spark".

Sparkling Water (H2O + Spark) is H2O's integration of their platform within the Spark project, which combines the machine learning capabilities of H2O with all the functionality of Spark. This means that users can run H2O algorithms on Spark RDD/DataFrame for both exploration and deployment purposes. This is made possible because H2O and Spark share the same JVM, which allows for seamless transitions between the two platforms. H2O stores data in the H2O frame, which is a columnar-compressed representation of your dataset that can be created from Spark RDD and/or DataFrame. Throughout much of this book, we will be referencing algorithms from Spark's MLlib library and H2O's platform, showing how to use both the libraries to get the best results possible for a given task.

The following is a summary of the features Sparkling Water comes equipped with:

- Use of H2O algorithms within a Spark workflow
- Transformations between Spark and H2O data structures
- Use of Spark RDD and/or DataFrame as inputs to H2O algorithms
- Use of H2O frames as inputs into MLlib algorithms (will come in handy when we do feature engineering later)
- Transparent execution of Sparkling Water applications on top of Spark (for example, we can run a Sparkling Water application within a Spark stream)
- The H2O user interface to explore Spark data

Design of Sparkling Water

Sparkling Water is designed to be executed as a regular Spark application. Consequently, it is launched inside a Spark executor created after submitting the application. At this point, H2O starts services, including a distributed key-value (K/V) store and memory manager, and orchestrates them into a cloud. The topology of the created cloud follows the topology of the underlying Spark cluster.

As stated previously, Sparkling Water enables transformation between different types of RDDs/DataFrames and H2O's frame, and vice versa. When converting from a hex frame to an RDD, a wrapper is created around the hex frame to provide an RDD-like API. In this case, data is not duplicated but served directly from the underlying hex frame. Converting from an RDD/DataFrame to a H2O frame requires data duplication because it transforms data from Spark into H2O-specific storage. However, data stored in an H2O frame is heavily compressed and does not need to be preserved as an RDD anymore:

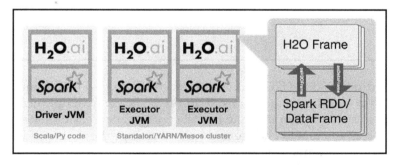

Data sharing between sparkling water and Spark

What's the difference between H2O and Spark's MLlib?

As stated previously, MLlib is a library of popular machine learning algorithms built using Spark. Not surprisingly, H2O and MLlib share many of the same algorithms but differ in both their implementation and functionality. One very handy feature of H2O is that it allows users to visualize their data and perform feature engineering tasks, which we will cover in depth in later chapters. The visualization of data is accomplished by a web-friendly GUI and allows users a friendly interface to seamlessly switch between a code shell and a notebook-friendly environment. The following is an example of the H2O notebook - called *Flow* - that you will become familiar with soon:

One other nice addition is that H2O allows data scientists to grid search many hyper-parameters that ship with their algorithms. Grid search is a way of optimizing all the hyperparameters of an algorithm to make model configuration easier. Often, it is difficult to know which hyperparameters to change and how to change them; the grid search allows us to explore many hyperparameters simultaneously, measure the output, and help select the best models based on our quality requirements. The H2O grid search can be combined with model cross-validation and various stopping criteria, resulting in advanced strategies such as *picking 1000 random parameters from a huge parameters hyperspace and finding the best model that can be trained under two minutes and with AUC greater than 0.7*

Data munging

Raw data for problems often comes from multiple sources with different and often incompatible formats. The beauty of the Spark programming model is its ability to define data operations that process the incoming data and transform it into a regular form that can be used for further feature engineering and model building. This process is commonly referred to as data munging and is where much of the battle is won with respect to data science projects. We keep this section intentionally brief because the best way to showcase the power--and necessity!--of data munging is by example. So, take heart; we have *plenty* of practice to go through in this book, which emphasizes this essential process.

Data science - an iterative process

Often, the process flow of many big data projects is iterative, which means a lot of back-and-forth testing new ideas, new features to include, tweaking various hyper-parameters, and so on, with a *fail fast* attitude. The end result of these projects is usually a model that can answer a question being posed. Notice that we didn't say *accurately* answer a question being posed! One pitfall of many data scientists these days is their inability to generalize a model for new data, meaning that they have overfit their data so that the model provides poor results when given new data. Accuracy is extremely task-dependent and is usually dictated by the business needs with some sensitivity analysis being done to weigh the cost-benefits of the model outcomes. However, there are a few standard accuracy measures that we will go over throughout this book so that you can compare various models to see *how* changes to the model impact the result.

H2O is constantly giving meetup talks and inviting others to give machine learning meetups around the US and Europe. Each meetup or conference slides is available on SlideShare (`http://www.slideshare.com/0xdata`) or YouTube. Both the sites serve as great sources of information not only about machine learning and statistics but also about distributed systems and computation. For example, one of the most interesting presentations highlights the "Top 10 pitfalls in a data scientist job" (`http://www.slideshare.net/0xdata/h2o-world-top-10-data-science-pitfalls-mark-landry`)

Summary

In this chapter, we wanted to give you a brief glimpse into the life of a data scientist, what this entails, and some of the challenges that data scientists consistently face. In light of these challenges, we feel that the Apache Spark project is ideally positioned to help tackle these topics, which range from data ingestion and feature extraction/creation to model building and deployment. We intentionally kept this chapter short and light on verbiage because we feel working through examples and different use cases is a better use of time as opposed to speaking abstractly and at length about a given data science topic. Throughout the rest of this book, we will focus solely on this process while giving best-practice tips and recommended reading along the way for users who wish to learn more. Remember that before embarking on your next data science project, be sure to clearly define the problem beforehand, so you can ask an intelligent question of your data and (hopefully) get an intelligent answer!

One awesome website for all things data science is KDnuggets (`http://www.kdnuggets.com`). Here's a great article on the language all data scientists must learn in order to be successful (`http://www.kdnuggets.com/2015/09/one-language-data-scientist-must-master.html`).

2
Detecting Dark Matter - The Higgs-Boson Particle

True or false? Positive or negative? Pass or no pass? User clicks on the ad versus not clicking the ad? If you've ever asked/encountered these questions before then you are already familiar with the concept of *binary classification*.

At it's core, binary classification - also referred to as *binomial classification* - attempts to categorize a set of elements into two distinct groups using a classification rule, which in our case, can be a machine learning algorithm. This chapter shows how to deal with it in the context of Spark and big data. We are going to explain and demonstrate:

- Spark MLlib models for binary classification including decision trees, random forest, and the gradient boosted machine
- Binary classification support in H2O
- Searching for the best model in a hyperspace of parameters
- Evaluation metrics for binomial models

Type I versus type II error

Binary classifiers have intuitive interpretation since they are trying to separate data points into two groups. This sounds simple, but we need to have some notion of measuring the quality of this separation. Furthermore, one important characteristic of a binary classification problem is that, often, the proportion of one group of labels versus the other can be disproportionate. That means the dataset may be imbalanced with respect to one label which necessitates careful interpretation by the data scientist.

Suppose, for example, we are trying to detect the presence of a particular rare disease in a population of 15 million people and we discover that - using a large subset of the population - only 10,000 or 10 million individuals actually carry the disease. Without taking this huge disproportion into consideration, the most naive algorithm would guess "no presence of disease" on the remaining five million people simply because 0.1% of the subset carried the disease. Suppose that of the remaining five million people, the same proportion, 0.1%, carried the disease, then these 5,000 people would not be correctly diagnosed because the naive algorithm would simply guess no one carries the disease. Is this acceptable? In this situation, the *cost* of the errors posed by binary classification is an important factor to consider, which is relative to the question being asked.

Given that we are only dealing with two outcomes for this type of problem, we can create a 2-D representation of the different types of errors that are possible. Keeping our preceding example of the people carrying / not carrying the disease, we can think about the outcome of our classification rule as follows:

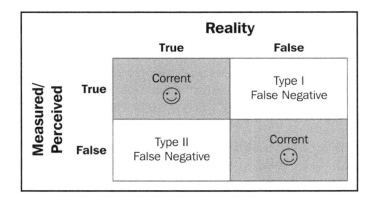

Figure 1 - Relation between predicted and actual values

From the preceding table, the green area represents where we are *correctly* predicting the presence / absence of disease in the individual whereas the white areas represent where our prediction was incorrect. These false predictions fall into two categories known as **Type I** and **Type II** errors:

- **Type I error**: When we reject the null hypothesis (that is, a person not carrying the disease) when in fact, it is true in actuality
- **Type II error**: Where we predict the presence of the disease when the individual does *not* carry the disease

Clearly, both errors are not good but often, in practice, some errors are more acceptable than others.

Consider the situation where our model makes significantly more Type II errors than Type I errors; in this case, our model would be predicting more people are carrying the disease than actually are - a conservative approach may be *more acceptable* than a Type II error where we are failing to identify the presence of the disease. Determining the *cost* of each type of error is a function of the question being asked and is something the data scientist must consider. We will revisit this topic of errors and some other metrics of model quality after we build our first binary classification model which tries to predict the presence / non-presence of the Higgs-Boson particle.

Finding the Higgs-Boson particle

On July 4, 2012, scientists from Europe's CERN lab in Geneva, Switzerland, presented strong evidence of a particle they believe is the Higgs-Boson, sometimes referred to as the *God-particle*. Why is this discovery so meaningful and important? As popular physicist and author Michio Kaku wrote:

"In quantum physics, it was a Higgs-like particle that sparked the cosmic explosion (that is, the big bang). In other words, everything we see around us, including galaxies, stars, planets, and us, owes its existence to the Higgs-Boson."

In layman's terms, the Higgs-Boson is the particle that gives mass to matter and offers a possible explanation for how the Earth was originally created and hence, its huge popularity in mainstream media channels.

The LHC and data creation

To test for the presence of the Higgs-Boson, scientists constructed the largest human-made machine called the **Large Hadron Collider** (**LHC**) near Geneva, close to the Franco-Swiss border. The LHC is a ring-shaped tunnel that runs 27 kilometers long (equivalent to the Circle Line from London's Underground) and lies 100 meters underground.

Through this tunnel, subatomic particles are fired in opposite directions with the help of the aforementioned magnets with speeds approaching the speed of light. Once a critical speed is reached, the particles are put on a collision course where detectors monitor and record the collisions. There are literally millions upon millions of collisions and sub-collisions! - and the resultant *particle debris* give in hope of detecting the Higgs-Boson.

The theory behind the Higgs-Boson

For quite some time, physicists have known that some fundamental particles have mass which contradicts the mathematics underlying the Standard Model which states these particles should be mass-less. In the 1960s, Peter Higgs and his colleagues challenged this mass conundrum by studying the universe after the big bang. At the time, it was largely believed that particles should be thought of as ripples in a quantum jelly as opposed to tiny billiard balls bouncing off one another. Higgs believed that during this early period, all particle jellies were runny with a consistency like water; but as the universe began to *cool down*, one particle jelly, known first as the *Higgs field*, began to condense and become thick. Consequently, other particle jellies, when interacting with the Higgs field, are drawn towards it thanks to inertia; and, according to Sir Isaac Newton, any particle with inertia should contain mass. This mechanism offers an explanation to how particles that makeup the Standard Model - born massless at first - may have acquired mass. It follows then that the amount of mass acquired by each particle is proportional to the strength with which it feels the effects of the Higgs field.

The article
`https://plus.maths.org/content/particle-hunting-lhc-higgs-boson`
is a great source of information for curious readers.

Measuring for the Higgs-Boson

Testing this theory goes back to the original notion of particle jelly ripples and in particular, the Higgs jelly which a) can ripple and b) would resemble a particle in an experiment: the infamous Higgs-Boson. So how do scientists detect this ripple using the LHC?

To monitor the collisions and the resulting post-collisions, scientists set up detectors which act like three-dimensional digital cameras which measure the tracks of particles coming from the collisions. Properties from these tracks - that is, how much they curve in magnetic fields - are used to infer various properties of the particles that generated them; one extremely common property that can be measured is an electric charge where it is believed the Higgs exists somewhere between 120 and 125 giga-electronvolts. Meaning, if the detectors find an event with an electric charge that exists between these two ranges, this would indicate a new particle which may be indicative of the Higgs-Boson.

The dataset

Upon releasing their findings to the scientific community in 2012, researchers later made the data public from the LHC experiments where they observed - and identified - a signal which is indicative of the Higgs-Boson particle. However, amidst the positive findings is a lot of background noise which causes an imbalance within the dataset. Our task as data scientist is to build a machine learning model which can accurately identify the Higgs-Boson particle from background noise. Already, you should be thinking about how this question is phrased which would be indicative of binary classification (that is, is this example the Higgs-Boson versus background noise?).

 You can download the dataset from `https://archive.ics.uci.edu/ml/datasets/HIGGS` or use the script `getdata.sh` located in the `bin` folder of this chapter.

This file is 2.6 gigs (uncompressed) and contains 11 million examples that have been labeled as 0 - background noise and 1 - Higgs-Boson. First, you will need to uncompress this file and then we will begin loading the data into Spark for processing and analysis. There are 29 total fields which make up the dataset:

- Field 1: Class label (1 = signal for Higgs-Boson, 2 = background noise)
- Fields 2-22: 21 "low-level" features that come from the collision detectors
- Fields 23-29: seven "high-level" features that have been hand-derived by particle physicists to help classify the particle into its appropriate class (Higgs or background noise)

Later in this chapter, we cover a **Deep Neural Network (DNN)** example that will attempt to *learn* these hand-derived features through layers of non-linear transformations to the input data.

Note that for the purposes of this chapter, we will work with a subset of the data, the first 100,000 rows, but all the code we show would also work on the original dataset.

Spark start and data load

Now it's time to fire up a Spark cluster which will give us all the functionality of Spark while simultaneously allowing us to use H2O algorithms and visualize our data. As always, we must download Spark 2.1 distribution from http://spark.apache.org/downloads.html and declare the execution environment beforehand. For example, if you download spark-2.1.1-bin-hadoop2.6.tgz from the Spark download page, you can prepare the environment in the following way:

```
tar -xvf spark-2.1.1-bin-hadoop2.6.tgz
export SPARK_HOME="$(pwd)/spark-2.1.1-bin-hadoop2.6
```

When the environment is ready, we can start the interactive Spark shell with Sparkling Water packages and this book package:

```
export SPARKLING_WATER_VERSION="2.1.12"
export SPARK_PACKAGES=\
"ai.h2o:sparkling-water-core_2.11:${SPARKLING_WATER_VERSION},\
ai.h2o:sparkling-water-repl_2.11:${SPARKLING_WATER_VERSION},\
ai.h2o:sparkling-water-ml_2.11:${SPARKLING_WATER_VERSION},\
com.packtpub:mastering-ml-w-spark-utils:1.0.0"
$SPARK_HOME/bin/spark-shell \
            --master 'local[*]' \
            --driver-memory 4g \
            --executor-memory 4g \
            --packages "$SPARK_PACKAGES"
```

H2O.ai is constantly keeping up with the latest releases of the Spark project to match the version of Sparkling Water. The book is using Spark 2.1.1 distribution and Sparkling Water 2.1.12. You can find the latest version of Sparkling Water for your version of Spark at http://h2o.ai/download/

This case is using the provided Spark shell which downloads and uses Spark packages of Sparkling Water version 2.1.12. The packages are identified by Maven coordinates - in this case ai.h2o represents organization ID, sparkling-water-core identifies Sparkling Water implementation (for Scala 2.11, since Scala versions are not binary compatible), and, finally, 2.1.12 is a version of the package. Furthermore, we are using this book -specific package which provides handful utilities.

The list of all published Sparkling Water versions is also available on Maven central: http://search.maven.org

The command starts Spark in a local mode - that is, the Spark cluster has a single node running on your computer. Assuming you did all this successfully, you should see the standard Spark shell output like this:

```
Spark context Web UI available at http://192.168.1.65:4040
Spark context available as 'sc' (master = local[*], app id = local-1500785309326).
Spark session available as 'spark'.
Welcome to
      ____              __
     / __/__  ___ _____/ /__
    _\ \/ _ \/ _ `/ __/  '_/
   /___/ .__/\_,_/_/ /_/\_\   version 2.1.1
      /_/

Using Scala version 2.11.8 (Java HotSpot(TM) 64-Bit Server VM, Java 1.7.0_60)
Type in expressions to have them evaluated.
Type :help for more information.

scala> []
```

Figure 2 - Notice how the shell starts up showing you the version of Spark you are using.

The provided book source code provides for each chapter the command starting the Spark environment; for this chapter, you can find it in the chapter2/bin folder.

The Spark shell is a Scala - based console application that accepts Scala code and executes it in an interactive way. The next step is to prepare the computation environment by importing packages which we are going to use during our example.

```
import org.apache.spark.mllib
import org.apache.spark.mllib.regression.LabeledPoint
import org.apache.spark.mllib.linalg._
import org.apache.spark.mllib.linalg.distributed.RowMatrix
import org.apache.spark.mllib.util.MLUtils
import org.apache.spark.mllib.evaluation._
import org.apache.spark.mllib.tree._
import org.apache.spark.mllib.tree.model._
import org.apache.spark.rdd._
```

Let's first ingest the .csv file that you should have downloaded and do a quick count to see how much data is in our subset. Here, please notice, that the code expects the data folder "data" relative to the current process working directory or location specified:

```
val rawData =
sc.textFile(s"${sys.env.get("DATADIR").getOrElse("data")}/higgs100k.csv")
println(s"Number of rows: ${rawData.count}")
```

The output is as follows:

```
Number of rows: 100000
```

You can observe that execution of the command `sc.textFile(...)` took no time and returned instantly, while executing `rawData.count` took the majority amount of time. This exactly demonstrates the difference between Spark **transformations** and **actions**. By design, Spark adopts **lazy evaluation** - it means that if a transformation is invoked, Spark just records it directly into its so-called **execution graph/plan**. That perfectly fits into the big data world, since users can pile up transformations without waiting. On the other hand, an action evaluates the execution graph - Spark instantiates each recorded transformation and applies it onto the output of previous transformations. This concept also helps Spark to analyze and optimize an execution graph before its execution - for example, Spark can reorganize the order of transformations or can decide to run transformations in parallel if they are independent.

Right now, we defined a transformation which loads data into the Spark data structure `RDD[String]` which contains all the lines of input data file. So, let's look at the first two rows:

```
rawData.take(2)
```

```
Rows
1.000000000000000000e+00,8.692932128906250000e-01,-6.350818276405334473e-01,2.2569026(
485731393098831177e-01,-1.092063903808593750e+00,0.000000000000000000e+00,1.374992132
138904333114624023e+00,-1.578198313713073730e+00,-1.046985387802124023e+00,0.00000000(
101961374282836914e+00,1.353760004043579102e+00,9.795631170272827148e-01,9.7807615995
766783475875854492e-01
1.000000000000000000e+00,9.075421094894409180e-01,3.291472792625427246e-01,3.59411865
575249195098876953e-01,-1.588229775428771973e+00,2.173076152801513672e+00,8.125811815.
999939501285552979e-01,-1.261431813240051270e+00,7.321561574935913086e-01,0.0000000000
000000000000000000e+00,3.022198975086212158e-01,8.330481648445129395e-01,9.8569965362!
983425855636596680e-01
```

The first two lines contain raw data as loaded from the file. You can see that a row is composed of a response column having the value 0,1 (the first value of the row) and other columns having real values. However, the lines are still represented as strings and require parsing and transformation into regular rows. Hence, based on the knowledge of the input data format, we can define a simple parser which splits an input line into numbers based on a comma:

```
val data = rawData.map(line => line.split(',').map(_.toDouble))
```

Now we can extract a response column (the first column in the dataset) and the rest of data representing the input features:

```
val response: RDD[Int] = data.map(row => row(0).toInt)
val features: RDD[Vector] = data.map(line => Vectors.dense(line.slice(1,
line.size)))
```

After this transformation, we have two RDDs:

- One representing the response column
- Another which contains dense vectors of numbers holding individual input features

Next, let's look in more detail at the input features and perform some very rudimentary data analysis:

```
val featuresMatrix = new RowMatrix(features)
val featuresSummary = featuresMatrix.computeColumnSummaryStatistics()
```

We converted this vector into a distributed *RowMatrix*. This gives us the ability to perform simple summary statistics (for example, compute mean, variance, and so on:)

```
import org.apache.spark.utils.Tabulizer._
println(s"Higgs Features Mean Values = ${table(featuresSummary.mean, 8)}")
```

The output is as follows:

```
Higgs Features Mean Values =
+------+------+------+------+------+------+------+------+
|0.990|-0.004|-0.002| 0.995|-0.008|0.987|-0.003|0.000|
|0.998| 0.991|-0.001| 0.004| 1.004|0.993| 0.002|0.001|
|1.006| 0.986|-0.008|-0.004| 0.993|1.033| 1.023|1.050|
|1.010| 0.973| 1.032| 0.959|    -|    -|    -|    -|
+------+------+------+------+------+------+------+------+
```

Take a look at following code:

```
println(s"Higgs Features Variance Values =
${table(featuresSummary.variance, 8)}")
```

The output is as follows:

```
Higgs Features Variance Values =
+-----+-----+-----+-----+-----+-----+-----+-----+
|0.316|1.010|1.012|0.354|1.014|0.224|1.017|1.017|
|1.056|0.248|1.010|1.014|1.101|0.238|1.017|1.011|
|1.431|0.255|1.018|1.014|1.951|0.426|0.138|0.027|
|0.159|0.274|0.132|0.098|    -|    -|    -|    -|
+-----+-----+-----+-----+-----+-----+-----+-----+
```

In the next step, let's explore columns in more details. We can get directly the number of non-zeros in each column to figure out if the data is dense or sparse. Dense data contains mostly non-zeros, sparse data the opposite. The ratio between the number of non-zeros in the data and the number of all values represents the sparsity of data. The sparsity can drive our selection of the computation method, since for sparse data it is more efficient to iterate over non-zeros only:

```
val nonZeros = featuresSummary.numNonzeros
println(s"Non-zero values count per column: ${table(nonZeros, cols = 8,
format = "%.0f")}")
```

The output is as follows:

```
Non-zero values count per column:
+------+------+------+------+------+------+------+------+
|100000|100000|100000|100000|100000|100000|100000|100000|
| 50907|100000|100000|100000| 50023|100000|100000|100000|
| 43176|100000|100000|100000| 34973|100000|100000|100000|
|100000|100000|100000|100000|    -|    -|    -|    -|
+------+------+------+------+------+------+------+------+
```

However, the call just gives us the number of non-zeros for all column, which is not so interesting. We are more curious about columns that contain some zero values:

```
val numRows = featuresMatrix.numRows
val numCols = featuresMatrix.numCols
val colsWithZeros = nonZeros
  .toArray
  .zipWithIndex
  .filter { case (rows, idx) => rows != numRows }
println(s"Columns with zeros:\n${table(Seq("#zeros", "column"),
```

```
colsWithZeros, Map.empty[Int, String])}")
```

In this case, we augmented the original vector of non-zeros by the index of each value and then filter out all the values which are equal to the number of rows in the original matrix. And we get:

```
Columns with zeros:

+-------+------+
| #zeros|column|
+-------+------+
|50907.0|    8|
|50023.0|   12|
|43176.0|   16|
|34973.0|   20|
+-------+------+
```

We can see that columns 8, 12, 16, and 20 contain some zero numbers, but still not enough to consider the matrix as sparse. To confirm our observation, we can compute the overall sparsity of the matrix (remainder: the matrix does not include the response column):

```
val sparsity = nonZeros.toArray.sum / (numRows * numCols)
println(f"Data sparsity: ${sparsity}%.2f")
```

The output is as follows:

```
Data sparsity: 0.92
```

And the computed number confirms our former observation - the input matrix is dense.

Now it is time to explore the response column in more detail. As the first step, we verify that the response contains only the values 0 and 1 by computing the unique values inside the response vector:

```
val responseValues = response.distinct.collect
 println(s"Response values: ${responseValues.mkString(", ")}")
```

```
Response values: 0, 1
```

The next step is to explore the distribution of labels in the response vector. We can compute the rate directly via Spark:

```
val responseDistribution = response.map(v => (v,1)).countByKey
 println(s"Response distribution:\n${table(responseDistribution)}")
```

The output is as follows:

```
Response distribution:

+-----+-----+
|   0|    1|
+-----+-----+
|47166|52834|
+-----+-----+
```

In this step, we simply transform each row into a tuple representing the row value and 1 expressing that the value occurs once in the row. Having RDDs of pairs, the Spark method `countByKey` aggregates pairs by a key and gives us a summary of the keys count. It shows that the data surprisingly contains slightly more cases which do represent Higgs-Boson but we can still consider the response nicely balanced.

We can also explore labels distribution visually with help of the H2O library. For that we need to start H2O services represented by `H2OContext`:

```
import org.apache.spark.h2o._
val h2oContext = H2OContext.getOrCreate(sc)
```

The code initializes the H2O library and starts H2O services on each node of the Spark clusters. It also exposes an interactive environment called Flow, which is useful for data exploration and model building. In the console, `h2oContext` prints the location of the exposed UI:

```
h2oContext: org.apache.spark.h2o.H2OContext =
Sparkling Water Context:
 * H2O name: sparkling-water-user-303296214
 * number of executors: 1
 * list of used executors:
  (executorId, host, port)
  ------------------------
  (driver,192.168.1.65,54321)
  ------------------------
  Open H2O Flow in browser: http://192.168.1.65:54321 (CMD + click in Mac
OSX)
```

Now we can directly open the Flow UI address and start exploring the data. However, before doing that, we need to publish the Spark data as an H2O frame called `response`:

```
val h2oResponse = h2oContext.asH2OFrame(response, "response")
```

If you import implicit conversions exposed by `H2OContext`, you will be able to invoke transformation transparently based on the defined type on the left-side of assignment:

For example:

```
import h2oContext.implicits._
val h2oResponse: H2OFrame = response
```

Now it is time to open the Flow UI. You can open it directly by accessing the URL reported by `H2OContext` or by typing `h2oContext.openFlow` in the Spark shell.

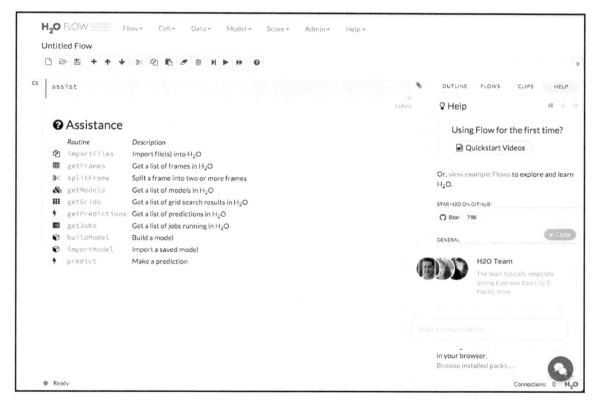

Figure 3 - Interactive Flow UI

The Flow UI allows for interactive work with the stored data. Let,s look at which data is exposed for the Flow by typing `getFrames` into the highlighted cell:

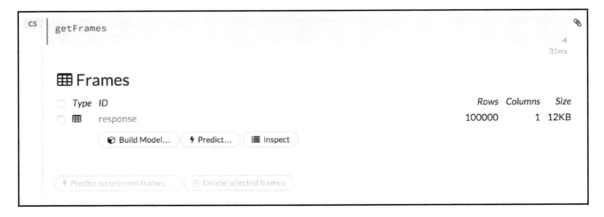

Figure 4 - Get list of available H2O frames

Figure 4 - Get list of available H2O frames

By clicking on the response field or typing `getColumnSummary "response", "values"`, we can get visual confirmation about the distribution of values in the response column and see that the problem is slightly imbalanced:

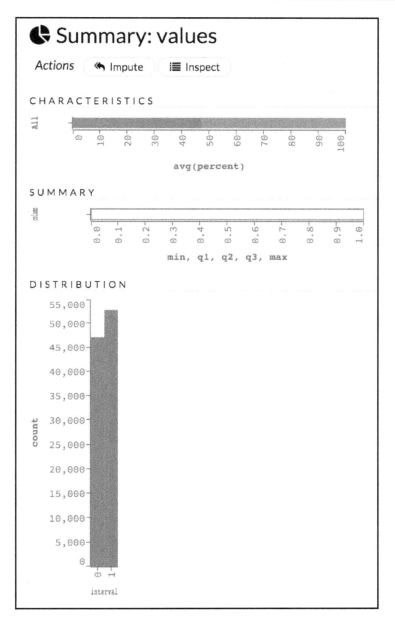

Figure 5 - Statistical properties of column named "response".

Labeled point vector

Prior to running any supervised machine learning algorithm using Spark MLlib, we must convert our dataset into a labeled point vector which maps features to a given label/response; labels are stored as doubles which facilitates their use for both classification and regression tasks. For all binary classification problems, labels should be stored as either 0 or 1, which we confirmed from the preceding summary statistics holds true for our example.

```
val higgs = response.zip(features).map {
case (response, features) =>
LabeledPoint(response, features) }

higgs.setName("higgs").cache()
```

An example of a labeled point vector follows:

```
(1.0, [0.123, 0.456, 0.567, 0.678, ..., 0.789])
```

In the preceding example, all doubles inside the bracket are the features and the single number outside the bracket is our label. Note that we are yet to tell Spark that we are performing a classification task and not a regression task which will happen later.

In this example, all input features contain only numeric values, but in many situations data that contains categorical values or string data. All this non-numeric representation needs to be converted into numbers, which we will show later in this book.

Data caching

Many machine learning algorithms are iterative in nature and thus require multiple passes over the data. However, all data stored in Spark RDD are by default transient, since RDD just stores the transformation to be executed and not the actual data. That means each action would recompute data again and again by executing the transformation stored in RDD.

Hence, Spark provides a way to persist the data in case we need to iterate over it. Spark also publishes several StorageLevels to allow storing data with various options:

- NONE: No caching at all
- MEMORY_ONLY: Caches RDD data only in memory
- DISK_ONLY: Write cached RDD data to a disk and releases from memory

- `MEMORY_AND_DISK`: Caches RDD in memory, if it's not possible to offload data to a disk
- `OFF_HEAP`: Use external memory storage which is not part of JVM heap

Furthermore, Spark gives users the ability to cache data in two flavors: *raw* (for example, `MEMORY_ONLY`) and *serialized* (for example, `MEMORY_ONLY_SER`). The later uses large memory buffers to store serialized content of RDD directly. Which one to use is very task and resource dependent. A good rule of thumb is if the dataset you are working with is less than 10 gigs then raw caching is preferred to serialized caching. However, once you cross over the 10 gigs soft-threshold, raw caching imposes a greater memory footprint than serialized caching.

Spark can be forced to cache by calling the `cache()` method on RDD or directly via calling the method persist with the desired persistent target - `persist(StorageLevels.MEMORY_ONLY_SER)`. It is useful to know that RDD allows us to set up the storage level only once.

The decision on what to cache and how to cache is part of the Spark magic; however, the golden rule is to use caching when we need to access RDD data several times and choose a destination based on the application preference respecting speed and storage. A great blogpost which goes into far more detail than what is given here is available at:

`http://sujee.net/2015/01/22/understanding-spark-caching/#.VpU1nJMrLdc`

Cached RDDs can be accessed as well from the H2O Flow UI by evaluating the cell with `getRDDs`:

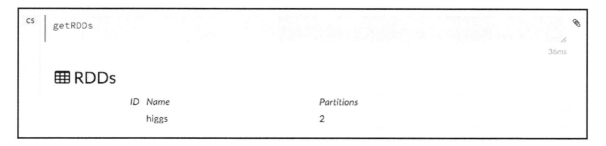

Creating a training and testing set

As with most supervised learning tasks, we will create a split in our dataset so that we *teach* a model on one subset and then test its ability to generalize on new data against the holdout set. For the purposes of this example, we split the data 80/20 but there is no hard rule on what the ratio for a split should be - or for that matter - how many splits there should be in the first place:

```
// Create Train & Test Splits
val trainTestSplits = higgs.randomSplit(Array(0.8, 0.2))
val (trainingData, testData) = (trainTestSplits(0), trainTestSplits(1))
```

By creating our 80/20 split on the dataset, we are taking a random sample of 8.8 million examples as our training set and the remaining 2.2 million as our testing set. We could just as easily take another random 80/20 split and generate a new training set with the same number of examples (8.8 million) but with different data. Doing this type of *hard* splitting of our original dataset introduces a sampling bias, which basically means that our model will learn to fit the training data but the training data may not be representative of "reality". Given that we are working with 11 million examples already, this bias is not as prominent versus if our original dataset is 100 rows, for example. This is often referred to as the **holdout method** for model validation.

You can also use the H2O Flow to split the data:

1. Publish the Higgs data as H2OFrame:

```
val higgsHF = h2oContext.asH2OFrame(higgs.toDF, "higgsHF")
```

2. Split data in the Flow UI using the command splitFrame (see *Figure 07*).
3. And then publish the results back to RDD.

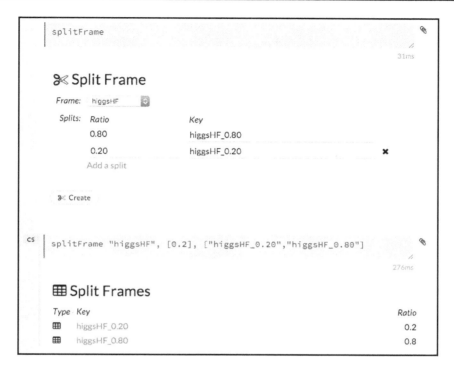

Figure 7 - Splitting Higgs dataset into two H2O frames representing 80 and 20 percent of data.

In contrast to Spark lazy evaluation, the H2O computation model is eager. That means the `splitFrame` invocation processes the data right away and creates two new frames, which can be directly accessed.

What about cross-validation?

Often, in the case of smaller datasets, data scientists employ a technique known as cross-validation, which is also available to you in Spark. The `CrossValidator` class starts by splitting the dataset into N-folds (user declared) - each fold is used N-1 times as part of the training set and once for model validation. For example, if we declare that we wish to use a **5-fold cross-validation**, the `CrossValidator` class will create five pairs (training and testing) of datasets using four-fifths of the dataset to create the training set with the final fifth as the test set, as shown in the following figure.

The idea is that we would see the performance of our algorithm across different, randomly sampled datasets to account for the inherent sampling bias when we create our training/testing split on 80% of the data. An example of a model that does not generalize well would be one where the accuracy - as measured by overall error, for example - would be all over the map with wildly different error rates, which would suggest we need to rethink our model.

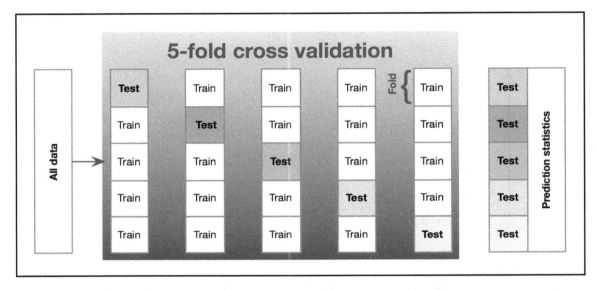

Figure 8 - Conceptual schema of 5-fold cross-validation.

There is no set rule on how many folds you should perform, as these questions are highly individual with respect to the type of data being used, the number of examples, and so on. In some cases, it makes sense to have extreme cross-validation where N is equal to the number of data points in the input dataset. In this case, the **Test** set contains only one row. This method is called as **Leave-One-Out (LOO)** validation and is more computationally expensive.

In general, it is recommended that you perform some cross-validation (often 5-folds, or 10-folds cross-validation is recommended) during the model construction to validate the quality of a model - especially when the dataset is small.

Our first model – decision tree

Our first attempt at trying to classify the Higgs-Boson from background noise will use a decision tree algorithm. We purposely eschew from explaining the intuition behind this algorithm as this has already been well documented with plenty of supporting literature for the reader to consume (http://www.saedsayad.com/decision_tree.htm, http://spark. apache.org/docs/latest/mllib-decision-tree.html). Instead, we will focus on the hyper-parameters and how to interpret the model's efficacy with respect to certain criteria / error measures. Let's start with the basic parameters:

```
val numClasses = 2
val categoricalFeaturesInfo = Map[Int, Int]()
val impurity = "gini"
val maxDepth = 5
val maxBins = 10
```

Now we are explicitly telling Spark that we wish to build a decision tree classifier that looks to distinguish between two classes. Let's take a closer look at some of the hyper-parameters for our decision tree and see what they mean:

numClasses: How many classes are we trying to classify? In this example, we wish to distinguish between the Higgs-Boson particle and background noise and thus there are four classes:

- categoricalFeaturesInfo: A specification whereby we declare what features are categorical features and should not be treated as numbers (for example, ZIP code is a popular example). There are no categorical features in this dataset that we need to worry about.
- impurity: A measure of the homogeneity of the labels at the node. Currently in Spark, there are two measures of impurity with respect to classification: Gini and Entropy and one impurity for regression: variance.
- maxDepth: A stopping criterion which limits the depth of constructed trees. Generally, deeper trees lead to more accurate results but run the risk of overfitting.
- maxBins: Number of bins (think "values") for the tree to consider when making splits. Generally, increasing the number of bins allows the tree to consider more values but also increases computation time.

Gini versus Entropy

In order to determine which one of the impurity measures to use, it's important that we cover some foundational knowledge beginning with the concept of **information gain**.

At it's core, information gain is as it sounds: the gain in information from moving between two states. More accurately, the information gain of a certain event is the difference between the amount of information known before and after the event takes place. One common measure of this information is looking at the **Entropy** which can be defined as:

$$Entropy = \sum_j -p_j \log_2 p_j$$

Where p_j is the frequency of label j at a node.

Now that you are familiar with the concept of information gain and Entropy, we can move on to what is meant by the **Gini Index** (there is no correlation whatsoever to the Gini coefficient).

The **Gini Index**: is a measure of how often a randomly chosen element would be misclassified if it were randomly given a label according to the distribution of labels at a given node.

$$Gini\ Index = 1 - \sum_j p_j^2$$

Compared with the equation for Entropy, the Gini Index should be computed slightly faster due to the absence of a log computation which may be why it is the **default** option for many other machine learning libraries including MLlib.

But does this make it a **better** measure for which to make splits for our decision tree? It turns out that the choice of impurity measure has little effect on performance with respect to single decision tree algorithms. The reason for this, according to Tan et. al, in the book *Introduction to Data Mining*, is that:

> "...This is because impurity measures are quite consistent with each other [...]. Indeed, the strategy used to prune the tree has a greater impact on the final tree than the choice of impurity measure."

Now it's time we train our decision tree classifier on the training data:

```
val dtreeModel = DecisionTree.trainClassifier(
trainingData,
numClasses,
categoricalFeaturesInfo,
impurity,
maxDepth,
maxBins)

// Show the tree
println("Decision Tree Model:\n" + dtreeModel.toDebugString)
```

This should yield a final output which looks like this (note that your results will be slightly different due to the random split of the data):

```
DecisionTreeModel classifier of depth 5 with 63 nodes
  If (feature 25 <= 1.0579049587249756)
   If (feature 25 <= 0.6132826209068298)
    If (feature 27 <= 0.8709201216697693)
     If (feature 5 <= 0.8882235884666443)
      If (feature 26 <= 0.7871721386909485)
       Predict: 0.0
      Else (feature 26 > 0.7871721386909485)
       Predict: 1.0
     Else (feature 5 > 0.8882235884666443)
      If (feature 27 <= 0.7900190353393555)
       Predict: 1.0
      Else (feature 27 > 0.7900190353393555)
       Predict: 1.0
    Else (feature 27 > 0.8709201216697693)
     If (feature 22 <= 1.0433123111724854)
      If (feature 24 <= 1.0797673463821411)
       Predict: 0.0
      Else (feature 24 > 1.0797673463821411)
       Predict: 0.0
     Else (feature 22 > 1.0433123111724854)
      If (feature 5 <= 1.535428524017334)
       Predict: 0.0
      Else (feature 5 > 1.535428524017334)
       Predict: 1.0
   Else (feature 25 > 0.6132826209068298)
    If (feature 26 <= 0.7871721386909485)
     If (feature 5 <= 0.8882235884666443)
      If (feature 25 <= 0.8765085935592651)
       Predict: 0.0
      Else (feature 25 > 0.8765085935592651)
       Predict: 0.0
     Else (feature 5 > 0.8882235884666443)
      If (feature 27 <= 0.7900190353393555)
       Predict: 1.0
      Else (feature 27 > 0.7900190353393555)
       Predict: 0.0
```

The output shows that decision tree has depth 5 and 63 nodes organized in an hierarchical decision predicate. Let's go ahead and interpret it looking at the first five *decisions*. The way it reads is: *"If feature 25's value is less than or equal to 1.0559 AND is less than or equal to 0.61558 AND feature 27's value is less than or equal to 0.87310 AND feature 5's value is less than or equal to 0.89683 AND finally, feature 22's value is less than or equal to 0.76688, then the prediction is 1.0 (the Higgs-Boson). BUT, these five conditions must be met in order for the prediction to hold."* Notice that if the last condition is not held (feature 22's value is > 0.76688) but the previous four held conditions remain true, then the prediction changes from 1 to 0, indicating background noise.

Now, let's score the model on our test dataset and print the prediction error:

```
val treeLabelAndPreds = testData.map { point =>
   val prediction = dtreeModel.predict(point.features)
   (point.label.toInt, prediction.toInt)
 }

 val treeTestErr = treeLabelAndPreds.filter(r => r._1 !=
r._2).count.toDouble / testData.count()
 println(f"Tree Model: Test Error = ${treeTestErr}%.3f")
```

The output is as follows:

```
Tree Model: Test Error = 0.337
```

After some period of time, the model will score all of the test set data and then compute an error rate which we defined in the preceding code. Again, your error rate will be slightly different than ours but as we show, our simple decision tree model has an error rate of ~33%. However, as you know, there are different kinds of errors that we can possibly make and so it's worth exploring what those types of error are by constructing a confusion matrix:

```
val cm = treeLabelAndPreds.combineByKey(
   createCombiner = (label: Int) => if (label == 0) (1,0) else (0,1),
   mergeValue = (v:(Int,Int), label:Int) => if (label == 0) (v._1 +1, v._2)
else (v._1, v._2 + 1),
   mergeCombiners = (v1:(Int,Int), v2:(Int,Int)) => (v1._1 + v2._1, v1._2 +
v2._2)).collect
```

The preceding code is using advanced the Spark method `combineByKey` which allows us to map each (K,V)-pair to a value, which is going to represent the output of the group by the key operation. In this case, the (K,V)-pair represents the actual value K and prediction V. We map each prediction to a tuple by creating a combiner (parameter `createCombiner`) - if the predicted values is 0, then we map to (1,0); otherwise, we map to (0,1). Then we need to define how combiners accept a new value and how combiners are merged together. At the end, the method produces:

```
cm: Array[(Int, (Int, Int))] = Array((0,(5402,4131)), (1,(2724,7846)))
```

The resulting array contains two tuples - one for the actual value 0 and another for the actual value 1. Each tuple contains the number of predictions 0 and 1. Hence, it is easy to extract all necessary to present a nice confusion matrix.

```
val (tn, tp, fn, fp) = (cm(0)._2._1, cm(1)._2._2, cm(1)._2._1, cm(0)._2._2)
println(f"""Confusion Matrix
   |   ${0}%5d ${1}%5d   ${"Err"}%10s
   |0  ${tn}%5d ${fp}%5d ${tn+fp}%5d ${fp.toDouble/(tn+fp)}%5.4f
   |1  ${fn}%5d ${tp}%5d ${fn+tp}%5d ${fn.toDouble/(fn+tp)}%5.4f
   |   ${tn+fn}%5d ${fp+tp}%5d ${tn+fp+fn+tp}%5d
${(fp+fn).toDouble/(tn+fp+fn+tp)}%5.4f
   |""".stripMargin)
```

The code extracts all true negatives and positives predictions and also missed predictions and outputs of the confusion matrix based on the template shown on *Figure 9*:

```
Confusion Matrix
      0     1        Err
0  5494  4090  9584 0.4268
1  2655  7762 10417 0.2549
   8149 11852 20001 0.3372
```

In the preceding code, we are using a powerful Scala feature, which is called *string interpolation*: `println(f"...")`. It allows for the easy construction of the desired output by combining a string output and actual Scala variables. Scala supports different string "interporlators", but the most used are *s* and *f*. The *s* interpolator allows for referencing any Scala variable or even code: `s"True negative: ${tn}"`. While, the *f* interpolator is type-safe - that means the user is required to specify the type of variable to show: `f"True negative: ${tn}%5d"` - and references the variable `tn` as decimal type and asks for printing on five decimal spaces.

Going back to our first example in this chapter, we can see that our model is making most of the errors in detecting the actual Boson particle. In this case, all data points representing detection of Boson are wrongly missclassified as non-Boson. However, the overall error rate is pretty low! This is a nice example of how the overall error rate can be misleading for a dataset with an imbalanced response.

	Predicted 0	Predicted 1	Totals	Missclasification error
Actual 0	true negatives (TN)	false positives (FP)	$TN + FP$	$\dfrac{FP}{TN + FP}$
Actual 1	false negatives (FN)	true positives (TP)	$FN + TP$	$\dfrac{FN}{(FN + TP)}$
Totals	$TN + FN$	$FP + TP$		$\dfrac{FN + FP}{TN + FP + FN + TP}$

Figure 9 - Confusion matrix schema.

Next, we will consider another modeling metric used to judge classification models, called the **Area Under the** (Receiver Operating Characteristic) **Curve** (**AUC**) (see the following figure for an example). The **Receiver Operating Characteristic** (**ROC**) curve is a graphical representation of the **True Positive Rate** versus the **False Positive Rate**:

- **True Positive Rate**: The total number of true positives divided by the sum of true positives and false negatives. Expressed differently, it is the ratio of the true signals for the Higgs-Boson particle (where the actual label was 1) to all the predicted signals for the Higgs-Boson (where our model predicted label is 1). The value is shown on the y-axis.
- **False Positive Rate**: The total number of false positives divided by the sum of false positives and true negatives, which is plotted on the x-axis.
- For more metrics, please see the figure for "Metrics derived from confusion matrix".

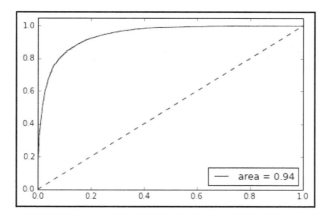

Figure 10 - Sample AUC Curve with an AUC value of 0.94

It follows that the ROC curve portrays our model's tradeoff of TPR against FPR for a given decision threshold (the decision threshold is the cutoff point whereby we say it is label 0 or label 1). Therefore, the area under the ROC curve can be thought of as an *average model accuracy* whereby a value of 1.0 would represent perfect classification, 0.5 would be a coin-flip (meaning our model is doing a 50-50 job at guessing 1 or 0), and anything less than 0.5 would mean flipping a coin is more accurate than our model! This is an incredibly useful metric which we will see can be used to compare against different hyper-parameter tweaks and different models altogether! Let's go ahead and create a function which will allow us to calculate the AUC for our decision tree model which we will use to compare against other models:

```
type Predictor = {
  def predict(features: Vector): Double
}

def computeMetrics(model: Predictor, data: RDD[LabeledPoint]):
BinaryClassificationMetrics = {
    val predAndLabels = data.map(newData =>
(model.predict(newData.features), newData.label))
      new BinaryClassificationMetrics(predAndLabels)
}

val treeMetrics = computeMetrics(dtreeModel, testData)
println(f"Tree Model: AUC on Test Data =
${treeMetrics.areaUnderROC()}%.3f")
```

The output is as follows:

```
Tree Model: AUC on Test Data = 0.659
```

 Spark MLlib models do not share a common definition of interfaces; hence in the preceding example, we have to define the type `Predictor` exposing the method predict and use Scala structural typing in the definition of the method `computeMetrics`. Later in the book, we will show the Spark ML package, which is based on a unified pipeline-based API.

Rate	Formula
Accuracy	$\dfrac{TP + TN}{TN + FP + FN + TP}$
Missclasification error	$\dfrac{FN + FP}{TN + FP + FN + TP}$
True positive rate (Recall or Sensitivity)	$\dfrac{TP}{FN + TP}$
False positive Rate	$\dfrac{FP}{TN + FP}$
Specificity	$\dfrac{TN}{TN + TP}$
Precision	$\dfrac{TP}{FP + TP}$
Prevalence	$\dfrac{TP + FN}{TN + FP + FN + TP}$

Figure 11 - Metrics derived from confusion matrix.

Interested in a great read on this subject? There is no holy bible that is the be-all-end-all. The book, *The Elements of Statistical Learning,* by Trevor Hastie - renowned statistics professor from Stanford University - is a great source of information. This book offers useful nuggets for both beginners and advanced practitioners of machine learning and is highly recommended.

It is important to keep in mind that results between runs can be slightly different, since the Spark decision tree implementation is using internally the `RandomForest` algorithm, which is non-deterministic if a seed for a random generator is not specified. The problem is that the MLLib API for Spark `DecisionTree` does not allow to pass a seed as a parameter.

Next model – tree ensembles

Algorithms such as **Random Forest (RF)** or **Gradient Boosted Machine (GBM)** (also referred to as Gradient Boosted Trees) are two examples of ensemble tree-based models which are currently available in MLlib; you can think of an ensemble as an *uber-model* which represents a collection of base models. The best way to think about what an ensemble is doing behind the scenes is to consider a simple analogy:

"Suppose that you are the head coach of a famous soccer club and you have heard rumors of an incredible athlete from Brazil and it may be advantageous to sign this young athlete to your club before the other teams do; but your schedule is incredibly busy and instead, you send 10 of your assistant coaches to assess the player. Each one of your assistant coaches grades the player based on his/her coaching philosophy - maybe one coach wants to measure how fast the player can run 40 yards while another coach thinks height and arm-reach are important. Regardless of how each coach defines "athlete potential" you, as head coach, just want to know if you should sign the player to a contract now or wait. And so it goes that your coaches fly down to Brazil and each coach makes an assessment; upon arrival you go up to each of your coaches and ask "should we draft this player now or wait?" and, based on a simple rule like majority vote, you can make your decision. This an example of what an ensemble is doing behind the scenes with respect to a classification task."

You can think of each coach as a decision tree and, therefore, you will have an ensemble of 10 trees (for 10 coaches). How each coach assesses the player is highly specific and this holds true for our trees as well; for each of the 10 trees created features are selected randomly at each node (hence the random, in RF. Forest because there are many trees!). The reason for introducing this randomness and other base models is to prevent over-fitting the data. While RF and GBM are both tree-based ensembles, the manner in which they go about training is slightly different and deserves mention.

GBMs must be trained one tree at a time in order to minimize a `loss` function (for example, `log-loss`, squared error, and so on) and usually take longer to train than an RF which can generate multiple trees in parallel.

However, when training a GBM, it is recommended to make shallow trees which in turn lends itself to faster training.

- RFs generally do not overfit the data compared to a GBM; that is, we can add more trees to our forest and be less prone to over-fitting than if we added more trees to our GBM.
- Hyper-parameter tuning for an RF is much simpler than GBM. In his paper, *Influence of Hyperparameters on Random Forest Accuracy*, Bernard et al. show via experimentation that the number of K random features to select at each node is a key influencer with respect to model accuracy (https://hal.archives-ouvertes.fr/hal-00436358/document) Conversely, a GBM has much more hyper-parameters that must be considered, such as loss function, learning rate, number of iterations, and so on.

As with most *which is better* questions in data science, choosing between an RF and a GBM is open-ended and very task and dataset dependent.

Random forest model

Now, let's try building a random forest using 10 decision trees.

```
val numClasses = 2
val categoricalFeaturesInfo = Map[Int, Int]()
val numTrees = 10
val featureSubsetStrategy = "auto"
val impurity = "gini"
val maxDepth = 5
val maxBins = 10
val seed = 42


val rfModel = RandomForest.trainClassifier(trainingData, numClasses,
categoricalFeaturesInfo,
  numTrees, featureSubsetStrategy, impurity, maxDepth, maxBins, seed)
```

Just like our single decision tree model, we start by declaring the hyper-parameters, many of which should be familiar to you already from the decision tree example. In the preceding code, we will start by creating a random forest of 10 trees, solving a two-class problem. One key feature that is different is the feature subset strategy described as follows:

The `featureSubsetStrategy` object gives the number of features to use as candidates for making splits at each node. Can either be a fraction (for example, 0.5) or a function based on the number of features in your dataset. The setting `auto` allows the algorithm to choose this number for you but a common soft-rule states to use the square-root of the number of features you have.

Now that we have trained our model, let's score it against our hold-out set and compute the total error:

```
def computeError(model: Predictor, data: RDD[LabeledPoint]): Double = {
  val labelAndPreds = data.map { point =>
    val prediction = model.predict(point.features)
    (point.label, prediction)
  }
  labelAndPreds.filter(r => r._1 != r._2).count.toDouble/data.count
}
val rfTestErr = computeError(rfModel, testData)
println(f"RF Model: Test Error = ${rfTestErr}%.3f")
```

The output is as follows:

```
RF Model: Test Error = 0.349
```

And also compute AUC by using the already defined method `computeMetrics`:

```
val rfMetrics = computeMetrics(rfModel, testData)
println(f"RF Model: AUC on Test Data = ${rfMetrics.areaUnderROC}%.3f")
```

```
RF Model: AUC on Test Data = 0.644
```

Our RF - where we hardcode the hyper-parameters - performs much better than our single decision tree with respect to the overall model error and AUC. In the next section, we will introduce the concept of a grid search and how we can try varying hyper-parameter values / combinations and measure the impact on the model performance.

Again, results can slightly differ between runs. However, in contrast to the decision tree, it is possible to make a run deterministic by passing a seed as a parameter of the method `RandomForest.trainClassifier`.

Grid search

As with most algorithms in MLlib and H2O, there are many hyper-parameters to choose from which can have a significant effect on the performance of the model. Given the endless amount of combinations that are possible, is there an intelligent way we can begin looking at what combinations look more promising than others? Thankfully, the answer is an emphatic "YES!" and the solution is known as a grid search, which is ML-speak for running many models that use different combinations of hyper-parameters.

Let's try running a simple grid search using the RF algorithm. In this case, the RF model builder is invoked for each combination of parameters from a defined hyper-space of parameters:

```
val rfGrid =
    for (
    gridNumTrees <- Array(15, 20);
    gridImpurity <- Array("entropy", "gini");
    gridDepth <- Array(20, 30);
    gridBins <- Array(20, 50))
        yield {
    val gridModel = RandomForest.trainClassifier(trainingData, 2, Map[Int,
Int](), gridNumTrees, "auto", gridImpurity, gridDepth, gridBins)
    val gridAUC = computeMetrics(gridModel, testData).areaUnderROC
    val gridErr = computeError(gridModel, testData)
    ((gridNumTrees, gridImpurity, gridDepth, gridBins), gridAUC, gridErr)
    }
```

What we have just written is a `for`-loop that is going to try a number of different combinations with respect to the number of trees, impurity type, depth of the trees, and the bins (that is, values to try); And then, for each model created based on these hyper-parameter permutations, we are going to score the trained model against our hold-out set while computing the AUC metric and the overall error rate. In total we get 2*2*2*2=16 models. Again, your models will be slightly different than the ones we show here but your output should resemble something like this:

```
RF Model: Grid results:

+------------------------------+------+-----+
|trees, impurity, depth, bins| AUC|error|
+------------------------------+------+-----+
|        (15,entropy,20,20)|0.697|0.302|
|        (15,entropy,20,50)|0.698|0.301|
|        (15,entropy,30,20)|0.692|0.306|
|        (15,entropy,30,50)|0.689|0.309|
|           (15,gini,20,20)|0.691|0.308|
|           (15,gini,20,50)|0.693|0.306|
|           (15,gini,30,20)|0.687|0.312|
|           (15,gini,30,50)|0.692|0.306|
|        (20,entropy,20,20)|0.694|0.303|
|        (20,entropy,20,50)|0.701|0.297|
|        (20,entropy,30,20)|0.696|0.301|
|        (20,entropy,30,50)|0.693|0.304|
|           (20,gini,20,20)|0.694|0.303|
|           (20,gini,20,50)|0.701|0.296|
|           (20,gini,30,20)|0.689|0.308|
|           (20,gini,30,50)|0.694|0.303|
+------------------------------+------+-----+
```

Look at the first entry of our output:

```
| (15,entropy,20,20) |0.697|0.302|
```

We can interpret this as follows: for the combination of 15 decision trees, using Entropy as our impurity measure, along with a tree depth of 20 (for each tree) and a bin value of 20, our AUC is 0.695. Note that the results are shown in the order you wrote them initially. For our grid search using the RF algorithm, we can easily get a combination of hyper-parameters producing the highest AUC:

```
val rfParamsMaxAUC = rfGrid.maxBy(g => g._2)
println(f"RF Model: Parameters ${rfParamsMaxAUC._1}%s producing max AUC =
${rfParamsMaxAUC._2}%.3f (error = ${rfParamsMaxAUC._3}%.3f)")
```

The output is as follows:

```
RF Model: Parameters (20,gini,20,50) producing max AUC = 0.701 (error = 0.296)
```

Gradient boosting machine

So far, the best AUC we are able to muster is a 15-decision tree RF that has an AUC value of `0.698`. Now, let's go through the same process of running a single gradient boosted machine with hardcoded hyper-parameters and then doing a grid search over these parameters to see if we can get a higher AUC using this algorithm.

Recall that a GBM is slightly different than an RF due to its iterative nature of trying to reduce an overall `loss` function that we declare beforehand. Within MLlib there are three different loss functions to choose from as of 1.6.0:

- **Log-loss**: Use this `loss` function for classification tasks (note that GBM only supports binary classification for Spark. If you wish to use a GBM for multi-class classification, please use H2O's implementation, which we will show in the next chapter.
- **Squared-error**: Use this `loss` function for regression tasks it is is the current default `loss` function for this type of problem.
- **Absolute-error**: Another `loss` function that is available to use for regression tasks. Given that this function takes the absolute difference between the predicted and actual value, it controls for outliers much better than the squared error.

Given our task of binary classification, we will employ the `log-loss` function and begin building a 10 tree GBM model:

```
import org.apache.spark.mllib.tree.GradientBoostedTrees
 import org.apache.spark.mllib.tree.configuration.BoostingStrategy
 import org.apache.spark.mllib.tree.configuration.Algo

 val gbmStrategy = BoostingStrategy.defaultParams(Algo.Classification)
 gbmStrategy.setNumIterations(10)
 gbmStrategy.setLearningRate(0.1)
 gbmStrategy.treeStrategy.setNumClasses(2)
 gbmStrategy.treeStrategy.setMaxDepth(10)
 gbmStrategy.treeStrategy.setCategoricalFeaturesInfo(java.util.Collections.e
mptyMap[Integer, Integer])

 val gbmModel = GradientBoostedTrees.train(trainingData, gbmStrategy)
```

Notice that we must declare a boosting strategy before we can build our model. The reason is that MLlib does not know what type of problem we are tackling beforehand: classification or regression? So this strategy is letting Spark know that this is a binary classification problem and to use the declared hyper-parameters to build our model.

Following are some hyper-parameters to keep in mind when training GBMs:

- `numIterations`: By definition, a GBM builds trees one at a time in order to minimize a `loss` function we declare. This hyper-parameter controls the number of trees to build; be careful to not build too many trees as performance at test-time may not be ideal.
- `loss`: Where you declare which `loss` function to use depends on the question being asked and the dataset.
- `learningRate`: Optimizes speed of learning. Lower values (< 0.1) means slower learning, and improved generalization. However, it also needs a higher number of iterations and hence a longer computation time.

Let's score this model against the hold-out set and compute our AUC:

```
val gbmTestErr = computeError(gbmModel, testData)
println(f"GBM Model: Test Error = ${gbmTestErr}%.3f")
val gbmMetrics = computeMetrics(dtreeModel, testData)
println(f"GBM Model: AUC on Test Data = ${gbmMetrics.areaUnderROC()}%.3f")
```

The output is as follows:

```
GBM Model: Test Error = 0.305
GBM Model: AUC on Test Data = 0.659
```

As a final step, we will perform a grid-search over a few hyper-parameters and, similar to our previous RF grid-search example, output the combinations and their respective errors and AUC calculations:

```
val gbmGrid =
for (
  gridNumIterations <- Array(5, 10, 50);
  gridDepth <- Array(2, 3, 5, 7);
  gridLearningRate <- Array(0.1, 0.01))
yield {
  gbmStrategy.numIterations = gridNumIterations
  gbmStrategy.treeStrategy.maxDepth = gridDepth
  gbmStrategy.learningRate = gridLearningRate

  val gridModel = GradientBoostedTrees.train(trainingData, gbmStrategy)
  val gridAUC = computeMetrics(gridModel, testData).areaUnderROC
  val gridErr = computeError(gridModel, testData)
  ((gridNumIterations, gridDepth, gridLearningRate), gridAUC, gridErr)
}
```

We can print the first 10 lines of the result sorted by AUC:

```
println(
s"""GBM Model: Grid results:
      |${table(Seq("iterations, depth, learningRate", "AUC", "error"),
gbmGrid.sortBy(-_._2).take(10), format = Map(1 -> "%.3f", 2 -> "%.3f"))}
""".stripMargin)
```

The output is as follows:

```
GBM Model: Grid results:

+------------------------------------+-----+-----+
|iterations, depth, learningRate| AUC|error|
+------------------------------------+-----+-----+
|                   (50,7,0.1)|0.718|0.281|
|                   (50,5,0.1)|0.715|0.284|
|                   (10,7,0.1)|0.703|0.296|
|                   (50,3,0.1)|0.701|0.297|
|                  (50,7,0.01)|0.696|0.303|
|                    (5,7,0.1)|0.696|0.303|
|                   (10,5,0.1)|0.692|0.307|
|                   (50,2,0.1)|0.690|0.308|
|                  (10,7,0.01)|0.687|0.311|
|                   (5,7,0.01)|0.686|0.312|
+------------------------------------+-----+-----+
```

And we can easily get the model producing maximal AUC:

```
val gbmParamsMaxAUC = gbmGrid.maxBy(g => g._2)
println(f"GBM Model: Parameters ${gbmParamsMaxAUC._1}%s producing max AUC =
${gbmParamsMaxAUC._2}%.3f (error = ${gbmParamsMaxAUC._3}%.3f)")
```

The output is as follows:

```
GBM Model: Parameters (50,7,0.1) producing max AUC = 0.718 (error = 0.281)
```

Last model - H2O deep learning

So far we used the Spark MLlib for building different models; however, we can use also H2O algorithms as well. So let's try them!

At first, we are going to transfer our training and testing datasets over to H2O and create a DNN for our binary classification problem. To reiterate, this is made possible because Spark and H2O are sharing the same JVM which facilitates passing Spark RDDs over to H2O hex frames and vice versa.

All the models that we have run up to now have been in MLlib but now we are going to use H2O to build a DNN using the same training and testing sets that we used, which means we need to send this data over to our H2O cloud as follows:

```
val trainingHF = h2oContext.asH2OFrame(trainingData.toDF, "trainingHF")
val testHF = h2oContext.asH2OFrame(testData.toDF, "testHF")
```

To verify that we have successfully transferred our training and testing RDDs (which we converted to DataFrames), we can execute this command in our Flow notebook (all commands are executed with *Shift+Enter*). Notice that we have two H2O frames now called `trainingRDD` and `testRDD` which you can see in our H2O notebook by running the command `getFrames`.

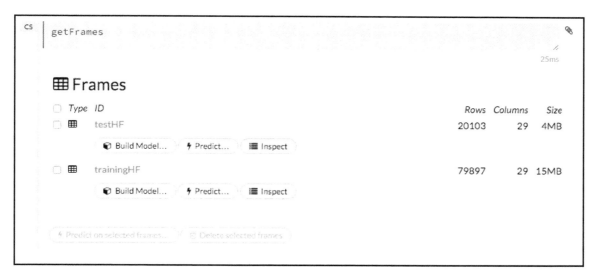

Figure 12 - List of available H2O frames is available by typing "getFrames" into Flow UI.

We can easily explore frames to see their structure by typing `getFrameSummary`
`"trainingHF"` into the Flow cell or just by clicking on the frame name (see *Figure 13*).

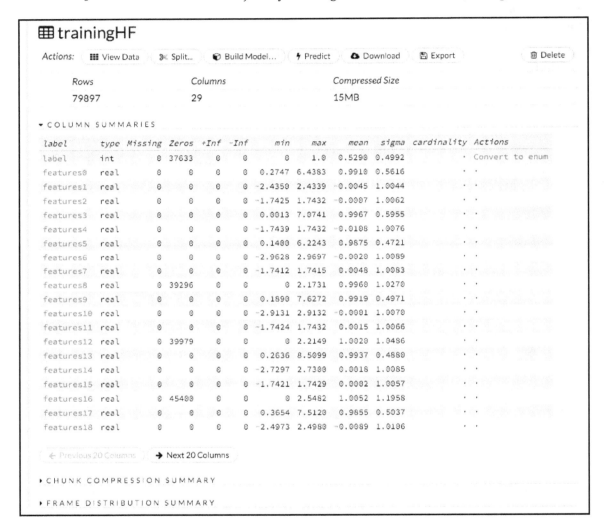

Figure 13 - Structure of training frame.

The preceding figure shows structure of the training frame - it has 80,491 rows and 29
columns; there are numeric columns named *features0, features1, ...* with real values and the
first column label containing integer values.

Since we would like to perform a binary classification, we need to transform the "label" column from the integer to categorical type. You can do that easily by clicking on the action *Convert to enum* in the Flow UI or in the Spark console by executing the following commands:

```
trainingHF.replace(0, trainingHF.vecs()(0).toCategoricalVec).remove()
trainingHF.update()

testHF.replace(0, testHF.vecs()(0).toCategoricalVec).remove()
testHF.update()
```

The code replaces the first vector by a transformed vector and removes the original vector from memory. Furthermore, the call `update` propagates changes into the shared distributed store, so they become visible by all the nodes in the cluster.

Build a 3-layer DNN

H2O exposes slightly different way of building models; however, it is unified among all H2O models. There are three basic building blocks:

- **Model parameters**: Defines inputs and algorithm specific parameters
- **Model builder**: Accepts model parameters and produces a model
- **Model**: Contains model definition but also technical information about model building such as score times or error rates for each iteration

Prior to building our model, we need to construct parameters for the DeepLearning algorithm:

```
import _root_.hex.deeplearning._
import DeepLearningParameters.Activation

val dlParams = new DeepLearningParameters()
dlParams._train = trainingHF._key
dlParams._valid = testHF._key
dlParams._response_column = "label"
dlParams._epochs = 1
dlParams._activation = Activation.RectifierWithDropout
dlParams._hidden = Array[Int](500, 500, 500)
```

Let's walk through the parameters and figure out the model we just initialized:

- `train` and `valid`: Specifying the training and testing set that we created. Note that these RDDs are in fact, H2O frames.
- `response_column`: Specifying the label that we use which we declared beforehand was the first element (indexes from 0) in each frame.
- `epochs`: An extremely important parameter which specifies how many times the network should pass over the training data; generally, models that are trained with higher `epochs` allow the network to *learn* new features and produce better model results. The caveat to this, however, is that these networks that have been trained for a long time suffer from overfitting and may not generalize well on new data.
- `activation`: These are the various non-linear functions that will be applied to the input data. In H2O there are three primary activations from which to choose from:
- `Rectifier`: Sometimes referred to as **rectified linear unit (ReLU)**, this is a function that has a lower limit of **0** but goes to positive infinity in a linear fashion. In terms of biology, these units are shown to be closer to actual neuron activations. Currently, this is the default activation function in H2O given its results for tasks such as image recognition and speed.

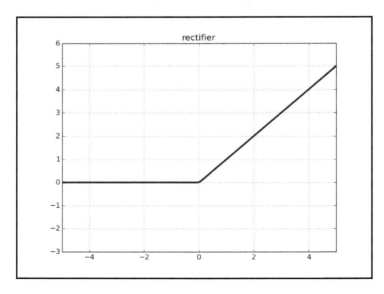

Figure 14 - Rectifier activation function

- `Tanh`: A modified logistic function that is bound between **-1** and **1** but goes through the origin at (0,0). Due to its symmetry around **0**, convergence is usually faster.

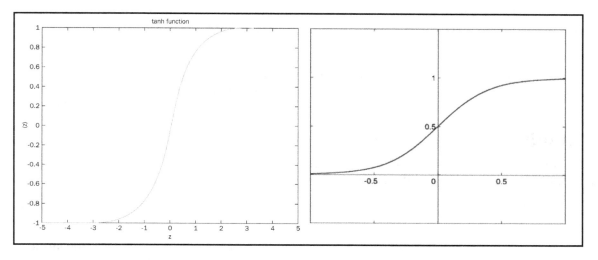

Figure 15 - Tanh activation function and Logistic function - note difference between Tanh.

- `Maxout`: A function whereby each neuron picks the largest value coming from k separate channels:
  - **hidden**: Another extremely important hyper-parameter, this is where we specify two things:
    - The number of layers (which you can create with additional commas). Note that in the GUI, the default parameter is a two-layers hidden network with 200 hidden neurons per layer.
    - The number of neurons per layer. As with most things regarding machine learning, there is no set rule on what this number should be and experimentation is usually best. However, there are some additional tuning parameters we will cover in the next chapter that will help you think about this, namely: L1 and L2 regularization and dropout.

Adding more layers

The reason for adding more layers to the network comes from our understanding of how the visual cortex works for humans. This is a dedicated area in the rear part of your brain that is used for recognizing objects/patterns/numbers, and so on, and is composed of complex layers of neurons that work to encode visual information and classify them accordingly based on prior knowledge.

Not surprisingly, there is no set rule on how many layers a network needs in order to produce good results and experimentation is highly recommended!

Building models and inspecting results

So now that you understand a little about the parameters and the model that we want to run, it's time to go ahead and train and inspect our network:

```
val dl = new DeepLearning(dlParams)
val dlModel = dl.trainModel.get
```

The code created the `DeepLearning` model builder and launched it. By default, the launch of `trainModel` is asynchronous (that is, it never blocks, but returns a job), but it is possible to wait until the end of computation by calling the method `get`. You can also explore the job progress in UI or even explore the unfinished model by typing `getJobs` into the Flow UI (see *Figure 18*).

Figure 18 - The command getJobs provides a list of executed jobs with their status.

The result of the computation is a DeepLearning model - we can directly explore the model and its details from the Spark shell:

```
println(s"DL Model: ${dlModel}")
```

We can also obtain a frame of predictions for the test data directly by calling the `score` method of the model:

```
val testPredictions = dlModel.score(testHF)

testPredictions: water.fvec.Frame =
Frame _95829d4e695316377f96db3edf0441ee (19912 rows and 3 cols):
         predict                   p0                    p1
    min          0.11323123896925524  0.017864442175851737
   mean          0.4856033079851807    0.5143966920148184
 stddev          0.1404849885490033    0.14048498854900326
    max          0.9821355578241482    0.8867687610307448
missing                         0.0                   0.0
      0        1  0.3908680007591152    0.6091319992408847
      1        1  0.3339873797352686    0.6660126202647314
      2        1  0.2958578897481016    0.7041421102518984
      3        1  0.2952981947808155    0.7047018052191846
      4        0  0.7523906949762337    0.24760930502376632
      5        1  0.53559438105240...
```

The table contains three columns:

- `predict`: Predicted value based on default threshold
- `p0`: Probability of selecting class 0
- `p1`: Probability of selecting class 1

We can also get model metrics for the test data:

```
import water.app.ModelMetricsSupport._
val dlMetrics = binomialMM(dlModel, testHF)
```

```
Model Metrics Type: Binomial
 Description: N/A
 model id: DeepLearning_model_1503814158569_1
 frame id: testHF
 MSE: 0.2219416
 RMSE: 0.4711068
 AUC: 0.70392555
 logloss: 0.6326101
 mean_per_class_error: 0.40489882
 default threshold: 0.44453179836273193
 CM: Confusion Matrix (Row labels: Actual class; Column labels: Predicted class):
            0       1    Error        Rate
     0   2374    7210   0.7523    7,210 / 9,584
     1    599    9818   0.0575     599 / 10,417
 Totals  2973   17028   0.3904    7,809 / 20,001
```

The output directly shows the AUC and accuracy (respective error rate). Please note that the model is really good at predicting Higgs-Boson; on the other hand, it has a high False Positive rate!

Finally, let's see how we can build a similar model using the GUI, only this time, we are going to exclude the physicist-hand-derived features from our model and use more neurons for inner layers:

1. Select the model to use for TrainingHF.

    As you can see, H2O and MLlib share many of the same algorithms with differing levels of functionality. Here we are going to select *Deep Learning* and then de-select the last eight hand-derived features.

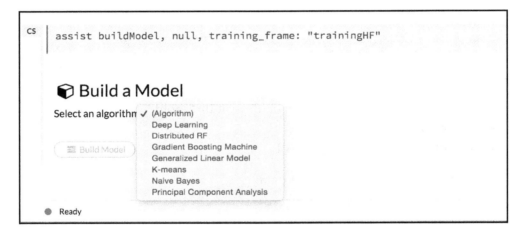

Figure 19- Selecting model algorithm

2. Build DNN and exclude hand-derived features.

    Here we are manually choosing to ignore features 21-27, which represent physicist-derived features in the hope that our network will learn them. Note also the ability to perform k-folds cross - validation should you choose to go this route as well.

model_id	deeplearning-839582	Destination id for this model; auto-generated if not specified
training_frame	trainingHF	Training frame
validation_frame	testHF	Validation frame
nfolds	0	Number of folds for N-fold cross-validation
response_column	label	Response column
ignored_columns	Search...	

Showing page 1 of 1. 7 ignored.

- features18 REAL
- features19 REAL
- ☐ features20 REAL
- ☑ features21 REAL
- ☑ features22 REAL
- ☑ features23 REAL
- ☑ features24 REAL
- ☑ features25 REAL
- ☑ features26 REAL
- ☑ features27 REAL

☑ All   ☐ None

Figure 20 - Selecting input features.

3. Specify the network topology.

As you can see, we are going to build a three-layer DNN using the rectifier activation function, where each layer will have 1,024 hidden neurons and this will run for 100 `epochs`.

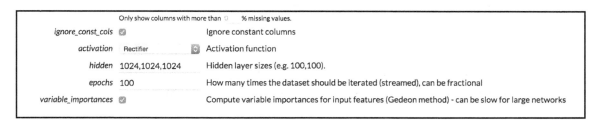

	Only show columns with more than 0 % missing values.	
ignore_const_cols	☑	Ignore constant columns
activation	Rectifier	Activation function
hidden	1024,1024,1024	Hidden layer sizes (e.g. 100,100).
epochs	100	How many times the dataset should be iterated (streamed), can be fractional
variable_importances	☑	Compute variable importances for input features (Gedeon method) - can be slow for large networks

Figure 21 - Configuring network topology with 3 layers, 1024 neurons per layer.

4. Explore the model results.

After running this model, which takes some time, we can click on the **View** button to inspect the AUC for both the training and testing set:

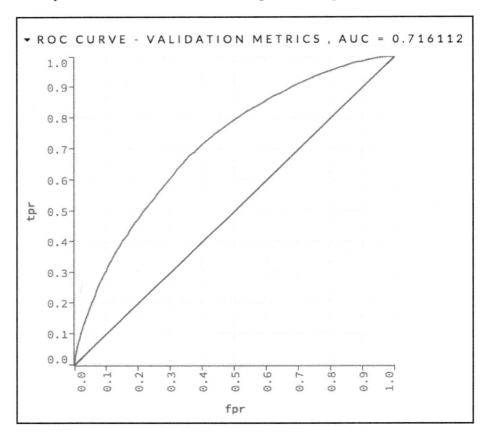

Figure 22 - AUC curve for validation data.

If you click your mouse and drag-and-drop on a section of the AUC curve, you can actually zoom in on that particular part of the curve and H2O gives summary statistics about the accuracy and precision at the various thresholds of the selected area.

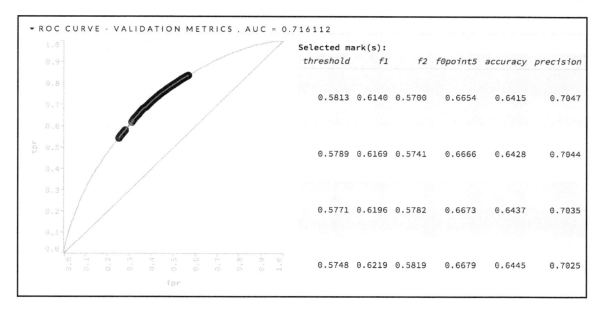

Figure 23 - ROC curve can be easily explored to find optimal threshold.

Also, there is a little button labeled Preview **Plain Old Java Object** (**POJO**), which we will explore in the latter chapters, which is how you will deploy your model into a production setting.

OK so we've built a few dozen models; it's time now to begin inspecting our results and figuring which one gives us the best results given the overall error and AUC metric. Interestingly, when we host the many meetups at our office and talk with top kagglers, these types of tables showing results are frequently constructed and it is a good way to keep track of a) what works and what doesn't and b) look back at what you have tried as a form of documentation.

Model	Error	AUC
Decision Tree	0.332	0.665
Grid-Search: Random Forest	0.294	0.704
Grid-Search: GBM	**0.287**	**0.712**
Deep Learning - all features	0.376	0.705
Deep Learning - subset feat.	0.301	0.716

So, which one do we go with? In this case, we like the the GBM model since it provides the second highest AUC value with the lowest accuracy. But always this decision is driven by the modeling goal - in this example, we were strictly motivated by accuracy of the model in finding Higgs-Bosons; however, in other cases, selection of the right model or models can be influenced by various aspects - for example, the time to find and build the best model.

Summary

This chapter was all about the binary classification problem: true or false and, for our example, the signal indicative of the Higgs-Boson or background noise? We have explored four different algorithms: **single decision tree**, **random forest**, **gradient boosted machine**, and DNN. For this exact problem, DNNs are the current world-beaters as the models can continue to train for longer (that is, increase the number of epochs) and more layers can be added
(http://papers.nips.cc/paper/5351-searching-for-higgs-boson-decay-modes-with-deep-learning.pdf)

In addition to exploring four algorithms and how to perform a grid-search against many hyper-parameters, we also looked at some important model metrics to help you better differentiate between models and understand ways to define how *good* is good. Our goal for this chapter was to expose you to a variety of different algorithms and tweaks within Spark and H2O to solve binary classification problems. In the next chapter, we will explore multi-class classification and how to create ensembles of models (sometimes called super-learners) to arrive at a good solution for our real-world example.

3
Ensemble Methods for Multi-Class Classification

Our modern world is already interconnected with many devices for collecting data about human behavior - for example, our cell phones are small spies in our pockets tracking number of steps, route, or our eating habits. Even the watches that we wear now can track everything from the number of steps we take to our heart rate at any given moment in time.

In all these situations, the gadgets try to guess what the user is doing based on collected data to provide reports of the user's activities through the day. From a machine learning perspective, the task can be viewed as a classification problem: detecting patterns in collected data and assigning the right activity category to them (that is, swimming, running, sleeping). But importantly, it is still supervised problem - that means to train a model, we need to provide observations annotated by actual categories.

In this section, we are going to focus on ensemble methods for modeling problems of multi-class classification - sometimes referred to as multinomial classification - using a sensor dataset provided by the UCI dataset library.

 Note that multi-class classification should not be confused with multi-label classification whereby multiple labels can be predicted for a given example. For example, a blog post can be tagged with multiple labels as one blog can encompass any number of topics; however, in multi-class classification, we are *forced* to choose one out of N possible topics where N > 2 possible labels.

The reader is going to learn in this chapter about the following topics:

- Preparing data for multi-class classification, including handling missing values
- Multi-class classification using the Spark RF algorithm
- Evaluating the quality of Spark classification models using different measures
- Building H2O tree-based classification models and exploring their quality

Data

In this chapter, we are going to use **Physical Activity Monitoring Data Set** (**PAMAP2**) published in the Machine Learning Repository by the University of Irvine: `https://archive.ics.uci.edu/ml/datasets/PAMAP2+Physical+Activity+Monitoring`

The full dataset contains **52** input features and **3,850,505** events describing 18 different physical activities (for example, walking, cycling, running, `watching TV`). The data was recorded by a heart rate monitor and three inertial measurement units located on the wrist, chest, and dominant side's ankle. Each event is annotated by an activity label describing the ground truth and also a timestamp. The dataset contains missing values indicated by the value `NaN`. Furthermore, some columns produced by sensors are marked as invalid ("orientation" - see dataset description):

PAMAP2 Physical Activity Monitoring Data Set
Download: Data Folder, Data Set Description

Data Set Characteristics:	Multivariate, Time-Series	Number of Instances:	3850505	Area:	Computer
Attribute Characteristics:	Real	Number of Attributes:	52	Date Donated	2012-08-06
Associated Tasks:	Classification	Missing Values?	Yes	Number of Web Hits:	30797

Figure 1: Properties of dataset as published in the Machine Learning Repository of the University of Irvine.

The dataset represents the perfect example for activity recognition: we would like to train a robust model which would be able to predict a performed activity based on incoming data from physical sensors.

Furthermore, the dataset is spread over multiple files, each file representing measurements of a single subject, which is another real-life aspect of data produced by multiple data sources so we will need to utilize Spark's ability to read from a directory and merge the files to make training/test datasets.

The following lines show a sample of the data. There are a couple of important observations that are worth noting:

- Individual values are separated by an empty space character
- The first value in each row represents a timestamp, while the second value holds the `activityId`

```
199.38 0 NaN 34.1875 1.54285 7.86975 5.88674 1.57679 7.65264 5.84959
-0.0855996 ... 1 0 0 0
199.39 11 NaN 34.1875 1.46513 7.94554 5.80834 1.5336 7.81914 5.92477
-0.0907069 ... 1 0 0 0
199.4 11 NaN 34.1875 1.41585 7.82933 5.5001 1.56628 8.03042 6.01488
-0.0399161 ... 1 0 0 0
```

The `activityId` is represented by a numeric value; hence, we need a translation table to transform an ID to a corresponding activity label which the dataset gives and we show as follows:

1 lying	2 sitting
3 standing	4 walking
5 running	6 cycling
7 Nordic walking	9 watching TV
10 computer work	11 car driving
12 ascending stairs	13 descending stairs
16 vacuum cleaning	17 ironing
18 folding laundry	19 house cleaning
20 playing soccer	24 rope jumping
0 other (transient activities)	

The example lines represent one "other activity" and then two measurements representing "car driving".

The third column contains heart rate measurements, while the rest of the columns represent data from three different inertia measurements units: columns 4-20 are from the hand sensor, 21-37 contain data from chest sensor and finally the columns 38-54 hold ankle sensor measurements. Each sensor measures 17 different values including temperature, 3-D acceleration, gyroscope and magnetometer data, and orientation. However, the orientation columns are marked as invalid in this dataset.

The input data pack contains two different folders - protocol, and optional measurements which contains data from a few subjects who performed some additional activities. In this chapter, we are going to use only data from optional folder.

Modeling goal

In this example, we would like to build a model based on information about physical activities to classify unseen data and annotate it with the corresponding physical activity.

Challenges

For the sensor data, there are numerous way to explore and build models. In this chapter, we mainly focus on classification; however, there are several aspects which would need deeper exploration, especially the following:

- Training data represents a time-ordered flow of events, but we are not going to reflect the time information but look at the data as one complete piece of information
- The same for test data -a single activity event is a part of an event stream captured during performing an activity and it can be easier to categorize it with knowledge of actual context

Nevertheless, for now, we ignore the time dimension and apply classification to explore possible patterns in the sensor data which would characterize performed activities.

Machine learning workflow

To build an initial model, our workflow includes several steps:

1. Data load and preprocessing, often referenced as **extract-transform-load** (**ETL**).
   - Load
   - Parse
   - Handle missing values

2. Unify data into a form expected by an algorithm.
   - Model training
   - Model evaluation
   - Model deployment

Starting Spark shell

The first step is to prepare the Spark environment to perform analysis. As in the previous chapter, we are going to start Spark shell; however, in this case, the command line is slightly more complicated:

```
export SPARKLING_WATER_VERSION="2.1.12"
export SPARK_PACKAGES=\
"ai.h2o:sparkling-water-core_2.11:${SPARKLING_WATER_VERSION},\
ai.h2o:sparkling-water-repl_2.11:${SPARKLING_WATER_VERSION},\
ai.h2o:sparkling-water-ml_2.11:${SPARKLING_WATER_VERSION},\
com.packtpub:mastering-ml-w-spark-utils:1.0.0"

$SPARK_HOME/bin/spark-shell \
        --master 'local[*]' \
        --driver-memory 8g \
        --executor-memory 8g \
        --conf spark.executor.extraJavaOptions=-XX:MaxPermSize=384M
        \
        --conf spark.driver.extraJavaOptions=-XX:MaxPermSize=384M \
        --packages "$SPARK_PACKAGES"
```

In this case, we require more memory since we are going to load larger data. We also need to increase the size of PermGen - a part of JVM memory which stores information about loaded classes. This is only necessary if you are using Java 7.

The memory settings for Spark jobs are an important part of job launching. In the simple `local[*]`-based scenario as we are using, there is no difference between the Spark driver and executor. However, for a larger job deployed on a standalone or YARN Spark cluster, the configuration of driver memory and executor memory needs to reflect the size of the data and performed transformations.

Moreover, as we discussed in the previous chapter, you can mitigate memory pressure by using a clever caching strategy and the right cache destination (for example, disk, off-heap memory).

Exploring data

The first step involves data load. In the case of multiple files, the SparkContext's method `wholeTextFiles` provides the functionality we need. It reads each file as a single record and returns it as a key-value pair, where the key contains the location of the file and the value holds the file content. We can reference input files directly via the wildcard pattern `data/subject*`. This is not only useful during loading files from a local filesystem but especially important for loading files from HDFS as well.

```
val path = s"${sys.env.get("DATADIR").getOrElse("data")}/subject*"
val dataFiles = sc.wholeTextFiles(path)
println(s"Number of input files: ${dataFiles.count}")
```

Since the names are not part of the input data, we define a variable that is going to hold the column names:

```
val allColumnNames = Array(
  "timestamp", "activityId", "hr") ++ Array(
  "hand", "chest", "ankle").flatMap(sensor =>
    Array(
      "temp",
      "accel1X", "accel1Y", "accel1Z",
      "accel2X", "accel2Y", "accel2Z",
      "gyroX", "gyroY", "gyroZ",
      "magnetX", "magnetY", "magnetZ",
      "orientX", "orientY", "orientZ").
    map(name => s"${sensor}_${name}"))
```

We simply defined the first three column names, and then column names for each of three position sensors. Furthermore, we also prepared a list of column indexes which are useless for modeling, including timestamp and orientation data:

```
val ignoredColumns =
  Array(0,
    3 + 13, 3 + 14, 3 + 15, 3 + 16,
    20 + 13, 20 + 14, 20 + 15, 20 + 16,
    37 + 13, 37 + 14, 37 + 15, 37 + 16)
```

The next step is to process the content of the referenced files and create an RDD which we use as input for data exploration and modeling. Since we are expecting to iterate over the data several times and perform different transformations, we are going to cache the data in memory:

```
val rawData = dataFiles.flatMap { case (path, content) =>
  content.split("\n")
}.map { row =>
  row.split(" ").map(_.trim).
  zipWithIndex.
  map(v => if (v.toUpperCase == "NAN") Double.NaN else v.toDouble).
  collect {
    case (cell, idx) if !ignoredColumns.contains(idx) => cell
  }
}
rawData.cache()

println(s"Number of rows: ${rawData.count}")
```

The output is as follows:

```
Number of rows: 977972
```

In this case, for each key-value pair we extract its content and split it based on line boundaries. Then we transform each line based on the file delimiter, which is a space between features. Since the files contains only numeric values and the string value NaN as a marker for missing values, we can simply transform all values into Java's Double, leaving Double.NaN as a representation for a missing value.

We can see our input file has 977,972 rows. During loading, we also skipped the timestamp column and columns which were marked as invalid in the dataset description (see the ignoredColumns array).

The RDD's interface follows the design principle of functional programming, the same principle which is adopted by the Scala programming language. This shared concept brings a uniform API for manipulating data structures; on the other hand, it is always good to know when an operation is invoked on a local object (array, list, sequence) and when it causes a distribution operation (RDD).

To keep our view of the dataset consistent, we also need to filter column names based on the list of ignored columns which was prepared in previous steps:

```
import org.apache.spark.utils.Tabulizer._
val columnNames = allColumnNames.
  zipWithIndex.
  filter { case (_, idx) => !ignoredColumns.contains(idx) }.
  map { case (name, _) => name }

println(s"Column names:${table(columnNames, 4, None)}")
```

The output is as follows:

```
Column names:
+--------------+--------------+--------------+--------------+
|    activityId|           hr|     hand_temp| hand_accel1X|
| hand_accel1Y| hand_accel1Z| hand_accel2X| hand_accel2Y|
| hand_accel2Z|   hand_gyroX|   hand_gyroY|   hand_gyroZ|
| hand_magnetX| hand_magnetY| hand_magnetZ|   chest_temp|
|chest_accel1X|chest_accel1Y|chest_accel1Z|chest_accel2X|
|chest_accel2Y|chest_accel2Z|  chest_gyroX|  chest_gyroY|
|  chest_gyroZ|chest_magnetX|chest_magnetY|chest_magnetZ|
|   ankle_temp|ankle_accel1X|ankle_accel1Y|ankle_accel1Z|
|ankle_accel2X|ankle_accel2Y|ankle_accel2Z|  ankle_gyroX|
|  ankle_gyroY|  ankle_gyroZ|ankle_magnetX|ankle_magnetY|
|ankle_magnetZ|           -|           -|           -|
+--------------+--------------+--------------+--------------+
```

It is always good to get rid of data which is useless for modeling. The motivation is to mitigate memory pressure during computation and modeling. For example, good targets for data removal are columns which contain random IDs, timestamps, constant columns, or columns which are already represented in the dataset.

From an intuitive point of view also, modelling ID terms, for example, doesn't make a lot of sense given the nature of the field. Feature selection is a hugely important topic and one that we will spend a great deal of time on later in the book.

Now let's look at the distribution of the individual activities in our dataset. We are going to use the same trick as in the previous chapter; however, we also would like to see actual names of activities instead of pure number-based representation. Hence, at first we define mapping describing a relation between an activity number and its name:

```
val activities = Map(
  1 -> "lying", 2 -> "sitting", 3 -> "standing", 4 -> "walking",
  5 -> "running", 6 -> "cycling", 7 -> "Nordic walking",
  9 -> "watching TV", 10 -> "computer work", 11 -> "car driving",
  12 -> "ascending stairs", 13 -> "descending stairs",
  16 -> "vacuum cleaning", 17 -> "ironing",
  18 -> "folding laundry", 19 -> "house cleaning",
  20 -> "playing soccer", 24 -> "rope jumping", 0 -> "other")
```

Then we compute the number of individual activities in the data with the help of the Spark method `reduceByKey`:

```
val dataActivityId = rawData.map(l => l(0).toInt)

val activityIdCounts = dataActivityId.
  map(n => (n, 1)).
  reduceByKey(_ + _)

val activityCounts = activityIdCounts.
  collect.
  sortBy { case (activityId, count) =>
    -count
}.map { case (activityId, count) =>
  (activitiesMap(activityId), count)
}

println(s"Activities distribution:${table({activityCounts})}")
```

The command computes the count of individual activities, translates the activity number to its label, and sorts the result in descending order based on counts:

```
Activities distribution:
+--------------+------+
|  computer work|309935|
|          other|195891|
| house cleaning|187188|
|folding laundry| 99878|
|    watching TV| 83646|
|    car driving| 54519|
| playing soccer| 46915|
+--------------+------+
```

Or visualized based on activity frequencies as shown in *Figure 2*.

Figure 2: Frequencies of different activities in input data.

It is always good to think about the order of the individual transformations which are applied on the data. In the preceding example, we applied the sortBy transformation after collecting all data locally with help of the Spark collect action. In this context, it makes perfect sense since we know that the result of the collect action is reasonably small (we have only 22 activity labels) and sortBy is applied on the local collection. On the other hand, putting sortBy before the collect action would force invocation of Spark RDD's transformation and scheduling sort as Spark distributed task.

Missing data

The data description mentions that sensors used for activity tracking were not fully reliable and results contain missing data. We need to explore them in more detail to see how this fact can influence our modeling strategy.

The first question is how many missing values are in our dataset. We know from the data description that all missing values are marked by the string NaN (that is, not a number), which is now represented as Double.NaN in the RDD rawData. In the next code snippet, we compute the number of missing values per row and the total number of missing values in the dataset:

```
val nanCountPerRow = rawData.map { row =>
  row.foldLeft(0) { case (acc, v) =>
    acc + (if (v.isNaN) 1 else 0)
  }
}
val nanTotalCount = nanCount.sum

val ncols = rawData.take(1)(0).length
val nrows = rawData.count

val nanRatio = 100.0 * nanTotalCount / (ncols * nrows)

println(f"""|NaN count = ${nanTotalCount}%.0f
            |NaN ratio = ${nanRatio}%.2f %%""".stripMargin)
```

The output is as follows:

```
NaN count = 937450
NaN ratio = 2.34 %
```

Right, now we have overall knowledge about the amount of missing values in our data. But we do not know how the missing values are distributed. Are they spread uniformly over the whole dataset? Or are there rows/columns which contain more missing values? In the following text, we will try to find answers to these questions.

> A common mistake is to compare a numeric value and `Double.NaN` with comparison operators. For example, the `if (v == Double.NaN) { ... }` is wrong, since the Java specification says:
> "NaN is unordered: (1) The numerical comparison operators <, <=, >, and >= return `false` if either or both operands are NaN, (2) The equality operator == returns `false` if either operand is NaN."
> Hence, `Double.NaN == Double.NaN` returns always `false`. The right way to compare numeric values with `Double.NaN` is to use the method isNaN: `if (v.isNaN) { ... }` (or use the corresponding static method `java.lang.Double.isNaN`).

At first, considering rows we have already computed numbers of missing values per row in the previous step. Sorting them and taking the unique values give us an understanding of how rows are affected by missing values:

```
val nanRowDistribution = nanCountPerRow.
  map( count => (count, 1)).
  reduceByKey(_ + _).sortBy(-_._1).collect
```

```
println(s"${table(Seq("#NaN","#Rows"), nanRowDistribution, Map.empty[Int,
String])}")
```

The output is as follows:

```
+----+------+
|#NaN| #Rows|
+----+------+
|  40|   104|
|  39|     3|
|  27|    40|
|  26|     4|
|  14|  3049|
|  13|   293|
|   1|885494|
|   0| 88985|
+----+------+
```

Now we can see that the majority of rows contain a single missing value. However, there are lot of rows containing 13 or 14 missing values, or even 40 rows containing 27 *NaNs* and 107 rows which contain more than 30 missing values (104 rows with 40 missing values, and 3 rows with 39 missing values). Considering that the dataset contains 41 columns, it means there are 107 rows which are useless (majority of values are missing), leaving 3,386 rows with at least two missing values which need attention, and 885,494 rows with a single missing value. We can now look at these rows in more detail. We select all rows which contain more missing values than a given threshold, for example, 26. We also collect the index of the rows (it is a zero-based index!):

```
val nanRowThreshold = 26
val badRows = nanCountPerRow.zipWithIndex.zip(rawData).filter(_._1._1 >
nanRowThreshold).sortBy(-_._1._1)
println(s"Bad rows (#NaN, Row Idx, Row):\n${badRows.collect.map(x => (x._1,
x._2.mkString(","))).mkString("\n")}")
```

Now we know exactly which rows are not useful. We have already observed that there are 107 bad rows which do not contain any useful information. Furthermore, we can see that lines which have 27 missing values have them in the places representing hand and ankle IMU sensors.

And finally, most of the lines have assigned `activityId` 10, 19, or 20, which represents `computer work`, `house cleaning`, and `playing soccer` activities, which are classes with top frequencies in dataset. That can lead us to theory that the "bad" lines were produced by explicitly rejecting a measurement device by subjects. Furthermore, we can also see the index of each wrong row and verify them in the input dataset. For now, we are going to leave the bad rows and focus on columns.

We can ask the same question about columns - are there any columns which contain a higher amount of missing values? Can we remove such columns? We can start by collecting the number of missing values per column:

```
val nanCountPerColumn = rawData.map { row =>
   row.map(v => if (v.isNaN) 1 else 0)
}.reduce((v1, v2) => v1.indices.map(i => v1(i) + v2(i)).toArray)

println(s"""Number of missing values per column:
      ^${table(columnNames.zip(nanCountPerColumn).map(t => (t._1, t._2,
"%.2f%%".format(100.0 * t._2 / nrows))).sortBy(-_._2))}
      ^""".stripMargin('^'))
```

The output is as follows:

```
Number of missing values per column:
+-------------+------+------+
|           hr|888687|90.87%|
|   ankle_temp|  1807| 0.18%|
| ankle_accel1X|  1807| 0.18%|
| ankle_accel1Y|  1807| 0.18%|
| ankle_accel1Z|  1807| 0.18%|
| ankle_accel2X|  1807| 0.18%|
| ankle_accel2Y|  1807| 0.18%|
| ankle_accel2Z|  1807| 0.18%|
|   ankle_gyroX|  1807| 0.18%|
|   ankle_gyroY|  1807| 0.18%|
|   ankle_gyroZ|  1807| 0.18%|
| ankle_magnetX|  1807| 0.18%|
| ankle_magnetY|  1807| 0.18%|
| ankle_magnetZ|  1807| 0.18%|
|    hand_temp|  1197| 0.12%|
|  hand_accel1X|  1197| 0.12%|
|  hand_accel1Y|  1197| 0.12%|
|  hand_accel1Z|  1197| 0.12%|
|  hand_accel2X|  1197| 0.12%|
|  hand_accel2Y|  1197| 0.12%|
|  hand_accel2Z|  1197| 0.12%|
|    hand_gyroX|  1197| 0.12%|
|    hand_gyroY|  1197| 0.12%|
|    hand_gyroZ|  1197| 0.12%|
|  hand_magnetX|  1197| 0.12%|
|  hand_magnetY|  1197| 0.12%|
|  hand_magnetZ|  1197| 0.12%|
|   chest_temp|   747| 0.08%|
| chest_accel1X|   747| 0.08%|
| chest_accel1Y|   747| 0.08%|
| chest_accel1Z|   747| 0.08%|
| chest_accel2X|   747| 0.08%|
| chest_accel2Y|   747| 0.08%|
| chest_accel2Z|   747| 0.08%|
|   chest_gyroX|   747| 0.08%|
|   chest_gyroY|   747| 0.08%|
|   chest_gyroZ|   747| 0.08%|
| chest_magnetX|   747| 0.08%|
| chest_magnetY|   747| 0.08%|
| chest_magnetZ|   747| 0.08%|
|   activityId|     0| 0.00%|
+-------------+------+------+
```

The result shows that the second column (do not forget that we have already removed invalid columns during data load), which represents subjects' heart rate, contains lot of missing values. More than 90% of values are marked by `NaN`, which was probably caused by a measurement process of the experiment (subjects probably do not wear the heart rate monitor during usual daily activities but only when practicing sport).

The rest of the columns contain sporadic missing values.

Another important observation is that the first column containing `activityId` does not include any missing values - that is good news and means that all observations were properly annotated and we do not need to drop any of them (for example, without a training target, we cannot train a model).

The RDD's `reduce` method represents action. That means it forces evaluation of the RDD and the result of the reduce is a single value and not RDD. Do not confuse it with `reduceByKey` which is an RDD operation and returns a new RDD of key-value pairs.

The next step is to decide what to do with missing data. There are many strategies to adopt; however we need to preserve the meaning of our data.

We can simply drop all rows or columns which contain missing data - a very common approach as a matter of fact! It makes good sense for rows which are polluted by too many missing values but this is not a good global strategy in this case since we observed that missing values are spread over almost all columns and rows. Hence, we need a better strategy for handling missing values.

A summary of missing values sources and imputation methods is available, for example, in the book *Data Analysis Using Regression and Mutlilevel/Hierarchical Models* by A. Gelman and J. Hill (`http://www.stat.columbia.edu/~gelman/arm/missing.pdf`) or in the presentation `https://www.amstat.org/sections/srms/webinarfiles/ModernMethodWebinarMay2012.pdf` or `https://www.utexas.edu/cola/prc/_files/cs/Missing-Data.pdf`.

Considering the heart rate column first, we cannot drop it since there is an obvious link between higher heart rate and practiced activity. However, we can still fill missing values with a reasonable constant. In the context of the heart rate, replacing missing values with the mean value of column values - a technique sometimes referred to as *mean computation of missing values* - can make good sense. We can compute it with the following lines of code:

```
val heartRateColumn = rawData.
  map(row => row(1)).
```

```
    filter(_.isNaN).
    map(_.toInt)

val heartRateValues = heartRateColumn.collect
val meanHeartRate = heartRateValues.sum / heartRateValues.count
scala.util.Sorting.quickSort(heartRateValues)
val medianHeartRate = heartRateValues(heartRateValues.length / 2)

println(s"Mean heart rate: ${meanHeartRate}")
println(s"Median heart rate: ${medianHeartRate}")
```

The output is as follows:

```
Mean heart rate: 92
Median heart rate: 87
```

We can see that `mean heart rate` is quite a high value, which reflects the fact that heart rate measurements are mainly associated with sport activities (a reader can verify that). But, for example, considering the activity `watching TV`, the value over 90 is slightly higher than the expected value, since the average resting rate is between 60 and 100 (based on Wikipedia).

So for this case, we can replace missing heart rate values with mean resting rate (80) or we can take the computed mean value of heart rate. Later, we will impute the computed mean value and compare or combine the results (this is called, multiple imputation method). Or we can append a column which marks a line with missing value (see, for example, https://www.utexas.edu/cola/prc/_files/cs/Missing-Data.pdf).

The next step is to replace missing values in the rest of the columns. We should perform the same analysis that we did for the heart rate column and see if there is a pattern in missing data or if they are just missing at random. For example, we can explore a dependency between missing value and our prediction target (in this case, `activityId`). Hence, we collect a number of missing values per column again; however, now we also remember `activityId` with each missing value:

```
def inc[K,V](l: Seq[(K, V)], v: (K, V)) // (3)
            (implicit num: Numeric[V]): Seq[(K,V)] =
  if (l.exists(_._1 == v._1)) l.map(e => e match {
    case (v._1, n) => (v._1, num.plus(n, v._2))
    case t => t
  }) else l ++ Seq(v)

val distribTemplate = activityIdCounts.collect.map { case (id, _) => (id,
0) }.toSeq
```

```
    val nanColumnDistribV1 = rawData.map { row => // (1)
      val activityId = row(0).toInt
      row.drop(1).map { v =>
        if (v.isNaN) inc(distribTemplate, (activityId, 1)) else
distribTemplate
      } // Tip: Make sure that we are returning same type
    }.reduce { (v1, v2) =>   // (2)
      v1.indices.map(idx => v1(idx).foldLeft(v2(idx))(inc)).toArray
    }

    println(s"""
          ^NaN Column x Response distribution V1:
          ^${table(Seq(distribTemplate.map(v => activitiesMap(v._1)))
                  ++ columnNames.drop(1).zip(nanColumnDistribV1).map(v =>
Seq(v._1) ++ v._2.map(_._2)), true)}
          """.stripMargin('^'))
```

The output is as follows:

```
NaN Column x Response distribution V1:

+--------------+---------------+---------------+--------------+---------------+-------------+-------------+
|              |other|folding laundry|playing soccer|computer work|house cleaning|car driving|watching TV|
+--------------+---------------+---------------+--------------+---------------+-------------+-------------+
|           hr|  178025|         90747|        42632|         281645|       170104|       49535|
|    hand_temp|     453|            64|          378|            172|          113|          15|
|  hand_accel1X|     453|            64|          378|            172|          113|          15|
|  hand_accel1Y|     453|            64|          378|            172|          113|          15|
|  hand_accel1Z|     453|            64|          378|            172|          113|          15|
|  hand_accel2X|     453|            64|          378|            172|          113|          15|
|  hand_accel2Y|     453|            64|          378|            172|          113|          15|
|  hand_accel2Z|     453|            64|          378|            172|          113|          15|
|    hand_gyroX|     453|            64|          378|            172|          113|          15|
|    hand_gyroY|     453|            64|          378|            172|          113|          15|
|    hand_gyroZ|     453|            64|          378|            172|          113|          15|
|  hand_magnetX|     453|            64|          378|            172|          113|          15|
|  hand_magnetY|     453|            64|          378|            172|          113|          15|
|  hand_magnetZ|     453|            64|          378|            172|          113|          15|
|    chest_temp|     109|            46|          256|            145|          122|          56|
|chest_accel1X|     109|            46|          256|            145|          122|          56|
|chest_accel1Y|     109|            46|          256|            145|          122|          56|
|chest_accel1Z|     109|            46|          256|            145|          122|          56|
|chest_accel2X|     109|            46|          256|            145|          122|          56|
|chest_accel2Y|     109|            46|          256|            145|          122|          56|
|chest_accel2Z|     109|            46|          256|            145|          122|          56|
```

The preceding code is slightly more complicated and deserves explanation. The call (1) transforms each value in a row into a sequence of (K, V) pairs where K represents the `activityId` stored in the row, and V is 1 if a corresponding column contains a missing value, else it is 0. Then the reduce method (2) recursively transforms row values represented by sequences into the final results, where each column has associated a distribution represented by a sequence of (K, V) pairs where K is `activityId` and V represents the number of missing values in rows with the `activityId`. The method is straightforward but overcomplicated using a non-trivial function `inc` (3). Furthermore, this naive solution is highly memory-inefficient, since for each column we duplicate information about `activityId`.

Hence, we can reiterate the naive solution by slightly changing the result representation by not computing distribution per column, but by counting all columns, missing value count per `activityId`:

```
val nanColumnDistribV2 = rawData.map(row => {
    val activityId = row(0).toInt
    (activityId, row.drop(1).map(v => if (v.isNaN) 1 else 0))
}).reduceByKey( (v1, v2) =>
    v1.indices.map(idx => v1(idx) + v2(idx)).toArray
).map { case (activityId, d) =>
    (activitiesMap(activityId), d)
}.collect

println(s"""
        ^NaN Column x Response distribution V2:
        ^${table(Seq(columnNames.toSeq) ++ nanColumnDistribV2.map(v =>
Seq(v._1) ++ v._2), true)}
        """.stripMargin('^'))
```

In this case, the result is an array of key-value pairs, where key is activity name, and value contains representing distribution of missing value in individual columns. Simply by running both samples, we can observe that the first one takes much more time than the second one. Also, the first one has higher memory demands and is much more complicated.

Finally, we can visualize the result as a heatmap where the x axis corresponds to columns and the y axis represents activities as shown in *Figure 3*. Such graphical representation gives us a comprehensible overview of how missing values are correlated with response column:

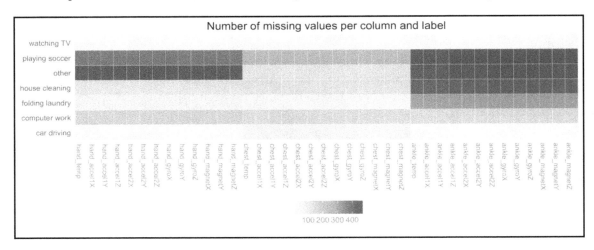

Figure 3: Heatmap showing number of missing values in each column grouped by activity.

The generated heatmap nicely shows the correlation of missing values. We can see that missing values are connected to sensors. If a sensor is not available or malfunctioning, then all measured values are not available. For example, this is visible for ankle sensor and playing soccer, other activities. On the other hand, the activity watching TV does not indicate any missing value pattern connected to a sensor.

Moreover, there is no other directly visible connection between missing data and activity. Hence, for now, we can decide to fill missing values with 0.0 to express that a missing sensor provides default values. However, our goal is to be flexible to experiment with different imputation strategies later (for example, imputing mean value of observation with the same activityId).

Summary of missing value analysis

We can now summarize all facts which we learned about missing values:

- There are 107 rows which are useless and need to be filtered out
- There are 44 rows with 26 or 27 missing values. These rows seem useless, so we are going to filter them out.

- The heart rate column contains the majority of missing values. Since we expect that the column contains important information which can help to distinguish between different sport activities, we are not going to ignore the column. However, we are going to impute the missing value based on different strategies:
  - Mean resting heart rate based on medical research
  - `mean heart rate` computed from available data
  - There is a pattern in the missing values in the rest of the columns - missing values are strictly linked to a sensor. We replace all these missing values with the value `0.0`.

Data unification

This exploratory analysis gives us an overview about shape of the data and the actions which we need to perform to deal with missing values. However, we still need to transform the data into a form expected by Spark algorithms. That includes:

- Handling missing values
- Handling categorical values

Missing values

The missing value handling step is easy, since we already performed missing value exploration and summarized the required transformations in the previous section. The following steps are going to implement them.

First, we define a list of imputed values - for each column, we assign a single `Double` value:

```
val imputedValues = columnNames.map {
  _ match {
    case "hr" => 60.0
    case _ => 0.0
  }
}
```

And a function which allow us to inject the values into our dataset:

```
import org.apache.spark.rdd.RDD
def imputeNaN(
  data: RDD[Array[Double]],
  values: Array[Double]): RDD[Array[Double]] = {
    data.map { row =>
      row.indices.map { i =>
        if (row(i).isNaN) values(i)
```

```
      else row(i)
    }.toArray
  }
}
```

The defined function accepts a Spark `RDD` where each row is represented as an array of `Double` numbers, and a parameter which contains values to replace the missing value for each column.

In the next step, we define a row filter - a method which removes all rows which contain more missing values than a given threshold. In this case, we can easily reuse the already computed value `nanCountPerRow`:

```
def filterBadRows(
  rdd: RDD[Array[Double]],
  nanCountPerRow: RDD[Int],
  nanThreshold: Int): RDD[Array[Double]] = {
    rdd.zip(nanCountPerRow).filter { case (row, nanCount) =>
      nanCount > nanThreshold
  }.map { case (row, _) =>
        row
  }
}
```

> Please notice that we parameterize defined transformations. It is good practice to keep code flexible enough to permit further experimentation with parameters. On the other hand, it is good to avoid building a complex framework. The rule of thumb is to parameterize functionality which we would like to use in different contexts or we need to have a freedom in configuring code constants.

Categorical values

Spark algorithms can handle different forms of categorical features, but they need to be transformed into a form expected by an algorithm. For example, decision trees can handle categorical features as they are; on the other hand, linear regression or neural networks need to expand categorical values into binary columns.

In this example, the good news is that all input features in our dataset are continuous. However, the target feature - `activityId` - represents multi-class features. The Spark MLlib classification guide (`https://spark.apache.org/docs/latest/mllib-linear-methods.html#classification`) says:

> *"The training data set is represented by an RDD of LabeledPoint in MLlib, where labels are class indices starting from zero."*

But our dataset contains different numbers of activityIds - see the computed variable `activityIdCounts`. Hence, we need to transform them into a form expected by MLlib by defining a map from `activityId` to `activityIdx`:

```
val activityId2Idx = activityIdCounts.
  map(_._1).
  collect.
  zipWithIndex.
  toMap
```

Final transformation

Finally, we can compose all the defined functionality together and prepare the data for model building. First, the `rawData` RDD is filtered and all bad rows are removed with the help of `filterBadRows`, then the result is processed by the `imputeNaN` method which injects given values at the location of missing values:

```
val processedRawData = imputeNaN(
  filterBadRows(rawData, nanCountPerRow, nanThreshold = 26),
  imputedValues)
```

At the end, verify that we invoked the right transformations by at least computing the number of rows:

```
println(s"Number of rows before/after: ${rawData.count} / ${
processedRawData.count}")
```

The output is as follows:

```
Number of rows before/after: 977972 / 977821
```

We can see that we filtered out 151 rows ,which corresponds to our preceding observations.

Understanding data is the key point of data science. It involves also understanding missing data. Never skip this stage since it can lead to biased models giving too good results. And, as we continuously point out, not understanding your data will lead you to ask poor questions which ultimately results in lackluster answers.

Modelling data with Random Forest

Random Forest is an algorithm which can be used for different problems - binomial as we showed in the previous chapter, regression, or multiclass classification. The beauty of Random Forest is that it combines multiple weak learners represented by decision trees into one ensemble.

Furthermore, to reduce variance of individual decision trees, the algorithms use the concept of bagging (Bootstrap aggregation). Each decision tree is trained on a subset of data generated by random selection with replacement.

Do not confuse bagging with boosting. Boosting incrementally builds an ensemble by training each new model to emphasize observations that previous model misclassified. Typically, after a weak model is added into the ensemble, the data is reweighted, observations that are misclassified gain weight, and vice versa. Furthermore, bagging can be invoked in parallel while boosting is a sequential process. Nevertheless, the goal of boosting is the same as of bagging - combine predictions of several weak models in order to improve generalization and robustness over a single model.

An example of a boosting method is a **Gradient Boosting Machine (GBM)** which uses the boosting method to combine weak models (decision trees) into an ensemble; however, it generalizes the approach by allowing the use of an arbitrary loss function: instead of trying to correct the previous weak model misclassified observations, the GBM allows you to minimize a specified loss function (for example, mean squared error for regression).

There are different variations of GBM - for example, stochastic GBM which combines boosting with bagging. The regular GBM and also stochastic GBM are available in H2O's machine learning toolbox. Furthermore, it is important to mention that GBM (as well as RandomForest) is an algorithm which builds pretty good models without extensive tuning.
More information about GBM is available in original paper of J.H. Friedman: *Greedy Function Approximation: A Gradient Boosting Machine* http://www-stat.stanford.edu/~jhf/ftp/trebst.pdf.

Moreover, RandomForest employs so-called "feature bagging" - while building a decision tree, it selects a random subset of feature to make a split decision. The motivation is to build a weak learner and enhance generalization - for example, if one of the features is a strong predictor for given target variable, it would be selected by the majority of trees, resulting in highly similar trees. However, by random selection of features, the algorithm can avoid the strong predictor and build trees which find a finer-grained structure of data.

RandomForest also helps easily select the most predictive feature since it allows for computation of variable importance in different ways. For example, computing an overall feature impurity gain over all trees gives a good estimate of how the strong feature is.

From an implementation point of view, RandomForest can be easily parallelized since the *built trees* step is independent. On the other hand, distributing RandomForest computation is slightly harder problem, since each tree needs to explore almost the full set of data.

The disadvantage of RandomForest is complicated interpretability. The resulting ensemble is hard to explore and explain interactions between individual trees. However, it is still one of the best models to use if we need to obtain a good model without advanced parameters tuning.

A good source of information about RandomForest is the original paper of Leo Breiman and Adele Cutler available, for example, here:
https://www.stat.berkeley.edu/~breiman/RandomForests/cc_home.htm
.

Building a classification model using Spark RandomForest

In the previous section, we explored data and unified it into a form without missing values. We still need to transform the data into a form expected by Spark MLlib. As explained in the previous chapter, it involves the creation of RDD of LabeledPoints. Each LabeledPoint is defined by a label and a vector defining input features. The label serves as a training target for model builders and it references the index of categorical variables (see prepared transformation activityId2Idx):

```
import org.apache.spark.mllib
import org.apache.spark.mllib.regression.LabeledPoint
import org.apache.spark.mllib.linalg.Vectors
import org.apache.spark.mllib.tree.RandomForest
import org.apache.spark.mllib.util.MLUtils

val data = processedRawData.map { r =>
    val activityId = r(0)
    val activityIdx = activityId2Idx(activityId)
    val features = r.drop(1)
    LabeledPoint(activityIdx, Vectors.dense(features))
}
```

The next step is to prepare data for training and model validation. We simply split the data into two parts: 80% for training and the remaining 20% for validation:

```
val splits = data.randomSplit(Array(0.8, 0.2))
val (trainingData, testData) =
    (splits(0), splits(1))
```

And after this step we are ready to invoke the modeling part of the workflow. The strategy for building a Spark RandomForest model is the same as GBM we showed in the previous chapter by calling the static method trainClassifier on object RandomForest:

```
import org.apache.spark.mllib.tree.configuration._
import org.apache.spark.mllib.tree.impurity._
val rfStrategy = new Strategy(
  algo = Algo.Classification,
  impurity = Entropy,
  maxDepth = 10,
  maxBins = 20,
  numClasses = activityId2Idx.size,
  categoricalFeaturesInfo = Map[Int, Int](),
  subsamplingRate = 0.68)

val rfModel = RandomForest.trainClassifier(
```

```
input = trainingData,
strategy = rfStrategy,
numTrees = 50,
featureSubsetStrategy = "auto",
seed = 42)
```

In this example, the parameters are split into two sets:

- Strategy which defines common parameters for building a decision tree
- RandomForest specific parameters

The strategy parameter list overlaps with the parameter list of decision tree algorithms discussed in the previous chapter:

- `input`: References training data represented by RDD of `LabeledPoints`.
- `numClasses`: Number of output classes. In this case we model only classes which are included in the input data.
- `categoricalFeaturesInfo`: Map of categorical features and their arity. We don't have categorical features in input data, that is why we pass an empty map.
- `impurity`: Impurity measure used for tree node splitting.
- `subsamplingRate`: A fraction of training data used for building a single decision tree.
- `maxDepth`: Maximum depth of a single tree. Deep trees have tendency to encode input data and overfit. On the other hand, overfitting in RandomForest is balanced by assembling multiple trees together. Furthermore, larger trees means longer training time and higher memory footprint.
- `maxBins`: Continuous features are transformed into ordered discretized features with at most `maxBins` possible values. The discretization is done before each node split.

The RandomForest - specific parameters are the following:

- `numTrees`: Number of trees in the resulting forest. Increasing the number of trees decreases model variance.
- `featureSubsetStrategy`: Specifies a method which produces a number of how many features are selected for training a single tree. For example: "sqrt" is normally used for classification, while "onethird" for regression problems. See value of `RandomForest.supportedFeatureSubsetStrategies` for available values.
- `seed`: Seed for random generator initialization, since RandomForest depends on random selection of features and rows.

The parameters `numTrees` and `maxDepth` are often referenced as stopping criteria. Spark also provides additional parameters to stop tree growing and produce fine-grained trees:

- `minInstancesPerNode`: A node is not split anymore, if it would provide left or right nodes which would contain smaller number of observations than the value specified by this parameter. Default value is 1, but typically for regression problems or large trees, the value should be higher.
- `minInfoGain`: Minimum information gain a split must get. Default value is 0.0.

Furthermore, Spark RandomForest accepts parameters which influence the performance of execution (see Spark documentation).

RandomForest is by definition an algorithm which depends on randomization. However, having non-deterministic runs is not the right behavior if you are trying to reproduce results or test corner cases. In this case, the seed parameter provides a way of fixing execution and providing deterministic results.

This is a common practice for non-deterministic algorithms; however, it is not enough if the algorithm is parallelized and its result depends on thread scheduling. In this case, ad-hoc methods need to be adopted (for example, limit parallelization by having only one computation thread, limit parallelization by limiting number of input partitions, or switching task scheduler to provide a fix schedule).

Classification model evaluation

Now, when we have a model, we need to evaluate the quality of the model to decide whether the model is good enough for our needs. Keep in mind, that all quality metrics connected to a model need to be considered in your specific context and evaluated with respect to your target objective (such as sales increase, fraud detection, and so on).

Spark model metrics

At first, use the embedded model metrics which the Spark API provides. We are going to use the same approach that we used in the previous chapter. We start by defining a method to extract model metrics for a given model and dataset:

```
import org.apache.spark.mllib.evaluation._
import org.apache.spark.mllib.tree.model._
def getMetrics(model: RandomForestModel, data: RDD[LabeledPoint]):
    MulticlassMetrics = {
```

```
        val predictionsAndLabels = data.map(example =>
            (model.predict(example.features), example.label)
        )
        new MulticlassMetrics(predictionsAndLabels)
    }
```

Then we can directly compute Spark `MulticlassMetrics`:

```
val rfModelMetrics = getMetrics(rfModel, testData)
```

And look at first interesting classification model metrics called `Confusion matrix`. It is represented by the type `org.apache.spark.mllib.linalg.Matrix` allowing you to perform algebraic operations:

```
println(s"""|Confusion matrix:
  |${rfModelMetrics.confusionMatrix}""".stripMargin)
```

The output is as follows:

```
Confusion matrix (Rows x Columns = Actual x Predicted):
36266.0  1409.0   454.0    14.0     1004.0   1.0      0.0
920.0    19026.0  0.0      0.0      67.0     0.0      0.0
53.0     0.0      9230.0   0.0      0.0      0.0      0.0
853.0    0.0      6.0      60960.0  119.0    0.0      0.0
1076.0   3.0      0.0      0.0      36177.0  0.0      0.0
198.0    0.0      0.0      0.0      1.0      10619.0  0.0
327.0    0.0      0.0      0.0      51.0     0.0      16231.0
```

In this case, Spark prints predicted classes in columns. The predicted classes are stored in the field `labels` of the object `rfModelMetrics`. However, the field contains only translated indexes (see the created variable `activityId2Idx`). Nevertheless, we can easily create a function to transform the label index to an actual label string:

```
def idx2Activity(idx: Double): String =
  activityId2Idx.
  find(e => e._2 == idx.asInstanceOf[Int]).
  map(e => activitiesMap(e._1)).
  getOrElse("UNKNOWN")

val rfCMLabels = rfModelMetrics.labels.map(idx2Activity(_))
println(s"""|Labels:
  |${rfCMLabels.mkString(", ")}""".stripMargin)
```

The output is as follows:

```
Labels:
other, folding laundry, playing soccer, computer work, house cleaning, car driving, watching TV
```

For example, we can see that other activity was mispredicted many times with other activities - it was predicted correctly for 36455 cases; however, for 1261 cases the model predicted the other activity, but actual activity was house cleaning. On the other hand, the model predicted the activity folding laundry instead of the other activity.

You can directly see that we can directly compute overall prediction accuracy based on correctly predicted activities located on the diagonal of the Confusion matrix:

```
val rfCM = rfModelMetrics.confusionMatrix
val rfCMTotal = rfCM.toArray.sum
val rfAccuracy = (0 until rfCM.numCols).map(i => rfCM(i,i)).sum / rfCMTotal
println(f"RandomForest accuracy = ${rfAccuracy*100}%.2f %%")
```

The output is as follows:

```
RandomForest accuracy = 96.64 %
```

However, the overall accuracy can be misleading in cases of classes are not evenly distributed (for example, most of the instances are represented by a single class). In such cases, overall accuracy can be confusing, since the model just predicting a dominant class would provide a high accuracy. Hence, we can look at our predictions in more detail and explore accuracy per individual class. However, first we look at the distribution of actual labels and predicted labels to see (1) if there is a dominant class and (2) if model preserves input distribution of classes and is not skewed towards predicting a single class:

```
import org.apache.spark.mllib.linalg.Matrix
 def colSum(m: Matrix, colIdx: Int) = (0 until m.numRows).map(m(_,
colIdx)).sum
 def rowSum(m: Matrix, rowIdx: Int) = (0 until m.numCols).map(m(rowIdx,
_)).sum
 val rfCMActDist = (0 until rfCM.numRows).map(rowSum(rfCM, _)/rfCMTotal)
 val rfCMPredDist = (0 until rfCM.numCols).map(colSum(rfCM, _)/rfCMTotal)

 println(s"""^Class distribution
            ^${table(Seq("Class", "Actual", "Predicted"),
                   rfCMLabels.zip(rfCMActDist.zip(rfCMPredDist)).map(p
=> (p._1, p._2._1, p._2._2)),
                   Map(1 -> "%.2f", 2 -> "%.2f"))}
```

```
""".stripMargin('^'))
```

The output is as follows:

```
Class distribution

+----------------+------+---------+
|           Class|Actual|Predicted|
+----------------+------+---------+
|           other| 0.20|     0.20|
|  folding laundry| 0.10|     0.10|
|   playing soccer| 0.05|     0.05|
|    computer work| 0.32|     0.31|
|   house cleaning| 0.19|     0.19|
|      car driving| 0.06|     0.05|
|      watching TV| 0.09|     0.08|
+----------------+------+---------+
```

We can easily see that there is no dominant class; however, the classes are not uniformly distributed. It is also worth noticing that the model preserves distribution of actual classes and there is no trend to prefer a single class. This just confirms our observation based on the Confusion matrix.

And finally, we can look at individual classes and compute precision (aka positive predictive value), recall (or so-called sensitivity) and F-1 score. To remind definitions from the previous chapter: precision is a fraction of the correct predictions for a given class (that is, TP/TP+TF), while recall is defined as a fraction of all class instances that were correctly predicted (that is, TP/TP+FN). And finally, the F-1 score combines both of them since it is computed as the weighted harmonic mean of precision and recall. We can easily compute them with the help of functions we already defined:

```
def rfPrecision(m: Matrix, feature: Int) = m(feature, feature) / colSum(m,
feature)
 def rfRecall(m: Matrix, feature: Int) = m(feature, feature) / rowSum(m,
feature)
 def rfF1(m: Matrix, feature: Int) = 2 * rfPrecision(m, feature) *
rfRecall(m, feature) / (rfPrecision(m, feature) + rfRecall(m, feature))

 val rfPerClassSummary = rfCMLabels.indices.map { i =>
   (rfCMLabels(i), rfRecall(rfCM, i), rfPrecision(rfCM, i), rfF1(rfCM, i))
 }

 println(s"""^Per class summary:
         ^${table(Seq("Label", "Recall", "Precision", "F-1"),
              rfPerClassSummary,
              Map(1 -> "%.4f", 2 -> "%.4f", 3 -> "%.4f"))}
         """.stripMargin('^'))
```

The output is as follows:

```
Per class summary:


+----------------+------+----------+------+
|           Label|Recall|Precision|   F-1|
+----------------+------+----------+------+
|           other|0.9264|    0.9137|0.9200|
| folding laundry|0.9507|    0.9309|0.9407|
|   playing soccer|0.9943|    0.9525|0.9730|
|    computer work|0.9842|    0.9998|0.9919|
|  house cleaning|0.9710|    0.9668|0.9689|
|      car driving|0.9816|    0.9999|0.9907|
|      watching TV|0.9772|    1.0000|0.9885|
+----------------+------+----------+------+
```

In our case, we deal with a quite good model since most of values are close to value 1.0. It means that the model performs well for each input category - generating a low number of false positives (precision) and also false negatives (recall).

The nice feature of the Spark API is that it already provides methods to compute all three metrics we computed manually. We can easily call methods `precision`, `recall`, `fMeasure` with the index of label to get the same values. However, in the Spark case, the `Confusion matrix` is collected for each call and hence increases overall computation time.

In our case, we use the already computed `Confusion matrix` and get the same results directly. Readers can verify that the following code gives us the same numbers as stored in `rfPerClassSummary`:

```
val rfPerClassSummary2 = rfCMLabels.indices.map { i =>
    (rfCMLabels(i), rfModelMetrics.recall(i), rfModelMetrics.precision(i),
rfModelMetrics.fMeasure(i))
}
```

By having statistics per class, we can compute macro-average metrics simply by computing the mean value for each of the computed metrics:

```
val rfMacroRecall = rfCMLabels.indices.map(i => rfRecall(rfCM,
i)).sum/rfCMLabels.size
val rfMacroPrecision = rfCMLabels.indices.map(i => rfPrecision(rfCM,
i)).sum/rfCMLabels.size
val rfMacroF1 = rfCMLabels.indices.map(i => rfF1(rfCM,
i)).sum/rfCMLabels.size

println(f"""|Macro statistics
  |Recall, Precision, F-1
```

```
   |${rfMacroRecall}%.4f, ${rfMacroPrecision}%.4f,
${rfMacroF1}%.4f""".stripMargin)
```

The output is as follows:

```
Macro statistics
Recall, Precision, F-1
0.9693, 0.9662, 0.9677
```

The `Macro` statistics give us an overall characteristic for all feature statistics. We can see expected values close to 1.0 since our model performs quite well on the testing data.

Moreover, the Spark ModelMetrics API provides also weighted precision, recall and `F-1` scores, which are mainly useful if we deal with unbalanced classes:

```
println(f"""|Weighted statistics
   |Recall, Precision, F-1
   |${rfModelMetrics.weightedRecall}%.4f,
${rfModelMetrics.weightedPrecision}%.4f,
${rfModelMetrics.weightedFMeasure}%.4f
   |""".stripMargin)
```

The output is as follows:

```
Weighted statistics
Recall, Precision, F-1
0.9664, 0.9669, 0.9666
```

And at the end, we are going to look at one more way of computing model metrics which is useful also in the cases when the classes are not well distributed. The method is called one-versus-all and it provides performance of the classifier with respect to one class at a time. That means we will compute a `Confusion matrix` for each output class - we can consider this approach as treating the classifier as a binary classifier predicting a class as positive case and any of other classes as negative case:

```
import org.apache.spark.mllib.linalg.Matrices
val rfOneVsAll = rfCMLabels.indices.map { i =>
    val icm = rfCM(i,i)
    val irowSum = rowSum(rfCM, i)
    val icolSum = colSum(rfCM, i)
    Matrices.dense(2,2,
      Array(
        icm, irowSum - icm,
        icolSum - icm, rfCMTotal - irowSum - icolSum + icm))
  }
```

```
println(rfCMLabels.indices.map(i =>
s"${rfCMLabels(i)}\n${rfOneVsAll(i)}").mkString("\n"))
```

This will give us performance of each class with respect to other classes represented by a simple binary `Confusion matrix`. We can sum up all matrices and get a `Confusion matrix` to compute average accuracy and micro-averaged metrics per class:

```
val rfOneVsAllCM = rfOneVsAll.foldLeft(Matrices.zeros(2,2))((acc, m) =>
  Matrices.dense(2, 2,
    Array(acc(0, 0) + m(0, 0),
          acc(1, 0) + m(1, 0),
          acc(0, 1) + m(0, 1),
          acc(1, 1) + m(1, 1)))
)
println(s"Sum of oneVsAll CM:\n${rfOneVsAllCM}")
```

The output is as follows:

```
Sum of oneVsAll CM:
188509.0  6556.0
6556.0    1163834.0
```

Having an overall `Confusion matrix`, we can compute average accuracy per class:

```
println(f"Average accuracy: ${(rfOneVsAllCM(0,0) +
rfOneVsAllCM(1,1))/rfOneVsAllCM.toArray.sum}%.4f")
```

The output is as follows:

```
Average accuracy: 0.9904
```

The matrix gives us also `Micro-averaged metrics` (recall, precision, F-1). However, it is worth mentioning that our `rfOneVsAllCM` matrix is symmetric. This means that `Recall`, `Precision` and `F-1` have the same value (since FP and FN are the same):

```
println(f"Micro-averaged metrics:
${rfOneVsAllCM(0,0)/(rfOneVsAllCM(0,0)+rfOneVsAllCM(1,0))}%.4f")
```

The output is as follows:

```
Micro-averaged metrics: 0.9664
```

An overview of the Spark ModelMetrics API is provided by the Spark documentation `https://spark.apache.org/docs/latest/mllib-evaluation-metrics.html`.

Furthermore, an understanding of model metrics and especially of a role of `Confusion matrix` in multiclass classification is crucial but not connected only to the Spark API. A great source of information is the Python scikit documentation (`http://scikit-learn.org/stable/modules/model_evaluation.html`) or various R packages (for example, `http://blog.revolutionanalytics.com/2016/03/com_class_eval_metrics_r.html`).

Building a classification model using H2O RandomForest

H2O provides multiple algorithms for building classification models. In this chapter, we will focus on tree ensembles again, but we are going to demonstrate their usage in the context of our sensor data problem.

We have already prepared data which we can use directly to build the H2O RandomForest model. To transfer it them into H2O format we need to create `H2OContext` and then call the corresponding transformation:

```
import org.apache.spark.h2o._
val h2oContext = H2OContext.getOrCreate(sc)

val trainHF = h2oContext.asH2OFrame(trainingData, "trainHF")
trainHF.setNames(columnNames)
trainHF.update()
val testHF = h2oContext.asH2OFrame(testData, "testHF")
testHF.setNames(columnNames)
testHF.update()
```

We created two tables referenced by the names `trainHF` and `testHF`. The code also updated names of columns by calling the method `setNames` since input `RDD` does not carry information about columns. The important step is call of the `update` method to save changes into H2O's distributed memory store. This is an important pattern exposed by the H2O API - all changes made on an object are done locally; to make them visible to other computation nodes, it is necessary to save them into the memory store (so-called **distributed key-value store (DKV)**)

Having data stored as H2O tables, we can open the H2O Flow user interface by calling `h2oContext.openFlow` and graphically explore the data. For example, the distribution of the `activityId` column as a numeric feature is shown in *Figure 4*:

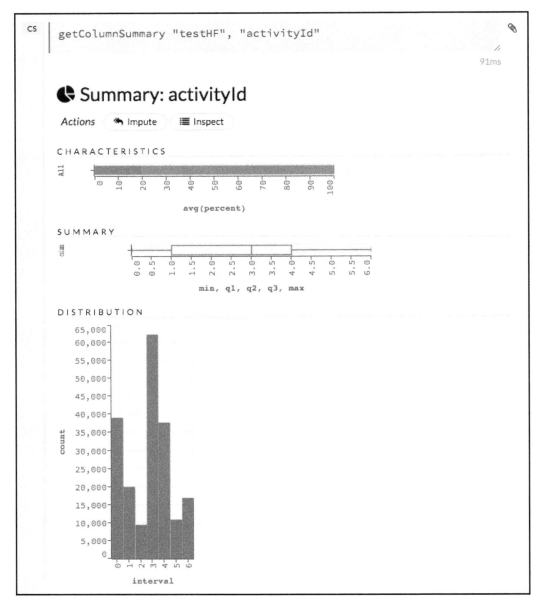

Figure 4: The view of numeric column activityId which needs transformation to categorical type.

We can directly compare the results and verify that we observe right distribution by a piece of Spark code:

```
println(s"""^Distribution of activityId:
             ^${table(Seq("activityId", "Count"),
                     testData.map(row => (row.label, 1)).reduceByKey(_ +
_).collect.sortBy(_._1),
                     Map.empty[Int, String])}
             """.stripMargin('^'))
```

The output is as follows:

The next step is to prepare the input data to run H2O algorithms. First we need to verify that column types are in the form expected by the algorithm. The H2O Flow UI provides a list of columns with basic attributes (*Figure 5*):

label	type	Missing	Zeros	+Inf	-Inf	min	max	mean	sigma	cardinality	Actions
activityId	int	0	39128	0	0	0	6.0	2.7128	1.8317	•	Convert to enum
hr	int	0	0	0	0	60.0	191.0	62.9525	11.7725	•	Convert to enum
hand_temp	real	0	214	0	0	0	35.5000	32.9545	2.4494	• •	
hand_accel1X	real	0	214	0	0	-145.6420	55.9555	-1.5868	5.6434	• •	
hand_accel1Y	real	0	214	0	0	-107.3120	154.3340	3.9780	5.5410	• •	
hand_accel1Z	real	0	214	0	0	-61.0048	53.3689	4.4181	4.4314	• •	
hand_accel2X	real	0	214	0	0	-61.4316	59.0598	-1.4879	5.6702	• •	
hand_accel2Y	real	0	214	0	0	-61.8133	62.1680	3.9753	5.5501	• •	
hand_accel2Z	real	0	214	0	0	-56.9831	50.6461	4.6147	4.4553	• •	
hand_gyroX	real	0	214	0	0	-26.8771	26.1856	-0.0008	1.1837	• •	
hand_gyroY	real	0	214	0	0	-9.4233	12.1368	0.0216	0.8829	• •	
hand_gyroZ	real	0	214	0	0	-13.1562	13.9000	-0.0118	0.9985	• •	
hand_magnetX	real	0	214	0	0	-125.5900	120.4470	10.6430	23.3746	• •	
hand_magnetY	real	0	214	0	0	-126.0850	60.5706	-23.2246	25.4803	• •	
hand_magnetZ	real	0	214	0	0	-149.1000	111.5870	-28.0218	27.9664	• •	
chest_temp	real	0	121	0	0	0	37.5625	35.2217	2.0143	• •	
chest_accel1X	real	0	121	0	0	-23.0343	45.5300	0.4331	1.4587	• •	
chest_accel1Y	real	0	121	0	0	-26.3759	78.2053	8.3267	2.8876	• •	
chest_accel1Z	real	0	121	0	0	-77.4224	18.1696	-1.5721	4.5279	• •	
chest_accel2X	real	0	121	0	0	-22.6737	37.4121	0.2799	1.4527	• •	

Figure 5: Columns of imported training dataset shown in Flow UI.

We can see that the `activityId` column is numeric; however, to perform classification, H2O requires columns to be categorical. So we need to transform the column by clicking on **Convert to enum** in UI or programmatically:

```
trainHF.replace(0, trainHF.vec(0).toCategoricalVec).remove
trainHF.update
testHF.replace(0, testHF.vec(0).toCategoricalVec).remove
testHF.update
```

Again, we need to update the modified frame in the memory store by calling the `update` method. Furthermore, we are transforming a vector to another vector type and we do not need the original vector anymore, hence we can call the `remove` method on the result of the `replace` call.

After transformation, the `activityId` column is categorical; however, the vector domain contains values "0", "1", ..."6" - they are stored in the field `trainHF.vec("activityId").domain`. Nevertheless, we can update the vector with actual category names. We have already prepared index to name transformation called `idx2Activity` - hence we prepare a new domain and update the `activityId` vector domain for training and test tables:

```
val domain = trainHF.vec(0).domain.map(i => idx2Activity(i.toDouble))
trainHF.vec(0).setDomain(domain)
water.DKV.put(trainHF.vec(0))
testHF.vec(0).setDomain(domain)
water.DKV.put(testHF.vec(0))
```

In this case, we need to update the modified vector in the memory store as well - instead of calling the `update` method, the code makes explicit call of the method `water.DKV.put` which directly saves the object into the memory store.

In the UI, we can again explore the `activityId` column of test dataset and compare it with the results computed - *Figure 6:*

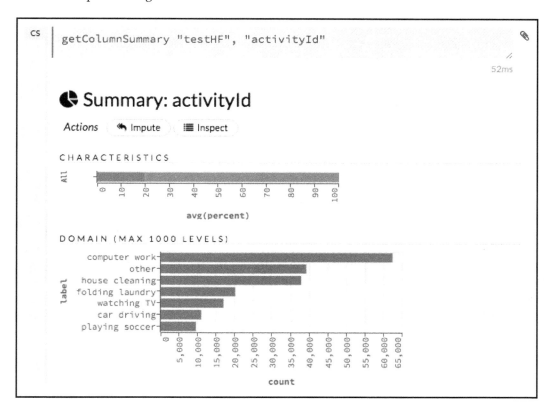

Figure 6: The column activityId values distribution in test dataset.

At this point, we have prepared the data to perform model building. The configuration of H2O RandomForest for a classification problem follows the same pattern we introduced in the previous chapter:

```
import _root_.hex.tree.drf.DRF
import _root_.hex.tree.drf.DRFModel
import _root_.hex.tree.drf.DRFModel.DRFParameters
import _root_.hex.ScoreKeeper._
import _root_.hex.ConfusionMatrix
import water.Key.make

val drfParams = new DRFParameters
drfParams._train = trainHF._key
drfParams._valid = testHF._key
```

```
drfParams._response_column = "activityId"
drfParams._max_depth = 20
drfParams._ntrees = 50
drfParams._score_each_iteration = true
drfParams._stopping_rounds = 2
drfParams._stopping_metric = StoppingMetric.misclassification
drfParams._stopping_tolerance = 1e-3
drfParams._seed = 42
drfParams._nbins = 20
drfParams._nbins_cats = 1024


val drfModel = new DRF(drfParams,
make[DRFModel]("drfModel")).trainModel.get
```

There are several important differences which distinguish the H2O algorithm from Spark. The first important difference is that we can directly specify a validation dataset as an input parameter (the _valid field). This is not necessary since we can perform validation after the model is built; however, when the validation dataset is specified, we can track the quality of the model in real-time during building and stop model building if we consider the model is good enough (see *Figure 7* - the "Cancel Job" action stops training but the model is still available for further actions). Furthermore, later we can continue model building and append more trees if it is demanded. The parameter _score_each_iteration controls how often scoring should be performed:

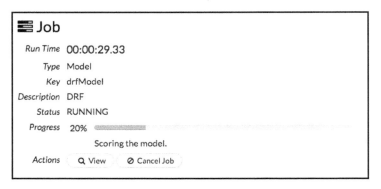

Figure 7: Model training can be tracked in Flow UI and also stopped by pressing "Cancel Job" button.

Another difference is represented by the parameters _nbins, _nbins_top_level, and _nbins_cats. The Spark RandomForest implementation accepts the parameter maxBins which controls discretization of continuous features. In the H2O case, it corresponds to the parameter _nbins. However, the H2O machine learning platform allows finer-grained tuning of discretization. Since top-level splits are the most important and can suffer from loss of information due to discretization, H2O permits temporary increase in the number of discrete categories for top-level splits via the parameter _nbins_top_level. Furthermore, high-value categorical features (> 1,024 levels) often degrades performance of computation by forcing an algorithm to consider all possible splits into two distinct subsets. Since there are 2^N subsets for N categorical levels, finding split points for these features can be expensive. For such cases, H2O brings the parameter _nbins_cats, which controls the number of categorical levels - if a feature contains more categorical levels than the value stored in the parameter, then the values are re-binned to fit into _nbins_cats bins.

The last important difference is that we specified an additional stopping criterion together with traditional depth and number of trees in ensemble. The criterion limits improvement of computed misclassification on validation data - in this case, we specified that model building should stop if two consecutive scoring measurements on validation data (the field _stopping_rounds) do not improve by 0.001 (the value of the field _stopping_tolerance). This is a perfect criterion if we know the expected quality of the model and would like to limit model training time. In our case, we can explore the number of trees in the resulting ensemble:

```
println(s"Number of trees: ${drfModel._output._ntrees}")
```

The output is as follows:

```
Number of trees: 14
```

Even we demanded 50 trees, the resulting model has only 14 trees since model training was stopped since the misclassification rate did not improve with respect to the given threshold.

H2O API exposes multiple stopping criteria which can be used by any of the algorithms - a user can use AUC value for binomial problems or MSE for regression problems. This is one of the most powerful feature which allow you to decrease computation time if huge space of hyper-parameters is explored

The quality of model can be explored in two ways: (1) directly by using the Scala API and accessing the model field _output which carries all output metrics, or (2) using the graphical interface to explore metrics in a more user-friendly way. For example, Confusion matrix on a specified validation set can be displayed as part of the model view directly in the Flow UI. Refer to the following figure:

▾ VALIDATION METRICS - CONFUSION MATRIX VERTICAL: ACTUAL; ACROSS: PREDICTED									
	other	folding laundry	playing soccer	computer work	house cleaning	car driving	watching TV	Error	Rate
other	39161	29	8	33	11	0	2	0.0021	83 / 39,244
folding laundry	47	19797	0	0	2	0	0	0.0025	49 / 19,846
playing soccer	6	0	9250	0	0	0	0	0.0006	6 / 9,256
computer work	71	0	0	61800	0	0	0	0.0011	71 / 61,871
house cleaning	215	0	0	0	37047	0	0	0.0058	215 / 37,262
car driving	6	0	0	0	0	10856	0	0.0006	6 / 10,862
watching TV	4	0	0	0	0	0	16592	0.0002	4 / 16,596
Total	39510	19826	9258	61833	37060	10856	16594	0.0022	434 / 194,937

Figure 8: Confusion matrix for initial RandomForest model composed of 14 trees.

It directly gives us error rate (0.22%) and misclassification per class and we can compare results directly with computed accuracy using Spark model. Furthermore, the Confusion matrix can be used to compute additional metrics which we explored.

For example, compute recall, precision, and F-1 metrics per class. We can simply transform H2O's Confusion matrix to Spark Confusion matrix and reuse all defined methods. But we have to be careful not to confuse actual and predicted values in the resulting Confusion matrix (the Spark matrix has predicted values in columns while the H2O matrix has them in rows):

```
val drfCM = drfModel._output._validation_metrics.cm
def h2oCM2SparkCM(h2oCM: ConfusionMatrix): Matrix = {
  Matrices.dense(h2oCM.size, h2oCM.size, h2oCM._cm.flatMap(x => x))
}
val drfSparkCM = h2oCM2SparkCM(drfCM)
```

You can see that computed metrics for the specified validation dataset are stored in model output field _output._validation_metrics. It contains Confusion matrix but also additional information about model performance tracked during training. Then we simply transformed the H2O representation into Spark matrix. Then we can easily compute macro-performance per class:

```
val drfPerClassSummary = drfCM._domain.indices.map { i =>
  (drfCM._domain(i), rfRecall(drfSparkCM, i), rfPrecision(drfSparkCM, i),
rfF1(drfSparkCM, i))
  }
```

```
println(s"""^Per class summary
           ^${table(Seq("Label", "Recall", "Precision", "F-1"),
                    drfPerClassSummary,
                    Map(1 -> "%.4f", 2 -> "%.4f", 3 -> "%.4f"))}
           """.stripMargin('^'))
```

The output is as follows:

```
Per class summary

+---------------+------+---------+------+
|          Label|Recall|Precision|   F-1|
+---------------+------+---------+------+
|          other|0.9901|   0.9985|0.9943|
|folding laundry|0.9991|   0.9966|0.9979|
| playing soccer|0.9987|   0.9992|0.9990|
|  computer work|0.9997|   0.9987|0.9992|
| house cleaning|0.9997|   0.9940|0.9968|
|    car driving|1.0000|   0.9997|0.9999|
|    watching TV|0.9999|   0.9995|0.9997|
+---------------+------+---------+------+
```

You can see that results are slightly better than the Spark results computed before, even though H2O used less trees. The explanation needs to explore H2O implementation of the RandomForest algorithm - H2O is using an algorithm based on generating a regression decision tree per output class - an approach which is often referenced as a "one-versus-all" scheme. This algorithm allows more fine-grained optimization with respect to individual classes. Hence in this case 14 RandomForest trees are internally represented by 14*7 = 98 internal decision trees.

The reader can find more explanation about the benefits of a "one-versus-all" scheme for multiclass classification problems in the paper *In Defense of One-Vs-All Classification* from Ryan Rifkin and Aldebaro Klautau. The authors show that the schema is as accurate as any other approaches; on the other hand, the algorithm forces the generation of more decision trees which can negatively influence computation time and memory consumption.

We can explore more properties about the trained model. One of the important RandomForest metrics is variable importance. It is stored under the model's field `_output._varimp`. The object contains raw values which can be scaled by calling the `scaled_values` method or obtain relative importance by calling the `summary` method. Nevertheless, they can be explored visually in the Flow UI as shown in *Figure 9*. The graph shows that the most significant features are measured temperatures from all three sensors followed by various movement data. And surprisingly to our expectation, the heart rate is not included among the top-level features:

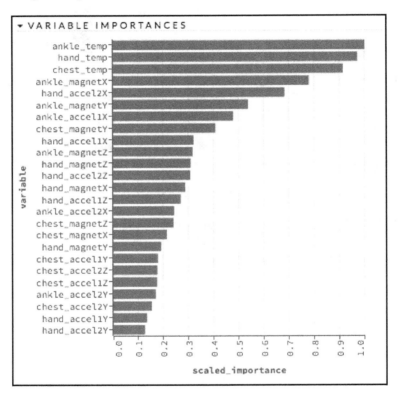

Figure 9: Variable importance for model "drfModel". The most important features include measured temperature.

If we are not satisfied with the quality of the model, it can be extended by more trees. We can reuse defined parameters and modify them in the following way:

- Set up the desired numbers of trees in the resulting ensemble (for example, 20).
- Disable early stopping criterion to avoid stopping model training before achieving the demanded number of trees.

- Configure a so called *model checkpoint* to point to the previously trained model. The model checkpoint is unique feature of the H2O machine learning platform available for all published models. It is useful in situations when you need to improve a given model by performing more training iterations.

After that, we can simply launch model building again. In this case, the H2O platform simply continues model training, reconstructs model state, and builds and appends new trees into a new model:

```
drfParams._ntrees = 20
drfParams._stopping_rounds = 0
drfParams._checkpoint = drfModel._key

val drfModel20 = new DRF(drfParams,
make[DRFModel]("drfMode20")).trainModel.get
println(s"Number of trees: ${drfModel20._output._ntrees}")
```

The output is as follows:

```
Number of trees: 20
```

In this case, only 6 trees were built - to see that, the user can explore the model training output in the console and find a line which ends model training output and reporting:

```
INFO: 6. tree was built in 00:00:05.145 (Wall: 23-Jul 13:44:44.530)
INFO: =================================================================
```

The 6th tree was generated in 2 seconds and it was the last tree appended into the existing ensemble creating a new model. We can again explore Confusion matrix of newly built model and see improvement in overall error rate from 0.23 to 0.2% (see *Figure 9*):

▼ VALIDATION METRICS - CONFUSION MATRIX VERTICAL: ACTUAL; ACROSS: PREDICTED

	other	folding laundry	playing soccer	computer work	house cleaning	car driving	watching TV	Error	Rate
other	39168	23	8	30	12	0	3	0.0019	76 / 39,244
folding laundry	35	19810	0	0	1	0	0	0.0018	36 / 19,846
playing soccer	6	0	9250	0	0	0	0	0.0006	6 / 9,256
computer work	70	0	0	61801	0	0	0	0.0011	70 / 61,871
house cleaning	197	0	0	0	37065	0	0	0.0053	197 / 37,262
car driving	6	0	0	0	0	10856	0	0.0006	6 / 10,862
watching TV	4	0	0	0	0	0	16592	0.0002	4 / 16,596
Total	39486	19833	9258	61831	37078	10856	16595	0.0020	395 / 194,937

Figure 10: Confusion matrix for RandomForest model with 20 trees.

Summary

This chapter introduced several important concepts including data cleanup and handling missing and categorical values, using Spark and H2O to train multi-classification models, and various evaluation metrics for classification models. Furthermore, the chapter brings the notion of model ensembles demonstrated on RandomForest as the ensemble of decision trees.

The reader should see the importance of data preparation, which plays a key role during every model training and evaluation process. Training and using a model without understanding the modeling context can lead to misleading decisions. Moreover, every model needs evaluation with respect to the modeling goal (for example, minimization of false positives). Hence understanding trade-offs of different model metrics of classification models is crucial.

In this chapter, we did not cover all possible modelling tricks for classification models, but there are a few of them still opened for curious readers:

We used a simple strategy to impute missing values in the heart rate column, but there are other possible solutions - for example, mean value imputation, or combining imputation with additional binary column which marks rows with the missing value. Both strategies can improve the accuracy of the model and we will use them later in this book.

Furthermore, the Occam's razor principle suggests that it is good idea to prefer a simpler model than a complex model providing the same accuracy. Hence, a good idea is to define a hyper-space of parameters and use an exploration strategy to find the simplest model (for example, fewer trees, less depth) which provides the same (or better) accuracy as the models trained in this chapter.

To conclude this chapter, it is important to mention that the tree ensemble presented in this chapter is a primitive instance powerful concept of ensembles and super-learners which we are going to introduce later in this book.

4
Predicting Movie Reviews Using NLP and Spark Streaming

In this chapter, we will take an in-depth look at the field of **Natural Language Processing** (**NLP**), not to be confused with Neuro-Linguistic Programming! NLP helps analyze raw textual data and extract useful information such as sentence structure, sentiment of text, or even translation of text between languages. Since many sources of data contain raw text, (for example, reviews, news articles, and medical records). NLP is getting more and more popular, thanks to providing an insight into the text and helps make automatized decisions easier.

Under the hood, NLP is often using machine-learning algorithms to extract and model the structure of text. The power of NLP is much more visible if it is applied in the context of another machine method, where, for example, text can represent one of the input features.

In this chapter, we will apply NLP to analyze the *sentiment* of movie reviews. Based on annotated training data, we will build a classification model that is going to distinguish between positive and negative movie reviews. It is important to mention that we do not extract sentiment directly from the text (based on words such as love, hate, and so on), but utilize a binary classification that we have already explored in the previous chapter.

In order to accomplish this, we will take raw movie reviews that have been manually scored beforehand and train an ensemble-a set of models-which are as follows:

1. Process the movie reviews to synthesize the features for our model.

   Here, we will explore the various features we can create with text data ranging from a bag-of-words approach to a weighted bag-of-words (for example, TF-IDF) and then briefly explore the word2vec algorithm, which we will explore in detail in `Chapter 5`, Word2vec for Prediction and Clustering.

   Alongside this, we will look at some basic ways of feature selection/omission, which include removing stopwords and punctuation, or stemming.

2. Using the generated features, we will run a variety of supervised, binary classification algorithms to help us classify positive and negative reviews, which include the following:
   - Classification decision tree
   - Naive Bayes
   - Random forest
   - Gradient boosted trees

3. Leveraging the combined predictive power of the four different learning algorithms, we will create a super-learner model, which takes all four "guesses" of the models as meta-features to train a deep neural network to output a final prediction.

4. Finally, we will create a Spark machine learning pipeline for this process, which does the following:
   - Extracts features from new movie reviews
   - Comes up with a prediction
   - Outputs this prediction inside of a Spark streaming application (yes, you will build your first machine learning application in every chapter for the remainder of this book!)

If this sounds a tad ambitious, take heart! We will step through each one of these tasks in a manner that is both methodical and purposeful so that you can have the confidence to build your own NLP application; but first, a little background history and some theory behind this exciting field.

NLP - a brief primer

Just like artificial neural networks, NLP is a relatively "old" subject, but one that has garnered a massive amount of attention recently due to the rise of computing power and various applications of machine learning algorithms for tasks that include, but are not limited to, the following:

- **Machine translation** (**MT**): In its simplest form, this is the ability of machines to translate one language of words to another language of words. Interestingly, proposals for machine translation systems pre-date the creation of the digital computer. One of the first NLP applications was created during World War II by an American scientist named Warren Weaver whose job was to try and crack German code. Nowadays, we have highly sophisticated applications that can translate a piece of text into any number of different languages we desire!

- **Speech recognition** (**SR**): These methodologies and technologies attempt to recognize and translate spoken words into text using machines. We see these technologies in smartphones nowadays that use SR systems in tasks ranging from helping us find directions to the nearest gas station to querying Google for the weekend's weather forecast. As we speak into our phones, a machine is able to recognize the words we are speaking and then translate these words into text that the computer can recognize and perform some task if need be.

- **Information retrieval** (**IR**): Have you ever read a piece of text, such as an article on a news website, for example, and wanted to see similar news articles like the one you just read? This is but one example of an information retrieval system that takes a piece of text as an "input" and seeks to obtain other relevant pieces of text similar to the input text. Perhaps the easiest and most recognizable example of an IR system is doing a search on a web-based search engine. We give some words that we want to "know" more about (this is the "input"), and the output are the search results, which are hopefully relevant to our input search query.

- **Information extraction** (**IE**): This is the task of extracting structured bits of information from unstructured data such as text, video and pictures. For example, when you read a blog post on some website, often, the post is tagged with a few keywords that describe the general topics about this posting, which can be classified using information extraction systems. One extremely popular avenue of IE is called *Visual Information Extraction,* which attempts to identify complex entities from the visual layout of a web page, for example, which would not be captured in typical NLP approaches.

- **Text summarization (darn, no acronym here!)**: This is a hugely popular area of interest. This is the task of taking pieces of text of various length and summarizing them by identifying topics, for example. In the next chapter, we will explore two popular approaches to text summarization via topic models such as **Latent Dirichlet Allocation (LDA)** and **Latent Semantic Analysis (LSA)**.

In this chapter, we will use NLP techniques to help us solve a binary classification problem for rating movie reviews from **International Movie Database (IMDb)**. Let's now shift our attention to the dataset we will use and learn more about feature extraction techniques with Spark.

The dataset

The Large Movie Review Database, originally published in the paper, *Learning Word Vectors for Sentiment Analysis,* by Andrew L. Maas et al, can be downloaded from `http://ai.stanford.edu/~amaas/data/sentiment/`.

The downloaded archive contains two folders labeled *train* and *test*. For train, there are 12,500 positive reviews and 12,500 negative reviews that we will train a classifier on. The test dataset contains the same amount of positive and negative reviews for a grand total of 50,000 positive and negative reviews amongst the two files.

Let's look at an example of one review to see what the data looks like:

> *"Bromwell High is nothing short of brilliant. Expertly scripted and perfectly delivered, this searing parody of students and teachers at a South London Public School leaves you literally rolling with laughter. It's vulgar, provocative, witty and sharp. The characters are a superbly caricatured cross-section of British society (or to be more accurate, of any society). Following the escapades of Keisha, Latrina, and Natella, our three "protagonists", for want of a better term, the show doesn't shy away from parodying every imaginable subject. Political correctness flies out the window in every episode. If you enjoy shows that aren't afraid to poke fun of every taboo subject imaginable, then Bromwell High will not disappoint!"*

It appears that the only thing we have to work with is the raw text from the movie review and review sentiment; we know nothing about the date posted, who posted the review, and other data that may/may not be helpful to us aside from the text.

Dataset preparation

Before running any data manipulation, we need to prepare the Spark environment as we did in the previous chapters. Let's start the Spark shell and request enough memory to process the downloaded dataset:

```
export SPARK_HOME="<path to your Spark2.0 distribution"
export SPARKLING_WATER_VERSION="2.1.12"
export SPARK_PACKAGES=\
"ai.h2o:sparkling-water-core_2.11:${SPARKLING_WATER_VERSION},\
ai.h2o:sparkling-water-repl_2.11:${SPARKLING_WATER_VERSION},\
ai.h2o:sparkling-water-ml_2.11:${SPARKLING_WATER_VERSION},\
com.packtpub:mastering-ml-w-spark-utils:1.0.0"
$SPARK_HOME/bin/spark-shell \
--master 'local[*]' \
--driver-memory 10g \
--executor-memory 10g \
--confspark.executor.extraJavaOptions=-XX:MaxPermSize=384M \
--confspark.driver.extraJavaOptions=-XX:MaxPermSize=384M \
--packages "$SPARK_PACKAGES" "$@"
```

 To avoid too much logging output from Spark, it is possible to control logging level at runtime directly by calling `setLogLevel` on SparkContext:
`sc.setLogLevel("WARN")`
The command decreases the verbosity of the Spark output.

The next challenge is to read in the training dataset, which is composed of 25,000 positive and negative movie reviews. The following lines of code will read in these files and then create our binary labels of 0 for a negative review and 1 for a positive review.

We directly utilize the exposed Spark `sqlContext` method, `textFile`, that allows for reading multiple files and returns Dataset[String]. This is the difference from the method mentioned in the previous chapters, which were using the method called `wholeTextFiles` and producing RDD[String]:

```
val positiveReviews=
spark.sqlContext.read.textFile("../data/aclImdb/train/pos/*.txt")
    .toDF("reviewText")
println(s"Number of positive reviews: ${positiveReviews.count}")
Number of positive reviews: 12500
```

We can directly show the first five lines using the dataset method `show` (you can modify the truncate parameter to show the full text of the review):

```
println("Positive reviews:")
positiveReviews.show(5, truncate = true)
```

```
Positive reviews:
+--------------------+
|          reviewText|
+--------------------+
|Match 1: Tag Team...|
|**Attention Spoil...|
|Titanic directed ...|
|By now you've pro...|
|*!!- SPOILERS - !...|
+--------------------+
only showing top 5 rows
```

Next, we will do the same thing for the negative reviews:

```
val negativeReviews=
spark.sqlContext.read.textFile("../data/aclImdb/train/neg/*.txt")
              .toDF("reviewText")
println(s"Number of negative reviews: ${negativeReviews.count}")
```

Take a look at the following screenshot:

```
Number of negative reviews: 12500
```

Now, each of the *positiveReview* and *negativeReviews* variables represents RDD of loaded reviews. Each row of dataset contains a string representing a single review. However, we still need to generate corresponding labels and merge both loaded datasets together.

The labeling is easy, since we loaded negative and positive reviews as separated Spark DataFrames. We can directly append a constant column representing the label 0 for negative reviews and 1 for positive reviews:

```
import org.apache.spark.sql.functions._
val pos= positiveReviews.withColumn("label", lit(1.0))
val neg= negativeReviews.withColumn("label", lit(0.0))
var movieReviews= pos.union(neg).withColumn("row_id",
monotonically_increasing_id)
println("All reviews:")
movieReviews.show(5)
```

Take a look at the following screenshot:

```
All reviews:
+--------------------+-----+------+
|          reviewText|label|row_id|
+--------------------+-----+------+
|Match 1: Tag Team...| 1.0|    0|
|**Attention Spoil...| 1.0|    1|
|Titanic directed ...| 1.0|    2|
|By now you've pro...| 1.0|    3|
|*!!- SPOILERS - !...| 1.0|    4|
+--------------------+-----+------+
only showing top 5 rows
```

In this case, we used the `withColumn` method, which appends a new column to an existing dataset. The definition of a new column `lit(1.0)` means a constant column defined by a numeric literal *1.0*. We need to use a real number to define the target value, since the Spark API expects it. Finally, we merged both datasets together using the `union` method.

We also appended the magic column `row_id`, which uniquely identifies each row in the dataset. This trick simplifies our workflow later when we need to join the output of several algorithms.

 Why did we use a double value instead of a string label representation? In the code labeling individual reviews, we defined a constant column with numeric literals representing double numbers. We could use also *lit("positive")* to label positive reviews, but using plain text labels would force us to transform the string value into numeric value in the later steps anyway. Hence, in this example, we will make our life easier using double value labels directly. Furthermore, we used double values directly since it is required by the Spark API.

Feature extraction

At this stage, we have only a raw text representing reviews, which is not sufficient to run any machine learning algorithm. We need to transform the text into a numeric format, aka perform the so-called "feature extraction" (it is as it sounds; we are taking the input data and extracting features which we will use to train a model). The method generates some new features based on input feature(s). There are many methods regarding how the text can be transformed into numeric features. We can count the number of words, length of text, or number of punctuations. However, to represent text in a systematic way that would reflect a text structure, we need more elaborate methods.

Feature extraction method– bag-of-words model

Now that we have ingested our data and created our labels, it's time to extract our features to build our binary classification model. As its name suggests, the bag-of-words approach is a very common feature-extraction technique whereby we take a piece of text, in this case a movie review, and represent it as a bag (aka multiset) of its words and grammatical tokens. Let's look at an example using a few movie reviews:

Review 1: *Jurassic World was such a flop!*

Review 2: *Titanic ... an instant classic. Cinematography was as good as the acting!!*

For each token (can be a word and/or punctuation), we will create a feature and then count the occurrence of that token throughout the document. Here's what our bag-of-words dataset would look like for the first review:

Review ID	a	Flop	Jurassic	such	World	!
Review 1	1	1	1	1	1	1

First, notice the arrangement of this dataset, often called a *document-term matrix* (each document [row] is composed of a certain set of words [terms] that make up this two-dimensional matrix). We can also arrange this differently and transpose the rows and columns to create-you guessed it-a *term-document matrix* whereby the columns now show the documents that have that particular term and the numbers inside the cells are the counts. Also, realize that the order of the words is alphabetical, which means we lose any sense of word order. This implies that the word "flop" is equidistant in similarity to the word "Jurassic," and while we know this is not true, this highlights one of the limitations of the bag-of-words approach: *the word order is lost, and sometimes, different documents can have the same representation but mean totally different things.*

In the next chapter, you will learn about an extremely powerful learning algorithm pioneered at Google and included in Spark called **word-to-vector** (**word2vec**), which essentially digitizes terms to "encode" their meaning.

Second, notice that for our given review of six tokens (including punctuation), we have six columns. Suppose we added the second review to our document-term-matrix; how would our original bag-of-words change?

Review ID	a	acting	an	as	Cinematography	classic	flop	good	instant	Jurassic	such	Titanic	was	World	.	!
Review 1	1	0	0	0	0	0	1	0	0	1	1	0	0	1	0	1
Review 2	0	1	1	2	1	1	0	1	1	0	0	1	1	0	1	2

We tripled our original number of features from five to 16 tokens, which brings us to another consideration with this approach. Given that we must create a feature for every token, it's not difficult to see we will soon have an extremely wide and very sparse matrix representation (sparse because one document will certainly not contain every word/symbol/emoticon, and so on, and therefore, most of the cell inputs will be zero). This poses some interesting problems with respect to the dimensionality for our algorithms.

Consider the situation where we are trying to train a random forest using a bag-of-words approach on a text document that has +200k tokens, whereby most of the inputs will be zero. Recall that in a tree-based learner, it is making determinations to "go left or go right", which is dependent on the feature type. In a bag-of-words example, we can count features as true or false (that is, the document has the term or not) or the occurrence of a term (that is, how many times does the document have this term). For each successive branch in our tree, the algorithm must consider all these features (or at least the square root of the number of features in the case of a random forest), which can be extremely wide and sparse, and make a decision that influences the overall outcome.

Luckily, you are about to learn how Spark deals with this type of dimensionality and sparsity along with some steps we can take to reduce the number of features in the next section.

Text tokenization

To perform feature extraction, we still need to provide individual words-tokens that are composing the original text. However, we do not need to consider all the words or characters. We can, for example, directly skip punctuations or unimportant words such as prepositions or articles, which mostly do not bring any useful information.

Furthermore, a common practice is to regularize tokens to a common representation. This can include methods such as unification of characters (for example, using only lowercase characters, removing diacritics, using common character encoding such as utf8, and so on) or putting words into a common form (so-called stemming, for example, "cry"/"cries"/"cried" is represented by "cry").

In our example, we will perform this process using the following steps:

1. Lowercase all words ("Because" and "because" are the same word).
2. Remove punctuation symbols with a regular expression function.
3. Remove stopwords. These are essentially injunctions and conjunctions such as *in, at, the, and, etc,* and so on, that add no contextual meaning to the review that we want to classify.

4. Find "rare tokens" that have a total number of occurrences less than three times in our corpus of reviews.

5. Finally, remove all "rare tokens."

Each of the steps in the preceding sequence represent our best practices when doing sentiment classification on text. For your situation, you may not want to lowercase all words (for example, "Python", the language and "python", the snake type, is an important distinction!). Furthermore, your stopwords list-if you choose to include one-may be different and incorporate more business logic given your task. One website that has done a fine job in collecting lists of stopwords is `http://www.ranks.nl/stopwords`.

Declaring our stopwords list

Here, we can directly reuse the list of generic English stopwords provided by Spark. However, we can enrich it by our specific stopwords:

```
import org.apache.spark.ml.feature.StopWordsRemover
val stopWords= StopWordsRemover.loadDefaultStopWords("english") ++
Array("ax", "arent", "re")
```

As stated earlier, this is an extremely delicate task and highly dependent on the business problem you are looking to solve. You may wish to add to this list terms that are relevant to your domain that will not help the prediction task.

Declare a tokenizer that tokenizes reviews and omits all stopwords and words that are too short:

```
val MIN_TOKEN_LENGTH = 3
val toTokens= (minTokenLen: Int, stopWords: Array[String],
    review: String) =>
      review.split("""\W+""")
            .map(_.toLowerCase.replaceAll("[^\\p{IsAlphabetic}]", ""))
            .filter(w =>w.length>minTokenLen)
            .filter(w => !stopWords.contains(w))
```

Let's take a look at this function step by step to see what it's doing. It accepts a single review as an input and then calls the following functions:

- `.split("""\W+""")`: This splits movie review text into tokens that are represented by alphanumeric characters only.
- `.map(_.toLowerCase.replaceAll("[^\\p{IsAlphabetic}]", ""))`: As a best practice, we lowercase the tokens so that at index time, *Java = JAVA = java*. However, this unification is not always the case, and it's important that you are aware of the implications lowercasing your text data can have on the model. As an example, "Python," the computing language would lowercase to "python," which is also a snake. Clearly, the two tokens are not the same; however, lowercasing would make it so! We will also filter out all numeric characters.
- `.filter(w =>w.length>minTokenLen)`: Only keep those tokens whose length is greater than a specified limit (in our case, three characters).
- `.filter(w => !stopWords.contains(w))`: Using the stopwords list that we declared beforehand, we can remove these terms from our tokenized data.

We can now directly apply the defined function on the corpus of reviews:

```
import spark.implicits._
val toTokensUDF= udf(toTokens.curried(MIN_TOKEN_LENGTH)(stopWords))
movieReviews= movieReviews.withColumn("reviewTokens",
                              toTokensUDF('reviewText))
```

In this case, we are marking the function `toTokens` as a Spark user-defined function by calling the `udf` marker, which exposes a common Scala function to be used in the context of the Spark DataFrame. After that, we can directly apply the defined `udf` function on the `reviewText` column in the loaded dataset. The output from the function creates a new column called `reviewTokens`.

We separated `toTokens` and `toTokensUDF` definitions since it would be easier to define them in one expression. This is a common practice that allows you to test the `toTokens` method in separation without the need of using and knowing Spark infrastructure.
Furthermore, you can reuse the defined `toTokens` method among different projects, which do not necessarily need to be Spark-based.

The following code finds all the rare tokens:

```
val RARE_TOKEN = 2
val rareTokens= movieReviews.select("reviewTokens")
        .flatMap(r =>r.getAs[Seq[String]]("reviewTokens"))
        .map((v:String) => (v, 1))
        .groupByKey(t => t._1)
        .reduceGroups((a,b) => (a._1, a._2 + b._2))
        .map(_._2)
        .filter(t => t._2 <RARE_TOKEN)
        .map(_._1)
        .collect()
```

Rare tokens computation is a complex operation. In our example, the input is represented by rows containing a list of tokens. However, we need to compute all the unique tokens and their occurrences.

Therefore, we flatten the structure into a new dataset where each row represents a token by using the `flatMap` method.

Then, we can use the same strategy that we used in the previous chapters. We can generate key-value pairs *(word, 1)* for each word.

The pair is expressing the number of occurrences of the given word. Then, we will just group all the pairs with the same word together (the `groupByKey` method) and compute the total number of occurrences of the word representing a group (`reduceGroups`). The following steps just filter out all too frequent words and finally collect the result as a list of words.

The next goal is to find rare tokens. In our example, we will consider each token with occurrences less than three as rare:

```
println(s"Rare tokens count: ${rareTokens.size}")
println(s"Rare tokens: ${rareTokens.take(10).mkString(", ")}")
```

The output is as following:

```
Rare tokens count: 26324
Rare tokens: adabted, akeem, apprehensions, auds, auteurist, baffel,
             ballbusting, baloons, bamrha, bargepoles
```

Now that we have our tokenization function, it is time to filter out rare tokens by defining another Spark UDF, which we will directly apply on the `reviewTokens` input data column:

```
val rareTokensFilter= (rareTokens: Array[String], tokens: Seq[String])
=>tokens.filter(token => !rareTokens.contains(token))
val rareTokensFilterUDF= udf(rareTokensFilter.curried(rareTokens))

movieReviews= movieReviews.withColumn("reviewTokens",
rareTokensFilterUDF('reviewTokens))

println("Movie reviews tokens:")
movieReviews.show(5)
```

Movie reviews tokens are as follows:

```
Movie reviews tokens:
+--------------------+-----+------+--------------------+
|          reviewText|label|row_id|        reviewTokens|
+--------------------+-----+------+--------------------+
|Match 1: Tag Team...|  1.0|     0|[match, team, tab...|
|**Attention Spoil...|  1.0|     1|[attention, spoil...|
|Titanic directed ...|  1.0|     2|[titanic, directe...|
|By now you've pro...|  1.0|     3|[probably, heard,...|
|*!!- SPOILERS - !...|  1.0|     4|[spoilers, begin,...|
+--------------------+-----+------+--------------------+
only showing top 5 rows
```

Depending on your particular task, you may wish to add or perhaps delete some stopwords or explore different regular expression patterns (teasing out email addresses using regular expressions, for example, is quite common). For now, we will take the tokens that we have to and use it to build our dataset.

Stemming and lemmatization

One extremely popular step in NLP is to stem words back to their root form. For example, "accounts" and "accounting" would both be stemmed to "account," which at first blush seems very reasonable. However, stemming falls prey to the following two areas, which you should be aware of:

1. **Over-stemming**: This is when stemming fails to keep two words with distinct meanings separate. For example, stem ("general," "genetic") = "gene".

2. **Under-stemming**: This is the inability to reduce words with the same meaning to their root forms. For example, stem ("jumping," "jumpiness") = *jumpi* but stem ("jumped," "jumps") = "jump." In this example, we know that each of the preceding terms are simply an inflection of the root word "jump;" however, depending on the stemmer you choose to employ (the two most common stemmers are Porter [oldest and most common] and Lancaster), you may fall into this error.

Given the possibilities of over and under-stemming words in your corpus, NLP practitioners cooked up the notion of lemmatization to help combat these known issues. The word "Lemming," is taking the canonical (dictionary) form of a *set of related words* based on the context of the word. For example, lemma ("paying," "pays," "paid") = "pay." Like stemming, lemmatization tries to group related words, but goes one step further by trying to group words by their word sense because, after all, the same two words can have entirely different meanings depending on the context! Given the depth and complexity of this chapter already, we will refrain from performing any lemmatization techniques, but interested parties can read further about this topic at `http://stanfordnlp.github.io/CoreNLP/`.

Featurization - feature hashing

Now, it is time to transform string representation into a numeric one. We adopt a bag-of-words approach; however, we use a trick called feature hashing. Let's look in more detail at how Spark employs this powerful technique to help us construct and access our tokenized dataset efficiently. We use feature hashing as a time-efficient implementation of a bag-of-words, as explained earlier.

At its core, feature hashing is a fast and space-efficient method to deal with high-dimensional data-typical in working with text-by converting arbitrary features into indices within a vector or matrix. This is best described with an example text. Suppose we have the following two movie reviews:

1. *The movie Goodfellas was well worth the money spent. Brilliant acting!*
2. *Goodfellas is a riveting movie with a great cast and a brilliant plot-a must see for all movie lovers!*

For each token in these reviews, we can apply a "hashing trick," whereby we assign the distinct tokens a number. So, the set of unique tokens (after lowercasing + text processing) in the preceding two reviews would be in alphabetical order:

```
{"acting": 1, "all": 2, "brilliant": 3, "cast": 4, "goodfellas": 5,
"great": 6, "lover": 7, "money": 8, "movie": 9, "must": 10, "plot": 11,
"riveting": 12, "see": 13, "spent": 14, "well": 15, "with": 16, "worth":
17}
```

We will then apply the hashes to create the following matrix:

```
[[1, 1, 0, 1, 0, 0, 0, 0, 1, 0, 0, 0, 0, 1, 1, 0, 1]
 [0, 1, 1, 1, 1, 1, 1, 0, 0, 1, 0, 1, 1, 0, 0, 1, 0]]
```

The matrix from the feature hashing is constructed as follows:

- Rows *represent* the movie review numbers.
- Columns *represent* the features (not the actual words!). The feature space is represented by a range of used hash functions. Note that for each row, there is the same number of columns and not just one ever-growing, wide matrix.
- Thus, every entry in the matrix $(i, j) = k$ means that in row i, feature j, appears k times. So, for example, the token "movie" which is hashed on feature 9, appears twice in the second review; therefore, matrix $(2, 9) = 2$.
- The used hashing function makes gaps. If the hashing function hashes a small set of words into large numeric space, the resulting matrix will have high sparsity.
- One important consideration to think about is the notion of hashing collisions, which is where two different features (tokens, in this case) are hashed into the same index number in our feature matrix. A way to guard against this is to choose a large number of features to hash, which is a parameter we can control in Spark (the default setting for this in Spark is 2^{20} ~ 1 million features).

Now, we can employ Spark's hashing function, which will map each token to a hash index that will make up our feature vector/matrix. As always, we will start with our imports of the necessary classes we will need and then change the default value for the number of features to create hashes against to roughly 4096 (2^{12}).

In the code, we will use the `HashingTF` transformer from the Spark ML package (you will learn more about transformations later in this chapter). It requires the names of input and output columns. For our dataset `movieReviews`, the input column is `reviewTokens`, which holds the tokens created in the previous steps. The result of the transformation is stored in a new column called `tf`:

```
val hashingTF= new HashingTF hashingTF.setInputCol("reviewTokens")
                    .setOutputCol("tf")
                    .setNumFeatures(1 <<12) // 2^12
                    .setBinary(false)
val tfTokens= hashingTF.transform(movieReviews)
println("Vectorized movie reviews:")
tfTokens.show(5)
```

The output is as follows:

```
Vectorized movie reviews:
+--------------------+-----+------+--------------------+--------------------+
|          reviewText|label|row_id|        reviewTokens|                  tf|
+--------------------+-----+------+--------------------+--------------------+
|Match 1: Tag Team...|  1.0|     0|[match, team, tab...|(4096,[0,14,30,46...|
|**Attention Spoil...|  1.0|     1|[attention, spoil...|(4096,[10,14,30,3...|
|Titanic directed ...|  1.0|     2|[titanic, directe...|(4096,[2,9,20,29,...|
|By now you've pro...|  1.0|     3|[probably, heard,...|(4096,[3,14,29,31...|
|*!!- SPOILERS - !...|  1.0|     4|[spoilers, begin,...|(4096,[3,14,24,31...|
+--------------------+-----+------+--------------------+--------------------+
only showing top 5 rows
```

After invoking the transformation, the resulting `tfTokens` dataset contains alongside original data a new column called `tf`, which holds an instance of `org.apache.spark.ml.linalg`. Vector for each input row. The vector in our case is a sparse vector (because the hash space is much larger than the number of unique tokens).

Term Frequency - Inverse Document Frequency (TF-IDF) weighting scheme

We will now use Spark ML to apply a very common weighting scheme called a TF-IDF to convert our tokenized reviews into vectors, which will be inputs to our machine learning models. The math behind this transformation is relatively straightforward:

$$w_{i,j} = tf_{i,j} \times \log\left(\frac{N}{df_i}\right)$$

For each token:

1. Find the term frequency within a given document (in our case, a movie review).
2. Multiply this count by the log of the inverse document frequency that looks at how common the token occurs among all of the documents (commonly referred to as the corpus).
3. Taking the inverse is useful, in that it will penalize tokens that occur too frequently in the document (for example, "movie") and boost those tokens that do not appear as frequently.

Now, we can scale terms based on the inverse term document frequency formula explained earlier. First, we need to compute a model-a prescription about how to scale term frequencies. In this case, we use the Spark `IDF` estimator to create a model based on the input data produced by the previous step `hashingTF`:

```
import org.apache.spark.ml.feature.IDF
val idf= new IDF idf.setInputCol(hashingTF.getOutputCol)
                    .setOutputCol("tf-idf")
val idfModel= idf.fit(tfTokens)
```

Now, we will build a Spark estimator that we trained (fitted) on the input data (= output of transformation in the previous step). The IDF estimator computes weights of individual tokens. Having the model, it is possible to apply it on any data that contains a column defined during fitting:

```
val tfIdfTokens= idfModel.transform(tfTokens)
println("Vectorized and scaled movie reviews:")
tfIdfTokens.show(5)
```

```
Vectorized and scaled movie reviews:
+--------------------+-----+------+--------------------+--------------------+--------------------+
|          reviewText|label|row_id|        reviewTokens|                  tf|              tf-idf|
+--------------------+-----+------+--------------------+--------------------+--------------------+
|Match 1: Tag Team...|  1.0|     0|[match, team, tab...|(4096,[0,14,30,46...|(4096,[0,14,30,46...|
|**Attention Spoil...|  1.0|     1|[attention, spoil...|(4096,[10,14,30,3...|(4096,[10,14,30,3...|
|Titanic directed ...|  1.0|     2|[titanic, directe...|(4096,[2,9,20,29,...|(4096,[2,9,20,29,...|
|By now you've pro...|  1.0|     3|[probably, heard,...|(4096,[3,14,29,31...|(4096,[3,14,29,31...|
|*!!- SPOILERS - !...|  1.0|     4|[spoilers, begin,...|(4096,[3,14,24,31...|(4096,[3,14,24,31...|
+--------------------+-----+------+--------------------+--------------------+--------------------+
only showing top 5 rows
```

Let's look in more detail at a single row and the difference between `hashingTF` and `IDF` outputs. Both operations produced a sparse vector the same length. We can look at non-zero elements and verify that both rows contain non-zero values at the same locations:

```
import org.apache.spark.ml.linalg.Vector
val vecTf= tfTokens.take(1)(0).getAs[Vector]("tf").toSparse
val vecTfIdf= tfIdfTokens.take(1)(0).getAs[Vector]("tf-idf").toSparse
println(s"Both vectors contains the same layout of non-zeros:
${java.util.Arrays.equals(vecTf.indices, vecTfIdf.indices)}")
```

We can also print a few non-zero values:

```
println(s"${vecTf.values.zip(vecTfIdf.values).take(5).mkString("\n")}")
```

```
Both vectors contains the same layout of non-zeros: true
(12.0,52.6425382904535)
(1.0,1.17600860711636)
(4.0,11.122643572548267)
(1.0,1.5708342880419173)
(1.0,4.309559943087155)
```

You can directly see that tokens with the same frequency in the sentence can have different resulting scores based on their frequencies over all the sentences.

Let's do some (model) training!

At this point, we have a numeric representation of textual data, which captures the structure of reviews in a simple way. Now, it is time for model building. First, we will select columns that we need for training and split the resulting dataset. We will keep the generated `row_id` column in the dataset. However, we will not use it as an input feature, but only as a simple unique row identifier:

```
valsplits = tfIdfTokens.select("row_id", "label",
idf.getOutputCol).randomSplit(Array(0.7, 0.1, 0.1, 0.1), seed = 42)
val(trainData, testData, transferData, validationData) = (splits(0),
splits(1), splits(2), splits(3))
Seq(trainData, testData, transferData, validationData).foreach(_.cache())
```

Notice that we have created four different subsets of our data: a training dataset, testing dataset, transfer dataset, and a final validation dataset. The transfer dataset will be explained later on in the chapter, but everything else should appear very familiar to you already from the previous chapters.

Also, the cache call is important since the majority of the algorithms are going to iteratively query the dataset data, and we want to avoid repeated evaluation of all the data preparation operations.

Spark decision tree model

First, let's start with a simple decision tree and perform a grid search over a few of the hyper-parameters. We will follow the code from Chapter 2, *Detecting Dark Matter: The Higgs-Boson Particle* to build our models that are trained to maximize the AUC statistic. However, instead of using models from the MLlib library, we will adopt models from the Spark ML package. The motivation of using the ML package will be clearer later when we will need to compose the models into a form of pipeline. Nevertheless, in the following code, we will use DecisionTreeClassifier, which we fit to trainData, generate prediction for testData, and evaluate the model's AUC performance with the help of BinaryClassificationEvaluato:

```
import org.apache.spark.ml.classification.DecisionTreeClassifier
import org.apache.spark.ml.classification.DecisionTreeClassificationModel
import org.apache.spark.ml.evaluation.BinaryClassificationEvaluator
import java.io.File
val dtModelPath = s" $ MODELS_DIR /dtModel"
val dtModel= {
  val dtGridSearch = for (
    dtImpurity<- Array("entropy", "gini");
    dtDepth<- Array(3, 5))
    yield {
      println(s"Training decision tree: impurity $dtImpurity,
              depth: $dtDepth")
      val dtModel = new DecisionTreeClassifier()
          .setFeaturesCol(idf.getOutputCol)
          .setLabelCol("label")
          .setImpurity(dtImpurity)
          .setMaxDepth(dtDepth)
          .setMaxBins(10)
          .setSeed(42)
          .setCacheNodeIds(true)
          .fit(trainData)
      val dtPrediction = dtModel.transform(testData)
      val dtAUC = new BinaryClassificationEvaluator().setLabelCol("label")
          .evaluate(dtPrediction)
      println(s" DT AUC on test data: $dtAUC")
      ((dtImpurity, dtDepth), dtModel, dtAUC)
    }
    println(dtGridSearch.sortBy(-_._3).take(5).mkString("\n"))
```

```
val bestModel = dtGridSearch.sortBy(-_._3).head._2
bestModel.write.overwrite.save(dtModelPath)
bestModel
}
```

```
Training decision tree: impurity entropy, depth: 3
DT AUC on test data: 0.5704125809734585
Training decision tree: impurity entropy, depth: 5
DT AUC on test data: 0.6123589190615425
Training decision tree: impurity gini, depth: 3
DT AUC on test data: 0.5704546494784851
Training decision tree: impurity gini, depth: 5
DT AUC on test data: 0.658750720212806
```

After selecting the best model, we will write it into a file. This is a useful trick since model training can be time and resource expensive, and the next time, we can load the model directly from the file instead of retraining it again:

```
val dtModel= if (new File(dtModelPath).exists()) {
  DecisionTreeClassificationModel.load(dtModelPath)
} else { /* do training */ }
```

Spark Naive Bayes model

Next, let's look to employ Spark's implementation of Naive Bayes. As a reminder, we purposely stay away from going into the algorithm itself as this has been covered in many machine learning books; instead, we will focus on the parameters of the model and ultimately, how we can "deploy" these models in a Spark streaming application later on in this chapter.

Spark's implementation of Naive Bayes is relatively straightforward, with just a few parameters we need to keep in mind. They are mainly as follows:

- **getLambda**: Sometimes referred to as "additive smoothing" or "laplace smoothing," this parameter allows us to smooth out the observed proportions of our categorical variables to create a more uniform distribution. This parameter is especially important when the number of categories you are trying to predict is very low and you don't want entire categories to be missed due to low sampling. Enter the lambda parameter that "helps" you combat this by introducing some minimal representation of some of the categories.

- **getModelType**: There are two options here: *"multinomial"* (default) or *"Bernoulli."* The *Bernoulli* model type would assume that our features are binary, which in our text example would be *"does review have word _____? Yes or no?"* The *multinomial* model type, however, takes discrete word counts. One other model type that is not currently implemented in Spark for Naive Bayes but is appropriate for you to know is a Gaussian model type. This gives our model features the freedom to come from a normal distribution.

Given that we only have one hyper-parameter to deal with in this case, we will simply go with the default value for our lamda, but you are encouraged to try a grid search approach as well for optimal results:

```
import org.apache.spark.ml.classification.{NaiveBayes, NaiveBayesModel}
val nbModelPath= s"$MODELS_DIR/nbModel"
val nbModel= {
  val model = new NaiveBayes()
      .setFeaturesCol(idf.getOutputCol)
      .setLabelCol("label")
      .setSmoothing(1.0)
      .setModelType("multinomial") // Note: input data are multinomial
      .fit(trainData)
  val nbPrediction = model.transform(testData)
  val nbAUC = new BinaryClassificationEvaluator().setLabelCol("label")
              .evaluate(nbPrediction)
  println(s"Naive Bayes AUC: $nbAUC")
  model.write.overwrite.save(nbModelPath)
  model
}
```

```
Naive Bayes AUC: 0.4843121496534903
```

It is interesting to compare the performance of different models for the same input dataset. Often, it turns out that even a simple Naive Bayes algorithm lends itself very well to text classification tasks. The reason partly has to do with the first adjective of this algorithm: "naive." Specifically, this particular algorithm assumes that our features-which in this case are globally weighted term frequencies-are mutually independent. Is this true in the real world? More often, this assumption is often violated; however, this algorithm still could perform just as well, if not better, than more complex models.

Spark random forest model

Next, we will move on to our random forest algorithm, which, as you will recall from the previous chapters, is an ensemble of various decision trees whereby we perform a grid search again alternating between various depths and other hyper-parameters, which will be familiar:

```
import org.apache.spark.ml.classification.{RandomForestClassifier,
RandomForestClassificationModel}
val rfModelPath= s"$MODELS_DIR/rfModel"
val rfModel= {
  val rfGridSearch = for (
    rfNumTrees<- Array(10, 15);
    rfImpurity<- Array("entropy", "gini");
    rfDepth<- Array(3, 5))
    yield {
      println( s"Training random forest: numTrees: $rfNumTrees,
              impurity $rfImpurity, depth: $rfDepth")
    val rfModel = new RandomForestClassifier()
        .setFeaturesCol(idf.getOutputCol)
        .setLabelCol("label")
        .setNumTrees(rfNumTrees)
        .setImpurity(rfImpurity)
        .setMaxDepth(rfDepth)
        .setMaxBins(10)
        .setSubsamplingRate(0.67)
        .setSeed(42)
        .setCacheNodeIds(true)
        .fit(trainData)
    val rfPrediction = rfModel.transform(testData)
    val rfAUC = new BinaryClassificationEvaluator()
                .setLabelCol("label")
                .evaluate(rfPrediction)
    println(s" RF AUC on test data: $rfAUC")
    ((rfNumTrees, rfImpurity, rfDepth), rfModel, rfAUC)
  }
  println(rfGridSearch.sortBy(-_._3).take(5).mkString("\n"))
  val bestModel = rfGridSearch.sortBy(-_._3).head._2
  // Stress that the model is minimal because of defined gird space^
  bestModel.write.overwrite.save(rfModelPath)
  bestModel
}
```

```
Training random forest: numTrees: 10, impurity entropy, depth: 3
RF AUC on test data: 0.7074721068984243
Training random forest: numTrees: 10, impurity entropy, depth: 5
RF AUC on test data: 0.765794536075256
Training random forest: numTrees: 10, impurity gini, depth: 3
RF AUC on test data: 0.710100883640532
Training random forest: numTrees: 10, impurity gini, depth: 5
RF AUC on test data: 0.7532190820046402
Training random forest: numTrees: 15, impurity entropy, depth: 3
RF AUC on test data: 0.7627100732866996
Training random forest: numTrees: 15, impurity entropy, depth: 5
RF AUC on test data: 0.7953145108745386
Training random forest: numTrees: 15, impurity gini, depth: 3
RF AUC on test data: 0.7639953502522747
Training random forest: numTrees: 15, impurity gini, depth: 5
RF AUC on test data: 0.806763586545605
```

From our grid search, the highest AUC we are seeing is `0.769`.

Spark GBM model

Finally, we will move on to our **gradient boosting machine** (**GBM**), which will be the final
model in our ensemble of models. Note that in the previous chapters, we used H2O's
version of GBM, but now, we will stick with Spark and use Spark's implementation of GBM
as follows:

```
import org.apache.spark.ml.classification.{GBTClassifier,
GBTClassificationModel}
val gbmModelPath= s"$MODELS_DIR/gbmModel"
val gbmModel= {
  val model = new GBTClassifier()
      .setFeaturesCol(idf.getOutputCol)
      .setLabelCol("label")
      .setMaxIter(20)
      .setMaxDepth(6)
      .setCacheNodeIds(true)
      .fit(trainData)
  val gbmPrediction = model.transform(testData)
  gbmPrediction.show()
  val gbmAUC = new BinaryClassificationEvaluator()
      .setLabelCol("label")
      .setRawPredictionCol(model.getPredictionCol)
      .evaluate(gbmPrediction)
  println(s" GBM AUC on test data: $gbmAUC")
  model.write.overwrite.save(gbmModelPath)
```

```
    model
}
```

```
GBM AUC on test data: 0.7549674490735507
```

So now, we have trained up four different learning algorithms: a (single) decision tree, a random forest, Naive Bayes, and a gradient boosted machine. Each provides a different AUC as summarized in the table here. We can see that the best performing model is RandomForest followed by GBM. However, it is fair to say that we did not perform any exhausted search for the GBM model nor did we use a high number of iterations as is usually recommended:

Decision tree	0.659
Naive Bayes	0.484
Random forest	0.769
GBM	0.755

Super-learner model

Now, we will combine the prediction power for all of these algorithms to generate a "super-learner" with the help of a neural network, which takes each model's prediction as input and then, tries to come up with a better prediction, given the guesses of the individually trained models. At a high level, the architecture would look something like this:

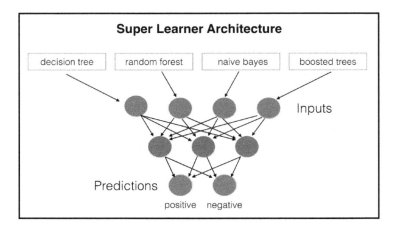

We will explain further the intuition behind building a "super-learner" and the benefits of this approach, and teach you how to build your Spark streaming application, which will take in your text (that is, a movie review that you will write) and run it through the prediction engine of each of your models. Using these predictions as input into your neural network, we will yield a positive or negative sentiment using the combined power of the various algorithms.

Super learner

In the preceding sections, we trained several models. Now, we will compose them into an ensemble called a super learner using a deep learning model. The process to build a super learner is straightforward (see the preceding figure):

1. Select base algorithms (for example, GLM, random forest, GBM, and so on).
2. Select a meta-learning algorithm (for example, deep learning).
3. Train each of the base algorithms on the training set.
4. Perform K-fold cross-validation on each of these learners and collect the cross-validated predicted values from each of the base algorithms.
5. The N cross-validated predicted values from each of the L-base algorithms can be combined to form a new NxL matrix. This matrix, along with the original response vector, is called the "level-one" data.
6. Train the meta-learning algorithm on the level-one data.
7. The super learner (or so-called "ensemble model") consists of the L-base learning models and the meta-learning model, which can then be used to generate predictions on a test set.

The key trick of ensembles is to combine a diverse set of strong learners together. We already discussed a similar trick in the context of the random forest algorithm.

The PhD thesis of Erin LeDell contains much more detailed information about super learners and their scalability. You can find it at http://www.stat.berkeley.edu/~ledell/papers/ledell-phd-thesis.pdf.

In our example, we will simplify the whole process by skipping cross-validation but using a single hold-out dataset. It is important to mention that this is not the recommended approach!

As the first step, we use trained models and a transfer dataset to get predictions and compose them into a new dataset, augmenting it by the actual labels.

This sounds easy; however, we cannot use the *DataFrame#withColumn* method directly and create a new `DataFrame` from multiple columns from different datasets, since the method accepts columns only from the left-hand side `DataFrame` or constant columns.

Nevertheless, we have already prepared the dataset for this situation by assigning a unique ID to each row. In this case, we will use it and join individual model predictions based on `row_id`. We also need to rename each model prediction column to uniquely identify the model prediction inside the dataset:

```
import org.apache.spark.ml.PredictionModel
import org.apache.spark.sql.DataFrame

val models = Seq(("NB", nbModel), ("DT", dtModel), ("RF", rfModel), ("GBM",
gbmModel))
def mlData(inputData: DataFrame, responseColumn: String, baseModels:
Seq[(String, PredictionModel[_, _])]): DataFrame= {
baseModels.map{ case(name, model) =>
model.transform(inputData)
    .select("row_id", model.getPredictionCol )
    .withColumnRenamed("prediction", s"${name}_prediction")
  }.reduceLeft((a, b) =>a.join(b, Seq("row_id"), "inner"))
    .join(inputData.select("row_id", responseColumn), Seq("row_id"),
"inner")
}
val mlTrainData= mlData(transferData, "label", models).drop("row_id")
mlTrainData.show()
```

```
+-------------+-------------+-------------+--------------+-----+
|NB_prediction|DT_prediction|RF_prediction|GBM_prediction|label|
+-------------+-------------+-------------+--------------+-----+
|          0.0|          1.0|          1.0|           1.0|  1.0|
|          1.0|          1.0|          1.0|           1.0|  0.0|
|          0.0|          0.0|          0.0|           0.0|  0.0|
|          0.0|          1.0|          1.0|           0.0|  0.0|
|          0.0|          1.0|          1.0|           1.0|  0.0|
|          0.0|          0.0|          0.0|           0.0|  0.0|
|          0.0|          1.0|          0.0|           1.0|  0.0|
|          0.0|          1.0|          0.0|           1.0|  0.0|
|          0.0|          1.0|          1.0|           1.0|  0.0|
|          1.0|          1.0|          1.0|           1.0|  0.0|
|          0.0|          0.0|          0.0|           0.0|  0.0|
|          1.0|          1.0|          1.0|           1.0|  1.0|
|          0.0|          1.0|          0.0|           1.0|  1.0|
|          1.0|          1.0|          1.0|           1.0|  1.0|
|          0.0|          0.0|          1.0|           0.0|  0.0|
|          0.0|          1.0|          1.0|           0.0|  0.0|
|          0.0|          0.0|          1.0|           0.0|  0.0|
|          0.0|          0.0|          1.0|           0.0|  0.0|
|          0.0|          1.0|          1.0|           0.0|  0.0|
|          0.0|          0.0|          0.0|           0.0|  0.0|
+-------------+-------------+-------------+--------------+-----+
only showing top 20 rows
```

The table is composed of the models' prediction and annotated by the actual label. It is interesting to see how individual models agree/disagree on the predicted value.

We can use the same transformation to prepare a validation dataset for our super learner:

```
val mlTestData = mlData(validationData, "label", models).drop("row_id")
```

Now, we can build our meta-learner algorithm. In this case, we will use the deep learning algorithm provided by the H2O machine learning library. However, it needs a little bit of preparation-we need to publish the prepared train and test data as H2O frames:

```
import org.apache.spark.h2o._
val hc= H2OContext.getOrCreate(sc)
val mlTrainHF= hc.asH2OFrame(mlTrainData, "metaLearnerTrain")
val mlTestHF= hc.asH2OFrame(mlTestData, "metaLearnerTest")
```

We also need to transform the `label` column into a categorical column. This is necessary; otherwise, the H2O deep learning algorithm would perform regression since the `label` column is numeric:

```
importwater.fvec.Vec
val toEnumUDF= (name: String, vec: Vec) =>vec.toCategoricalVec
mlTrainHF(toEnumUDF, 'label).update()
mlTestHF(toEnumUDF, 'label).update()
```

Now, we can build an H2O deep learning model. We can directly use the Java API of the algorithm; however, since we would like to compose all the steps into a single Spark pipeline, we will utilize a wrapper exposing the Spark estimator API:

```
val metaLearningModel= new H2ODeepLearning()(hc, spark.sqlContext)
    .setTrainKey(mlTrainHF.key)
    .setValidKey(mlTestHF.key)
    .setResponseColumn("label")
    .setEpochs(10)
    .setHidden(Array(100, 100, 50))
    .fit(null)
```

Since we directly specified the validation dataset, we can explore the performance of the model:

```
Model Metrics Type: Binomial
 Description: Metrics reported on full validation frame
 model id: DeepLearning_model_1500875766182_1
 frame id: metaLearnerTest
 MSE: 0.4889693
 RMSE: 0.6992634
 AUC: 0.8502772
 logloss: 2.5960147
 mean_per_class_error: 0.19902605
 default threshold: 0.0015407047467306256
 CM: Confusion Matrix (Row labels: Actual class; Column labels: Predicted class):
            0     1    Error       Rate
      0    943   309  0.2468   309 / 1,252
      1    188  1055  0.1512   188 / 1,243
 Totals  1131  1364  0.1992   497 / 2,495
```

Alternatively, we can open the H2O Flow UI (by calling `hc.openFlow`) and explore its performance in the visual form:

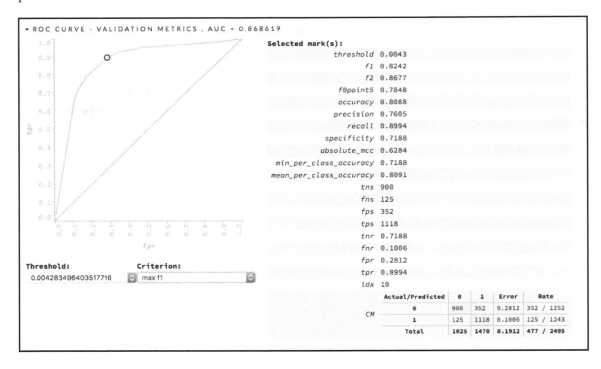

You can easily see that the AUC for this model on the validation dataset is 0.868619 - the value higher than all the AUC values of the individual models.

Composing all transformations together

In the previous section, we developed individual steps using Spark primitives, that is, UDFs, native Spark algorithms, and H2O algorithms. However, to invoke all these transformation on unseen data requires a lot of manual effort. Hence, Spark introduces the concept of pipelines, mainly motivated by Python scikit pipelines (`http://scikit-learn.org/stable/modules/generated/sklearn.pipeline.Pipeline.html`).

> To learn more about the design decision behind Python, we recommend that you read the excellent paper "API design for machine learning software: experiences from the scikit-learn project" by Lars Buitinck et al (`https://arxiv.org/abs/1309.0238`).

The pipeline is composed of stages that are represented by estimators and transformations:

- **Estimators**: These are the core elements that expose a fit method that creates a model. Most of the classification and regression algorithms are represented as an estimator.
- **Transformers**: These transform an input dataset into a new dataset. The transformers expose the method `transform`, which implements the logic of transformation. The transformers can produce single on multiple vectors. Most of the models produced by estimators are transformers-they transform an input dataset into a new dataset representing the prediction. Another example can be the TF transformer used in this section.

The pipeline itself exposes the same interface as the estimator. It has the fit method, so it can be trained and produces a "pipeline model", which can be used for data transformation (it has the same interface as transformers). Hence, the pipelines can be combined hierarchically together. Furthermore, the individual pipeline stages are invoked in a sequential order; however, they can still represent a directed acyclic graph (for example, a stage can have two input columns, each produced by a different stage). In this case, the sequential order has to follow the topological ordering of the graph.

In our example, we will compose all the transformation together. However, we will not define a training pipeline (that is, a pipeline that will train all the models), but we will use the already trained models to set up the pipeline stages. Our motivation is to define a pipeline that we can use to score a new movie review.

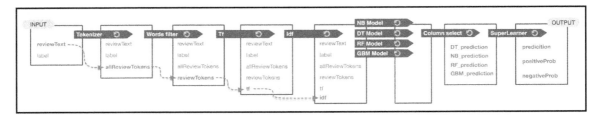

So, let's start from the beginning of our example-the first operation that we applied on the input data was a simple tokenizer. It was defined by a Scala function that we wrapped into a form of Spark UDF. However, to use it as a part of the pipeline we need to wrap the defined Scala function into a transformation. Spark does not provide any simple wrapper to do that, so it is necessary to define a generic transformation from scratch. We know that we will transform a single column into a new column. In this case, we can use UnaryTransformer, which exactly defines one-to-one column transformation. We can be a little bit more generic and define a generic wrapper for Scala functions (aka Spark UDFs):

```
import org.apache.spark.ml.{Pipeline, UnaryTransformer}
import org.apache.spark.sql.types._
import org.apache.spark.ml.param.ParamMap
import org.apache.spark.ml.util.{MLWritable, MLWriter}

class UDFTransformer[T, U](override valuid: String,
                           f: T =>U, inType: DataType,
                           outType: DataType)
extendsUnaryTransformer[T, U, UDFTransformer[T, U]] with MLWritable {

override protected defcreateTransformFunc: T =>U = f

override protected defvalidateInputType(inputType: DataType): Unit =
require(inputType == inType)

override protected defoutputDataType: DataType = outType

override defwrite: MLWriter = new MLWriter {
override protected defsaveImpl(path: String): Unit = {}
  }
}
```

The `UDFTransformer` class wraps a function `f`, which accepts a generic type `T`, and produces type `U`. At the Spark dataset level, it transforms an input column (see `UnaryTransformer`) of type `inType` into a new output column (again, the field is defined by `UnaryTransformer`) of the `outType` type. The class also has a dummy implementation of the trait `MLWritable`, which supports serialization of the transformer into a file.

Now, we just need to define our tokenizer transformer:

```
val tokenizerTransformer= new UDFTransformer[String, Array[String]](
  "tokenizer", toTokens.curried(MIN_TOKEN_LENGTH)(stopWords),
  StringType, new ArrayType(StringType, true))
```

The defined transformer accepts a string column (that is, a movie review) and produces a new column that contains an array of strings representing movie review tokens. The transformer is directly using the `toTokens` function, which we used at the beginning of the chapter.

The next transformation should remove rare words. In this case, we will use a similar approach as in the previous step and utilize the defined `UDFTransformer` function:

```
val rareTokensFilterTransformer= new UDFTransformer[Seq[String],
Seq[String]](
  "rareWordsRemover",
  rareTokensFilter.curried(rareTokens),
  newArrayType(StringType, true), new ArrayType(StringType, true))
```

This transformer accepts a column containing an array of tokens and produces a new column containing a filtered array of tokens. It is using the already defined `rareTokensFilter` Scala function.

 So far, we have not specified any input data dependencies, including names of input columns. We will keep it for the final pipeline definition.

The next steps include vectorization with the help of the `TF` method hashing string tokens into a large numeric space and followed by a transformation based on the built `IDF` model. Both transformations are already defined in the expected form-the first `hashingTF` transformation is already a transformer translating a set of tokens into numeric vectors, the second one `idfModel` accepts the numeric vector and scales it based on the computed coefficients.

These steps provide input for the trained binomial models. Each base model represents a transformer producing several new columns such as prediction, raw prediction, and probabilities. However, it is important to mention that not all models provide the full set of columns. For example, Spark GBM currently (Spark version 2.0.0) provides only the prediction column. Nevertheless, it is good enough for our example.

After generating predictions, our dataset contains many columns; for example, input columns, columns with tokens, transformed tokens, and so on. However, to apply the generated meta-learner, we need only columns with prediction generated by the base models. Hence, we will define a column selector transformation, which drops all the unnecessary columns. In this case, we have a transformation-accepting dataset with N-columns and producing a new dataset with M-columns. Therefore, we cannot use UnaryTransformer defined earlier, and we need to define a new ad-hoc transformation called ColumnSelector:

```
import org.apache.spark.ml.Transformer
class ColumnSelector(override valuid: String, valcolumnsToSelect:
Array[String]) extends Transformer with MLWritable {

  override deftransform(dataset: Dataset[_]): DataFrame= {
    dataset.select(columnsToSelect.map(dataset.col): _*)
  }

  override deftransformSchema(schema: StructType): StructType = {
    StructType(schema.fields.filter(col=>columnsToSelect
                          .contains(col.name)))
  }

  override defcopy(extra: ParamMap): ColumnSelector = defaultCopy(extra)

  override defwrite: MLWriter = new MLWriter {
    override protected defsaveImpl(path: String): Unit = {}
  }
}
```

ColumnSelector represents a generic transformer that selects only the given columns from the input dataset. It is important to mention the overall two-stages concept-the first stage transforms the schema (that is, the metadata associated with each dataset) and the second transforms the actual dataset. The separation allows Spark to invoke early checks on transformers to find incompatibilities before invoking actual data transformations.

We need to define the actual column selector transformer by creating an instance of `columnSelector`-be aware of specifying the right columns to keep:

```
val columnSelector= new ColumnSelector(
  "columnSelector",  Array(s"DT_${dtModel.getPredictionCol}",
  s"NB_${nbModel.getPredictionCol}",
  s"RF_${rfModel.getPredictionCol}",
  s"GBM_${gbmModel.getPredictionCol}")
```

At this point, our transformers are ready to be composed into the final "super-learning" pipeline. The API of the pipeline is straightforward-it accepts individual stages that are invoked sequentially. However, we still need to specify dependencies between individual stages. Mostly the dependency is described by input and output column names:

```
val superLearnerPipeline = new Pipeline()
 .setStages(Array(
// Tokenize
tokenizerTransformer
    .setInputCol("reviewText")
    .setOutputCol("allReviewTokens"),
// Remove rare items
rareTokensFilterTransformer
    .setInputCol("allReviewTokens")
    .setOutputCol("reviewTokens"),
hashingTF,
idfModel,
dtModel
    .setPredictionCol(s"DT_${dtModel.getPredictionCol}")
    .setRawPredictionCol(s"DT_${dtModel.getRawPredictionCol}")
    .setProbabilityCol(s"DT_${dtModel.getProbabilityCol}"),
nbModel
    .setPredictionCol(s"NB_${nbModel.getPredictionCol}")
    .setRawPredictionCol(s"NB_${nbModel.getRawPredictionCol}")
    .setProbabilityCol(s"NB_${nbModel.getProbabilityCol}"),
rfModel
    .setPredictionCol(s"RF_${rfModel.getPredictionCol}")
    .setRawPredictionCol(s"RF_${rfModel.getRawPredictionCol}")
    .setProbabilityCol(s"RF_${rfModel.getProbabilityCol}"),
gbmModel// Note: GBM does not have full API of PredictionModel
.setPredictionCol(s"GBM_${gbmModel.getPredictionCol}"),
columnSelector,
metaLearningModel
 ))
```

There are a few important concepts worth mentioning:

- The `tokenizerTransformer` and `rareTokensFilterTransformer` are connected via the column `allReviewTokens`-the first one is the column producer, and the second one is the column consumer.
- The `dtModel`, `nbModel`, `rfModel`, and `gbmModel` models have the same input column defined as `idf.getOutputColumn`. In this case, we have effectively used computation DAG, which is topologically ordered into a sequence
- All the models have the same output columns (with some exceptions, in the case of GBM), which cannot be appended into the resulting dataset all together since the pipeline expects unique names of columns. Hence, we need to rename the output columns of the models by calling `setPredictionCol`, `setRawPredictionCol`, and `setProbabilityCol`. It is important to mention that the GBM does not produce raw prediction and probabilities columns right now.

Now, we can fit the pipeline to get the pipeline model. This is, in fact, an empty operation, since our pipeline is composed only of transformers. However, we still need to call the `fit` method:

```
val superLearnerModel= superLearnerPipeline.fit(pos)
```

Voila, we have our super-learner model, composed of multiple Spark models and orchestrated by the H2O deep learning model. It is time to use the model to make a prediction!

Using the super-learner model

The usage of the model is easy-we need to provide a dataset with a single column called `reviewText` and transform it with `superLearnerModel`:

```
val review = "Although I love this movie, I can barely watch it, it is so
real....."
val reviewToScore= sc.parallelize(Seq(review)).toDF("reviewText")
val reviewPrediction= superLearnerModel.transform(reviewToScore)
```

The returned prediction `reviewPrediction` is a dataset with the following structure:

```
reviewPrediction.printSchema()
```

```
root
 |-- predict: string (nullable = false)
 |-- p0: double (nullable = false)
 |-- p1: double (nullable = false)
```

The first column contains the predicted value, which was decided based on the F1 threshold. The columns `p0` and `p1` represent probabilities of individual prediction classes.

If we explore the content of the returned dataset, it contains a single row:

```
reviewPrediction.show()
```

```
+-------+------------------+-------------------+
|predict|                p0|                 p1|
+-------+------------------+-------------------+
|      1|0.9853714258834393|0.01462857411656607393|
+-------+------------------+-------------------+
```

Summary

This chapter demonstrated three powerful concepts: the processing of text, Spark pipelines, and super learners.

The text processing is a powerful concept that is waiting to be largely adopted by the industry. Hence, we will go deeper into the topic in the following chapters and look at other approaches of natural language processing.

The same holds for Spark pipelines, which have become an inherent part of Spark and the core of the Spark ML package. They offer an elegant way of reusing the same concepts during training and scoring time. Hence, we would like to use the concept in the upcoming chapters as well.

Finally, with super learners, aka ensembles, you learned the basic concept of how to benefit from ensembling multiple models together with the help of a meta-learner. This offers a simple but powerful way of building strong learners, which are still simple enough to understand.

5
Word2vec for Prediction and Clustering

In the previous chapters, we covered some basic NLP steps, such as tokenization, stoplist removal, and feature creation, by creating a **Term Frequency - Inverse Document Frequency (TF-IDF)** matrix with which we performed a supervised learning task of predicting the sentiment of movie reviews. In this chapter, we are going to extend our previous example to now include the amazing power of word vectors, popularized by Google researchers, Tomas Mikolov and Ilya Sutskever, in their paper, *Distributed Representations of Words and Phrases and their Compositionality.*

We will start with a brief overview of the motivation behind word vectors, drawing on our understanding of the previous NLP feature extraction techniques, and we'll then explain the concept behind the family of algorithms that represent the word2vec framework (indeed, word2vec is not just one single algorithm). Then, we will discuss a very popular extension of word2vec called doc2vec, whereby we are interested in *vectorizing* entire documents into a single fixed array of N numbers. We'll further research on this hugely popular field of NLP, or cognitive computing research. Next, we will apply a word2vec algorithm to our movie review dataset, examine the resulting word vectors, and create document vectors by taking the average of the individual word vectors in order to perform a supervised learning task. Finally, we will use these document vectors to run a clustering algorithm to see how well our movie review vectors group together.

The power of word vectors is an exploding area of research that companies such as Google and Facebook have invested in heavily, given its power of encoding the semantic and syntactic meaning of individual words, which we will discuss shortly. It's no coincidence that Spark implemented its own version of word2vec, which can also be found in Google's Tensorflow library and Facebook's Torch. More recently, Facebook announced a new real-time text processing called deep text, using their pretrained word vectors, in which they showcased their belief in this amazing technology and the implications it has or is having on their business applications. However, in this chapter, we'll just cover a small portion of this exciting area, including the following:

- Explanation of the word2vec algorithm
- Generalization of the word2vec idea, resulting in doc2vec
- Application of both the algorithms on the movie reviews dataset

Motivation of word vectors

Similar to the work we did in the previous chapter, traditional NLP approaches rely on converting individual words--which we created via tokenization--into a format that a computer algorithm can learn (that is, predicting the movie sentiment). Doing this required us to convert a single review of N tokens into a fixed representation by creating a TF-IDF matrix. In doing so, we did two important things *behind the scenes*:

1. Individual words were assigned an integer ID (for example, a hash). For example, the word *friend* might be assigned to 39,584, while the word *bestie* might be assigned to 99,928,472. Cognitively, we know that *friend* is very similar to *bestie*; however, any notion of similarity is lost by converting these tokens into integer IDs.

2. By converting each token into an integer ID, we consequently lose the context with which the token was used. This is important because in order to understand the cognitive meaning of words, and thereby train a computer to learn that *friend* and *bestie* are similar, we need to understand how the two tokens are used (for example, their respective contexts).

Given this limited functionality of traditional NLP techniques with respect to encoding the semantic and syntactic meaning of words, Tomas Mikolov and other researchers explored methods that employ neural networks to better *encode* the meaning of words as a vector of *N* numbers (for example, vector *bestie* = [0.574, 0.821, 0.756, ... , 0.156]). When calculated properly, we will discover that the vectors for *bestie* and *friend* are close in space, whereby closeness is defined as a cosine similarity. It turns out that these vector representations (often referred to as *word embeddings*) give us the ability to capture a richer understanding of text.

Interestingly, using word embeddings also gives us the ability to learn the same semantics across multiple languages despite differences in the written form (for example, Japanese and English). For example, the Japanese word for movie is *eiga* (映画); therefore, it follows that using word vectors, these two words, *movie* and 映画, should be close in the vector space despite their differences in appearance. Thus, the word embeddings allow for applications to be language-agnostic--yet another reason why this technology is hugely popular!

Word2vec explained

First things first: word2vec does not represent a *single* algorithm but rather a family of algorithms that attempt to encode the semantic and syntactic *meaning* of words as a vector of *N* numbers (hence, word-to-vector = word2vec). We will explore each of these algorithms in depth in this chapter, while also giving you the opportunity to read/research other areas of *vectorization* of text, which you may find helpful.

What is a word vector?

In its simplest form, a word vector is merely a one-hot-encoding, whereby every element in the vector represents a word in our vocabulary, and the given word is *encoded* with 1 while all the other words elements are encoded with 0. Suppose our vocabulary only has the following movie terms: **Popcorn**, **Candy**, **Soda**, **Tickets**, and **Blockbuster**.

Following the logic we just explained, we could encode the term **Tickets** as follows:

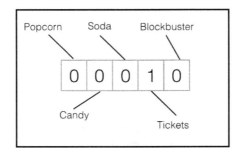

Using this simplistic form of encoding, which is what we do when we create a bag-of-words matrix, there is no meaningful comparison we can make between words (for example, *is Popcorn related to Soda; is Candy similar to Tickets?*).

Given these obvious limitations, word2vec attempts to remedy this via distributed representations for words. Suppose that for each word, we have a distributed vector of, say, 300 numbers that represent a single word, whereby each word in our vocabulary is also represented by a distribution of weights across those 300 elements. Now, our picture would drastically change to look something like this:

	Popcorn	**Candy**	**Soda**	**Tickets**	**Blockbuster**
element 1	0.573	0.805	0.402	0.805	0.311
element 2	0.199	0.573	0.294	0.311	0.199
element 3	0.805	0.199	0.805	0.924	0.573
element 4	0.311	0.402	0.311	0.294	0.004
element 5	0.294	0.004	0.573	0.199	0.924
⋮	⋮	⋮	⋮	⋮	⋮
element 299	0.402	0.294	0.199	0.004	0.805
element 300	0.924	0.311	0.924	0.573	0.402

Now, given this distributed representation of individual words as 300 numeric values, we can make meaningful comparisons among words using a cosine similarity, for example. That is, using the vectors for **Tickets** and **Soda**, we can determine that the two terms are not related, given their vector representations and their cosine similarity to one another. And that's not all we can do! In their ground-breaking paper, Mikolov et. al also performed mathematical functions of word vectors to make some incredible findings; in particular, the authors give the following *math problem* to their word2vec dictionary:

V(King) - V(Man) + V(Woman) ~ V(Queen)

It turns out that these distributed vector representations of words are extremely powerful in comparison questions (for example, is A related to B?), which is all the more remarkable when you consider that this semantic and syntactic learned knowledge comes from observing lots of words and their context with no other information necessary. That is, we did not have to tell our machine that *Popcorn* is a food, noun, singular, and so on.

How is this made possible? Word2vec employs the power of neural networks in a supervised fashion to learn the vector representation of words (which is an unsupervised task). If that sounds a bit like an oxymoron at first, fear not! Everything will be made clearer with a few examples, starting first with the **Continuous Bag-of-Words** model, commonly referred to as just the **CBOW** model.

The CBOW model

First, let's consider a simple movie review, which will act as our base example in the next few sections:

> *"An outstanding sci-fi film with plenty of smart ideas that forces us to consider the impact of alien life in our solar system."*

Now, imagine that we have a window that acts as a slider, which includes the main word currently in focus (highlighted in red in the following image), in addition to the five words before and after the focus word (highlighted in yellow):

> *"An outstanding sci-fi film with plenty of smart **ideas** regarding the impact of alien life in our solar system."*

The words in yellow form the context that surrounds the current focus word, *ideas*. These context words act as inputs to our feed-forward neural network, whereby each word is encoded via one-hot-encoding (all other elements are zeroed out) with one hidden layer and one output layer:

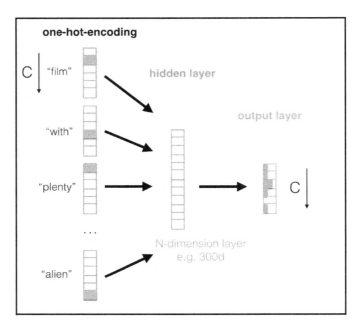

In the preceding diagram, the total size of our vocabulary (for example, post-tokenization) is denoted by a capital C, whereby we perform one-hot-encoding of each word within the context window--in this case, the five words before and after our focus word, *ideas*. At this point, we propagate our encoded vectors to our hidden layer via weighted sum--just like a *normal* feed-forward neural network--whereby, we specify beforehand the number of weights in our hidden layer. Finally, a sigmoid function is applied from the single hidden layer to the output layer, which attempts to predict the current focus word. This is achieved by maximizing the conditional probability of observing the focus word (*idea*), given the context of its surrounding words (**film**, **with**, **plenty**, **of**, **smart**, **regarding**, **the**, **impact**, **of**, and **alien**). Notice that the output layer is also of the same size as our initial vocabulary, C.

Herein lies the interesting property of both the families of the word2vec algorithm: it's an unsupervised learning algorithm at heart and relies on supervised learning to learn individual word vectors. This is true for the CBOW model and also the skip-gram model, which we will cover next. Note that at the time of writing this book, Spark's MLlib only incorporates the skip-gram model of word2vec.

The skip-gram model

In the previous model, we used a window of words before and after the focus word to predict the focus word. The skip-gram model takes a similar approach but reverses the architecture of the neural network. That is, we are going to start with the focus word as our input into our network and then try to predict the surrounding contextual words using a single hidden layer:

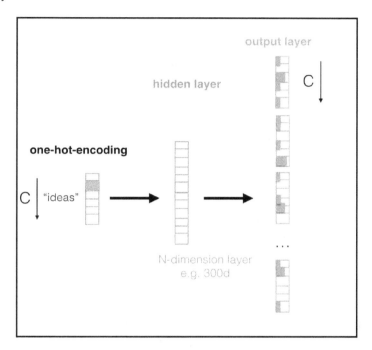

As you can see, the skip-gram model is the exact opposite of the CBOW model. The training goal of the network is to minimize the summed prediction error across all the context words in the output layer, which, in our example, is an input of *ideas* and an output layer that predicts *film, with, plenty, of, smart, regarding, the, impact, of,* and *alien.*

In the previous chapter, you saw that we used a tokenization function that removed stopwords, such as *the, with, to,* and so on, which we have not shown here intentionally to clearly convey our examples without losing the reader. In the example that follows, we will perform the same tokenization function as Chapter 4, *Predicting Movie Reviews Using NLP and Spark Streaming,* which will remove the stopwords.

Fun with word vectors

Now that we have condensed words (tokens) into vectors of numbers, we can have some fun with them. A few classic examples from the original Google paper that you can try for yourself are as follows:

- **Mathematical operations**: As mentioned earlier, the canonical example of this is *v(King) - v(Man) + v(Woman) ~ v(Queen)*. Using simple addition, such as *v(software) + v(engineer)*, we can come up with some fascinating relationships; here are a few more examples:

Czech + currency	Vietnam + capital	German + airlines	Russian + river	French + actress
koruna	Hanoi	airline Lufthansa	Moscow	Juliette Binoche
Check crown	Ho Chi Minh City	carrier Lufthansa	Volga River	Vanessa Paradis
Polish zolty	Viet Nam	flag carrier Lufthansa	upriver	Charlotte Gainsbourg
CTK	Vietnamese	Lufthansa	Russia	Cecile De

Table 5: Vector compositionality using element-wise addition. Four closest tokens to the sum of two vectors are shown, using the best Skip-gram model.

- **Similarity**: Given that we are working with a vector space, we can use the cosine similarity to compare one token against many in order to see similar tokens. For example, similar words to *v(Spark)* might be *v(MLlib)*, *v(scala)*, *v(graphex)*, and so on.
- **Matches/Not Matches**: Which words from a given list do not go together? For example, *doesn't_match[v(lunch, dinner, breakfast, Tokyo)] == v(Tokyo)*.
- **A is to B as C is to ?**: As per the Google paper, here is a list of word comparisons that are made possible by using the skip-gram implementation of word2vec:

Table 8:   *Examples of the word pair relationships, using the best word vectors from Table 4 (Skip-gram model trained on 783M words with 300 dimensionality).*

Relationship	Example 1	Example 2	Example 3
France - Paris	Italy: Rome	Japan: Tokyo	Florida: Tallahassee
big - bigger	small: larger	cold: colder	quick: quicker
Miami - Florida	Baltimore: Maryland	Dallas: Texas	Kona: Hawaii
Einstein - scientist	Messi: midfielder	Mozart: violinist	Picasso: painter
Sarkozy - France	Berlusconi: Italy	Merkel: Germany	Koizumi: Japan
copper - Cu	zinc: Zn	gold: Au	uranium: plutonium
Berlusconi - Silvio	Sarkozy: Nicolas	Putin: Medvedev	Obama: Barack
Microsoft - Windows	Google: Android	IBM: Linux	Apple: iPhone
Microsoft - Ballmer	Google: Yahoo	IBM: McNealy	Apple: Jobs
Japan - sushi	Germany: bratwurst	France: tapas	USA: pizza

Cosine similarity

Word similarity/dissimilarity is measured via cosine similarity, which has a very nice property of being bound between -1 and 1. Perfect similarity between two words will yield a score of 1, no relation will yield 0, and -1 means that they are opposites.

Note that the cosine similarity function for the word2vec algorithm (again, just the CBOW implementation in Spark, for now) is already baked into MLlib, which we will see shortly.

Take a look at the following diagram:

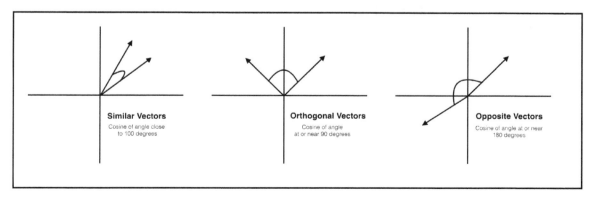

For those who are interested in other measures of similarity, a recent research has been published that makes a strong case for using **Earth-Mover's Distance** (**EMD**), which is a different method from cosine similarity, requiring some additional calculation, but shows promising early results.

Doc2vec explained

As we mentioned in the chapter's introduction, there is an extension of word2vec that encodes entire *documents* as opposed to individual words. In this case, a document is what you make of it, be it a sentence, a paragraph, an article, an essay, and so on. Not surprisingly, this paper came out after the original word2vec paper but was also, not surprisingly, coauthored by Tomas Mikolov and Quoc Le. Even though MLlib has yet to introduce doc2vec into their stable of algorithms, we feel it is necessary for a data science practitioner to know about this extension of word2vec, given its promise of and results with supervised learning and information retrieval tasks.

Like word2vec, doc2vec (sometimes referred to as *paragraph vectors*) relies on a supervised learning task to learn distributed representations of documents based on contextual words. Doc2vec is also a family of algorithms, whereby the architecture will look extremely similar to the CBOW and skip-gram models of word2vec that you learned in the previous sections. As you will see next, implementing doc2vec will require a parallel training of both individual word vectors and document vectors that represent what we deem as a *document*.

The distributed-memory model

This particular flavor of doc2vec closely resembles the CBOW model of word2vec, whereby the algorithm tries to predict a *focus word* given its surrounding *context words* but with the addition of a paragraph ID. Think of this as another individual contextual word vector that helps with the prediction task but is constant throughout what we consider to be a document. Continuing our previous example, if we have this movie review (we define one document as one movie review) and our focus word is *ideas*, we will now have the following architecture:

Document ID: 456

*"An outstanding sci-fi film with plenty of smart **ideas** regarding the impact of alien life in our solar system."*

...next word in document with a sliding window of 5 'context words'

Document ID: 456

*"An outstanding sci-fi film with plenty of smart ideas **regarding** the impact of alien life in our solar system."*

Note that as we move down the document and change the *focus word* from *ideas* to *regarding*, our context words will obviously change; however, **Document ID: 456** remains the same. This is a crucial point in doc2vec, as the document ID is used in the prediction task:

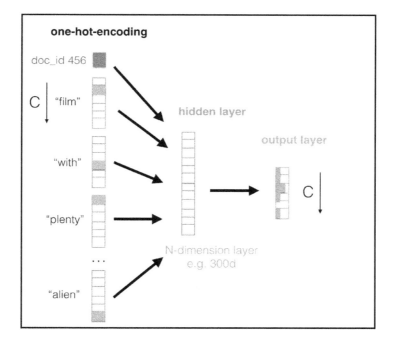

The distributed bag-of-words model

The last algorithm in doc2vec is modeled after the word2vec skip-gram model, with one exception--instead of using the *focus* word as the input, we will now take the document ID as the input and try to predict *randomly sampled* words from the document. That is, we will completely ignore the context words in our output altogether:

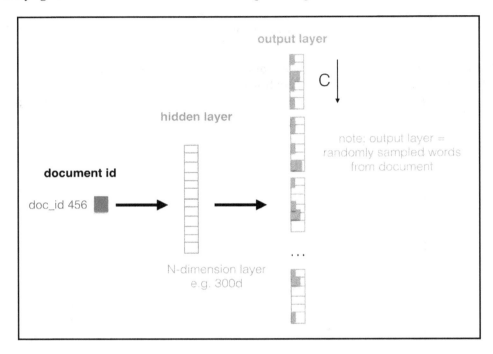

Like word2vec, we can take similarities of documents of N words using these *paragraph vectors*, which have proven hugely successful in both supervised and unsupervised tasks. Here are some of the experiments that Mikolov et. al ran using, notably, the supervised task that leverages the same dataset we used in the last two chapters!

Table 2. The performance of Paragraph Vector compared to other approaches on the IMDB dataset. The error rates of other methods are reported in (Wang & Manning, 2012).

Model	Error rate
BoW (bnc) (Maas et al., 2011)	12.20 %
BoW (bΔt'c) (Maas et al., 2011)	11.77%
LDA (Maas et al., 2011)	32.58%
Full+BoW (Maas et al., 2011)	11.67%
Full+Unlabeled+BoW (Maas et al., 2011)	11.11%
WRRBM (Dahl et al., 2012)	12.58%
WRRBM + BoW (bnc) (Dahl et al., 2012)	10.77%
MNB-uni (Wang & Manning, 2012)	16.45%
MNB-bi (Wang & Manning, 2012)	13.41%
SVM-uni (Wang & Manning, 2012)	13.05%
SVM-bi (Wang & Manning, 2012)	10.84%
NBSVM-uni (Wang & Manning, 2012)	11.71%
NBSVM-bi (Wang & Manning, 2012)	8.78%
Paragraph Vector	**7.42%**

Information-retrieval tasks (three paragraphs, the first should *sound* closer to the second than the third paragraph):

- **Paragraph 1:** calls from (000) 000 - 0000 . 3913 calls reported from this number . according to 4 reports the identity of this caller is american airlines .

- **Paragraph 2:** do you want to find out who called you from +1 000 - 000 - 0000 , +1 0000000000 or (000) 000 - 0000 ? see reports and share information you have about this caller

- **Paragraph 3:** allina health clinic patients for your convenience , you can pay your allina health clinic bill online . pay your clinic bill now , question and answers...

In the subsequent sections, we are going to create a *poor man's document vector* by taking the average of individual word vectors to form our document vector, which will encode entire movie reviews of n-length into vectors of dimension, 300.

At the time of writing this book, Spark's MLlib does not have an implementation of doc2vec; however, there are many projects that are leveraging this technology, which are in the incubation phase and which you can test out.

Applying word2vec and exploring our data with vectors

Now that you have a good understanding of word2vec, doc2vec, and the incredible power of word vectors, it's time we turned our focus to our original IMDB dataset, whereby we will perform the following preprocessing:

- Split words in each movie review by a space
- Remove punctuation
- Remove stopwords and all alphanumeric words
- Using our tokenization function from the previous chapter, we will end with an array of comma-separated words

Because we have already covered the preceding steps in Chapter 4, *Predicting Movie Reviews Using NLP and Spark Streaming*, we'll quickly reproduce them in this section.

As usual, we begin with starting the Spark shell, which is our working environment:

```
export SPARKLING_WATER_VERSION="2.1.12"
export SPARK_PACKAGES=\
"ai.h2o:sparkling-water-core_2.11:${SPARKLING_WATER_VERSION},\
ai.h2o:sparkling-water-repl_2.11:${SPARKLING_WATER_VERSION},\
ai.h2o:sparkling-water-ml_2.11:${SPARKLING_WATER_VERSION},\
com.packtpub:mastering-ml-w-spark-utils:1.0.0"

$SPARK_HOME/bin/spark-shell \
        --master 'local[*]' \
        --driver-memory 8g \
        --executor-memory 8g \
        --conf spark.executor.extraJavaOptions=-XX:MaxPermSize=384M \
        --conf spark.driver.extraJavaOptions=-XX:MaxPermSize=384M \
        --packages "$SPARK_PACKAGES" "$@"
```

In the prepared environment, we can directly load the data:

```
val DATASET_DIR =
s"${sys.env.get("DATADIR").getOrElse("data")}/aclImdb/train"
 val FILE_SELECTOR = "*.txt"

case class Review(label: Int, reviewText: String)

 val positiveReviews =
spark.read.textFile(s"$DATASET_DIR/pos/$FILE_SELECTOR")
     .map(line => Review(1, line)).toDF
 val negativeReviews =
spark.read.textFile(s"$DATASET_DIR/neg/$FILE_SELECTOR")
    .map(line => Review(0, line)).toDF
 var movieReviews = positiveReviews.union(negativeReviews)
```

We can also define the tokenization function to split the reviews into tokens, removing all the common words:

```
import org.apache.spark.ml.feature.StopWordsRemover
 val stopWords = StopWordsRemover.loadDefaultStopWords("english") ++
Array("ax", "arent", "re")

 val MIN_TOKEN_LENGTH = 3
 val toTokens = (minTokenLen: Int, stopWords: Array[String], review:
String) =>
    review.split("""\W+""")
      .map(_.toLowerCase.replaceAll("[^\\p{IsAlphabetic}]", ""))
      .filter(w => w.length > minTokenLen)
      .filter(w => !stopWords.contains(w))
```

With all the building blocks ready, we just apply them to the loaded input data, augmenting them by a new column, `reviewTokens`, which holds a list of words extracted from the review:

```
 val toTokensUDF = udf(toTokens.curried(MIN_TOKEN_LENGTH)(stopWords))
 movieReviews = movieReviews.withColumn("reviewTokens",
toTokensUDF('reviewText))
```

The `reviewTokens` column is a perfect input for the word2vec model. We can build it using the Spark ML library:

```
val word2vec = new Word2Vec()
   .setInputCol("reviewTokens")
   .setOutputCol("reviewVector")
   .setMinCount(1)
val w2vModel = word2vec.fit(movieReviews)
```

The Spark implementation has several additional hyperparameters:

- `setMinCount`: This is the minimum frequency with which we can create a word. It is another processing step so that the model is not running on super rare terms with low counts.
- `setNumIterations`: Typically, we see that a higher number of iterations leads to more *accurate* word vectors (think of these as the number of epochs in a traditional feed-forward neural network). The default value is set to 1.
- `setVectorSize`: This is where we declare the size of our vectors. It can be any integer with a default size of 100. Many of the *public* word vectors that come pretrained tend to favor larger vector sizes; however, this is purely application-dependent.
- `setLearningRate`: Just like a *regular* neural network, which we learned about in Chapter 2, *Detecting Dark Matter- The Higgs-Boson Particle*, discretion is needed in part by the data scientist--too little a learning rate and the model will take forever-and-a-day to converge. However, if the learning rate is too large, one risks a non-optimal set of learned weights in the network. The default value is 0.

Now that our model has finished, it's time to inspect some of our word vectors! Recall that whenever you are unsure of what values your model can produce, always hit the *tab* button, as follows:

```
w2vModel.findSynonyms("funny", 5).show()
```

The output is as follows:

```
+---------------+------------------+
|           word|        similarity|
+---------------+------------------+
|        unfunny|0.7436722528455839|
|          jokes|0.7124677827208712|
|      hilarious| 0.703418054119502|
|           joke|0.7005909410410399|
|unintentionally|0.6939198533161667|
+---------------+------------------+
```

Let's take a step back and consider what we just did here. First, we condensed the word, *funny*, to a vector composed of an array of 100 floating point numbers (recall that this is the default value for the Spark implementation of the word2vec algorithm). Because we have reduced all the words in our corpus of reviews to the same distributed representation of 100 numbers, we can make comparisons using the cosine similarity, which is what the second number in our result set reflects (the highest cosine similarity in this case is for the word *nutty*).

Note that we can also access the vector for *funny* or any other word in our dictionary using the `getVectors` function, as follows:

```
w2vModel.getVectors.where("word = 'funny'").show(truncate = false)
```

The output is as follows:

```
+-----+------------------------------------------------------------
|word |vector
+-----+------------------------------------------------------------
|funny|[-0.2903641164302826,0.17743447422981262,-0.15994349122047424,-0.0516541302204
+-----+------------------------------------------------------------
```

A lot of interesting research has been done on clustering similar words together based on these representations as well. We will revisit clustering later in this chapter when we'll try to cluster similar movie reviews after we perform a hacked version of doc2vec in the next section.

Creating document vectors

So, now that we can create vectors that encode the *meaning* of words, and we know that any given movie review post tokenization is an array of *N* words, we can begin creating a poor man's doc2vec by taking the average of all the words that make up the review. That is, for each review, by averaging the individual word vectors, we lose the specific sequencing of words, which, depending on the sensitivity of your application, can make a difference:

v(word_1) + v(word_2) + v(word_3) ... v(word_Z) / count(words in review)

Ideally, one would use a flavor of doc2vec to create document vectors; however, doc2vec has yet to be implemented in MLlib at the time of writing this book, so for now, we are going to use this simple version, which, as you will see, has surprising results. Fortunately, the Spark ML implementation of the word2vec model already averages word vectors if the model contains a list of tokens. For example, we can show that the phrase, *funny movie*, has a vector that is equal to the average of the vectors of the funny and movie tokens:

```
val testDf = Seq(Seq("funny"), Seq("movie"), Seq("funny",
"movie")).toDF("reviewTokens")
 w2vModel.transform(testDf).show(truncate=false)
```

The output is as follows:

```
+---------------+-------------------------------------------------------------------------------+
|reviewTokens   |reviewVector                                                                   |
+---------------+-------------------------------------------------------------------------------+
|[funny]        |[-0.2903641164302826,0.17743447422981262,-0.15994349122047424,-0.0516!
|[movie]        |[-0.13111236691474915,-0.10716702044010162,-0.3449690639972687,0.1149(
|[funny, movie]|[-0.21073824167251587,0.0351337268948555,-0.25245627760887146,0.03162!
+---------------+-------------------------------------------------------------------------------+
```

Hence, we can prepare our simple version of doc2vec by a simple model transformation:

```
val inputData = w2vModel.transform(movieReviews)
```

 As practitioners in this field, we have had the unique opportunity to work with various flavors of document vectors, including word averaging, doc2vec, LSTM auto-encoders, and skip-thought vectors. What we have found is that for small word snippets, where the sequencing of words isn't crucial, the simple word averaging does a surprisingly good job as supervised learning tasks. That is, not to say that it could be improved with doc2vec and other variants but is rather an observation based on the many use cases we have seen across various customer applications.

Supervised learning task

Like in the previous chapter, we need to prepare the training and validation data. In this case, we'll reuse the Spark API to split the data:

```
val trainValidSplits = inputData.randomSplit(Array(0.8, 0.2))
val (trainData, validData) = (trainValidSplits(0), trainValidSplits(1))
```

Now, let's perform a grid search using a simple decision tree and a few hyperparameters:

```
val gridSearch =
for (
    hpImpurity <- Array("entropy", "gini");
    hpDepth <- Array(5, 20);
    hpBins <- Array(10, 50))
yield {
println(s"Building model with: impurity=${hpImpurity}, depth=${hpDepth},
bins=${hpBins}")
val model = new DecisionTreeClassifier()
        .setFeaturesCol("reviewVector")
        .setLabelCol("label")
        .setImpurity(hpImpurity)
        .setMaxDepth(hpDepth)
        .setMaxBins(hpBins)
        .fit(trainData)

val preds = model.transform(validData)
val auc = new BinaryClassificationEvaluator().setLabelCol("label")
        .evaluate(preds)
    (hpImpurity, hpDepth, hpBins, auc)
    }
```

We can now inspect the result and show the best model AUC:

```
import com.packtpub.mmlwspark.utils.Tabulizer.table
println(table(Seq("Impurity", "Depth", "Bins", "AUC"),
            gridSearch.sortBy(_._4).reverse,
Map.empty[Int,String]))
```

The output is as follows:

```
+--------+-----+----+------------------+
|Impurity|Depth|Bins|               AUC|
+--------+-----+----+------------------+
| entropy|   20|  50|0.7054182687609908|
| entropy|   20|  10|0.7001480059428118|
|    gini|   20|  10|0.6960269296966128|
| entropy|    5|  10|0.6640498095868637|
|    gini|   20|  50|0.6401798806729296|
|    gini|    5|  50|0.6172009865557911|
| entropy|    5|  50|0.6122491001774006|
|    gini|    5|  10|0.5999167496804949|
+--------+-----+----+------------------+
```

Using this simple grid search on a decision tree, we can see that our *poor man's doc2vec* produces an AUC of 0.7054. Let's also expose our exact training and test data to H2O and try a deep learning algorithm using the Flow UI:

```
import org.apache.spark.h2o._
val hc = H2OContext.getOrCreate(sc)
val trainHf = hc.asH2OFrame(trainData, "trainData")
val validHf = hc.asH2OFrame(validData, "validData")
```

Now that we have successfully published our dataset as H2O frames, let's open the Flow UI and run a deep learning algorithm:

```
hc.openFlow()
```

First, note that if we run the `getFrames` command, we will see the two RDDs that we seamlessly passed from Spark to H2O:

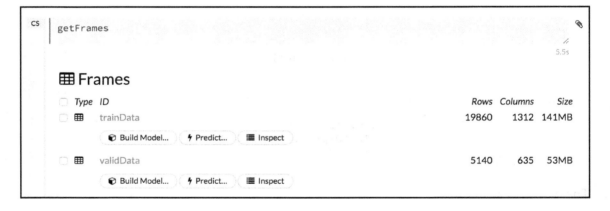

We need to change the type of column **label** from a numeric column to a categorical one by clicking on **Convert to enum** for both the frames:

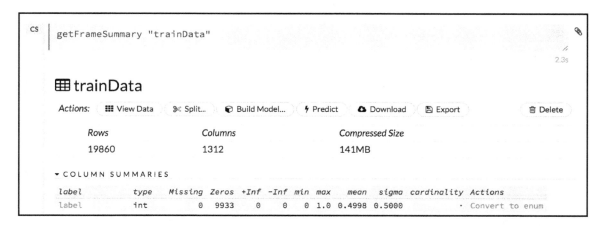

Next, we will run a deep learning model with all of the hyperparameters set to their default value and the first column set to be our label:

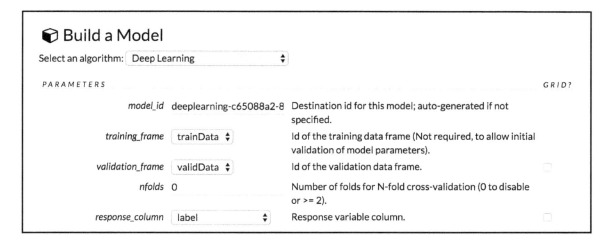

If you did not explicitly create a train/test dataset, you can also perform an *n folds cross-validation* using the *nfolds* hyperparameter previously:

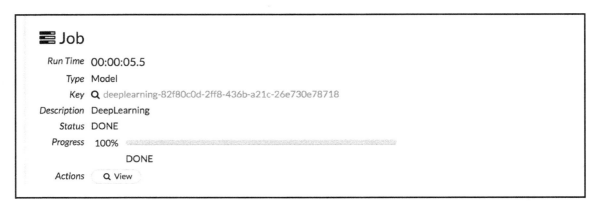

After running the model training, we can view the model output by clicking **View** to see the AUC on both the training and validation datasets:

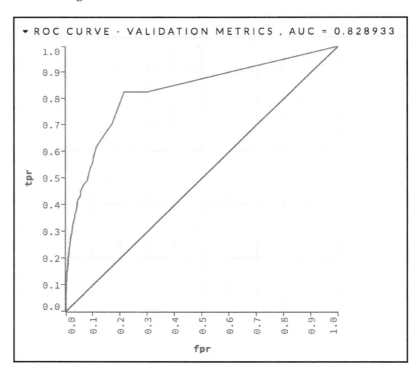

We see a higher AUC for our simple deep learning model of ~ 0.8289. This is a result without any tuning or hyperparameter searching.

What are some other steps that we can perform to improve the AUC even more? We could certainly try a new algorithm with grid searching for hyperparameters, but more interestingly, can we tune the document vectors? The answer is yes and no! It's a partial *no* because, as you will recall, word2vec is an unsupervised learning task at heart; however, we can get an idea of the strength of our vectors by observing some of the similar words returned. For example, let's take the word `drama`:

```
w2vModel.findSynonyms("drama", 5).show()
```

The output is as follows:

```
+--------+------------------+
|    word|        similarity|
+--------+------------------+
|romantic|0.5887061236424739|
|  comedy| 0.579466649385709|
|suspense|0.5774424230995622|
|thriller|0.5643072940714097|
| romance|0.5606321459552696|
+--------+------------------+
```

Intuitively, we can look at the results and ask whether these five words are *really the best* synonyms (that is, the best cosine similarities) of the the word *drama*. Let's now try rerunning our word2vec model by modifying its input parameters:

```
val newW2VModel = new Word2Vec()
    .setInputCol("reviewTokens")
    .setOutputCol("reviewVector")
    .setMinCount(3)
    .setMaxIter(250)
    .setStepSize(0.02)
    .fit(movieReviews)
    newW2VModel.findSynonyms("drama", 5).show()
```

The output is as follows:

```
+--------+------------------+
|    word|        similarity|
+--------+------------------+
|thriller| 0.6622763881272123|
|  comedy| 0.5814621487288816|
|suspense| 0.5144536036537819|
| romance| 0.5137010289175072|
|  action|0.47696545311978433|
+--------+------------------+
```

You should immediately notice that the synonyms are *better* in terms of similarity to the word in question, but also note that the cosine similarities are significantly higher for the terms as well. Recall that the default number of iterations for word2vec is 1 and now we have set it to 250, allowing our network to really triangulate on some quality word vectors, which can further be improved with more preprocessing steps and further tweaking of our hyperparameters for word2vec, which should produce document vectors of better quality.

Summary

Many companies such as Google freely give pretrained word vectors (trained on a subset of Google News, incorporating the top three million words/phrases) for various vector dimensions: for example, 25d, 50d, 100d, 300d, and so on. You can find the code (and the resulting word vectors) here. In addition to Google News, there are other sources of trained word vectors, which use Wikipedia and various languages. One question you might have is that if companies such as Google freely provide pretrained word vectors, why bother building your own? The answer to the question is, of course, application-dependent; Google's pretrained dictionary has three different vectors for the word *java* based on capitalization (JAVA, Java, and java mean different things), but perhaps, your application is just about coffee, so only one *version* of java is all that is really needed.

Our goal for this chapter was to give you a clear and concise explanation of the word2vec algorithms and very popular extensions of this algorithm, such as doc2vec and sequence-to-sequence learning models, which employ various flavors of recurrent neural networks. As always, one chapter is hardly enough time to cover this extremely exciting field in natural language processing, but hopefully, this is enough to whet your appetite for now!

As practitioners and researchers in this field, we (the authors) are constantly thinking of new ways of representing documents as fixed vectors, and there are a plenty of papers dedicated to this problem. You can consider *LDA2vec* and *Skip-thought Vectors* for further reading on the subject.

Some other blogs to add to your reading list regarding **Natural Language Processing** (**NLP**) and *Vectorizing* are as follows:

- Google's research blog (https://research.googleblog.com/)
- The NLP blog (always well thought out posts with a lot of links for further reading,) (http://nlpers.blogspot.com/))
- The Stanford NLP blog (http://nlp.stanford.edu/blog/)

In the next chapter, we will see word vectors again, where we'll combine all of what you have learned so far to tackle a problem that requires *the kitchen sink* with respect to the various processing tasks and model inputs. Stick around!

6
Extracting Patterns from Clickstream Data

When collecting real-world data between individual measures or events, there are usually very intricate and highly complex relationships to observe. The guiding example for this chapter is the observation of click events that users generate on a website and its subdomains. Such data is both interesting and challenging to investigate. It is interesting, as there are usually many *patterns* that groups of users show in their browsing behavior and certain *rules* they might follow. Gaining insights about user groups, in general, is of interest, at least for the company running the website and might be the focus of their data science team. Methodology aside, putting a production system in place that can detect patterns in real time, for instance, to find malicious behavior, can be very challenging technically. It is immensely valuable to be able to understand and implement both the algorithmic and technical sides.

In this chapter, we will look into two topics in depth: doing *pattern mining* and working with *streaming data* in Spark. The chapter is split up into two main sections. In the first, we will introduce the three available pattern mining algorithms that Spark currently comes with and apply them to an interesting dataset. In the second, we will take a more technical view on things and address the core problems that arise when deploying a streaming data application using algorithms from the first part. In particular, you will learn the following:

- The basic principles of frequent pattern mining.
- Useful and relevant data formats for applications.
- How to load and analyze a clickstream data set generated from user activity on http://MSNBC.com.
- Understanding and comparing three pattern mining algorithms available in Spark, namely *FP-growth*, *association rules*, and *prefix span*.

- How to apply these algorithms to MSNBC click data and other examples to identify the relevant patterns.
- The very basics of *Spark Streaming* and what use cases can be covered by it.
- How to put any of the preceding algorithms into production by deploying them with Spark Streaming.
- Implementing a more realistic streaming application with click events aggregated on the fly.

By construction, this chapter is more technically involved towards the end, but with *Spark Streaming* it also allows us to introduce yet another very important tool from the Spark ecosphere. We start off by presenting some of the basic questions of pattern mining and then discuss how to address them.

Frequent pattern mining

When presented with a new data set, a natural sequence of questions is:

- What kind of data do we look at; that is, what structure does it have?
- Which observations in the data can be found frequently; that is, which patterns or rules can we identify within the data?
- How do we assess what is frequent; that is, what are the good measures of relevance and how do we test for it?

On a very high level, frequent pattern mining addresses precisely these questions. While it's very easy to dive head first into more advanced machine learning techniques, these pattern mining algorithms can be quite informative and help build an intuition about the data.

To introduce some of the key notions of frequent pattern mining, let's first consider a somewhat prototypical example for such cases, namely shopping carts. The study of customers being interested in and buying certain products has been of prime interest to marketers around the globe for a very long time. While online shops certainly do help in further analyzing customer behavior, for instance, by tracking the browsing data within a shopping session, the question of what items have been bought and what patterns in buying behavior can be found applies to purely offline scenarios as well. We will see a more involved example of clickstream data accumulated on a website soon; for now, we will work under the assumption that only the events we can track are the actual payment transactions of an item.

Just this given data, for instance, for groceries shopping carts in supermarkets or online, leads to quite a few interesting questions, and we will focus mainly on the following three:

- *Which items are frequently bought together?* For instance, there is anecdotal evidence suggesting that beer and diapers are often bought together in one shopping session. Finding patterns of products that often go together may, for instance, allow a shop to physically place these products closer to each other for an increased shopping experience or promotional value even if they don't belong together at first sight. In the case of an online shop, this sort of analysis might be the base for a simple recommender system.

- Based on the previous question, *are there any interesting implications or rules to observe in shopping behaviour?*, continuing with the shopping cart example, can we establish associations such as *if bread and butter have been bought, we also often find cheese in the shopping cart*? Finding such association rules can be of great interest, but also need more clarification of what we consider to be *often*, that is, what does frequent mean.

- Note that, so far, our shopping carts were simply considered a *bag of items* without additional structure. At least in the online shopping scenario, we can endow data with more information. One aspect we will focus on is that of the *sequentiality* of items; that is, we will take note of the order in which the products have been placed into the cart. With this in mind, similar to the first question, one might ask, *which sequence of items can often be found in our transaction data?* For instance, larger electronic devices bought might be followed up by additional utility items.

The reason we focus on these three questions in particular is that Spark MLlib comes with precisely three pattern mining algorithms that roughly correspond to the aforementioned questions by their ability to answer them. Specifically, we will carefully introduce *FP-growth*, *association rules*, and *prefix span*, in that order, to address these problems and show how to solve them using Spark. Before doing so, let's take a step back and formally introduce the concepts we have been motivated for so far, alongside a running example. We will refer to the preceding three questions throughout the following subsection.

Pattern mining terminology

We will start with a set of items $I = \{a_1, ..., a_n\}$, which serves as the base for all the following concepts. A *transaction* T is just a set of items in I, and we say that T is a transaction of length l if it contains l item. A *transaction database* D is a database of transaction IDs and their corresponding transactions.

To give a concrete example of this, consider the following situation. Assume that the full item set to shop from is given by *I = {bread, cheese, ananas, eggs, donuts, fish, pork, milk, garlic, ice cream, lemon, oil, honey, jam, kale, salt}*. Since we will look at a lot of item subsets, to make things more readable later on, we will simply abbreviate these items by their first letter, that is, we'll write *I = {b, c, a, e, d, f, p, m, g, i, l, o, h, j, k, s}*. Given these items, a small transaction database D could look as follows:

Transaction ID	Transaction
1	a, c, d, f, g, i, m, p
2	a, b, c, f, l, m, o
3	b, f, h, j, o
4	b, c, k, s, p
5	a, c, e, f, l, m, n, p

Table 1: A small shopping cart database with five transactions

Frequent pattern mining problem

Given the definition of a transaction database, a *pattern* P is a *transaction contained in the transactions in D* and the support, *supp(P)*, of the pattern is the number of transactions for which this is true, divided or normalized by the number of transactions in D:

$$supp(s) = supp_D(s) = |\{\ s' \in S \mid s < s'\}| \ / \ |D|$$

We use the < symbol to denote *s* as a subpattern of *s'* or, conversely, call *s'* a superpattern of *s*. Note that in the literature, you will sometimes also find a slightly different version of support that does not normalize the value. For example, the pattern *{a, c, f}* can be found in transactions 1, 2, and 5. This means that *{a, c, f}* is a pattern of support *0.6* in our database D of five items.

Support is an important notion, as it gives us a first example of measuring the frequency of a pattern, which, in the end, is what we are after. In this context, for a given minimum support threshold *t*, we say *P* is a frequent pattern if and only if *supp(P)* is at least *t*. In our running example, the frequent patterns of length 1 and minimum support 0.6 are *{a}*, *{b}*, *{c}*, *{p}*, and *{m}* with support 0.6 and *{f}* with support 0.8. In what follows, we will often drop the brackets for items or patterns and write *f* instead of *{f}*, for instance.

Given a minimum support threshold, the problem of finding all the frequent patterns is called the *frequent pattern mining problem* and it is, in fact, the formalized version of the aforementioned first question. Continuing with our example, we have found all frequent patterns of length 1 for $t = 0.6$ already. How do we find longer patterns? On a theoretical level, given unlimited resources, this is not much of a problem, since all we need to do is count the occurrences of items. On a practical level, however, we need to be smart about how we do so to keep the computation efficient. Especially for databases large enough for Spark to come in handy, it can be very computationally intense to address the frequent pattern mining problem.

One intuitive way to go about this is as follows:

1. Find all the frequent patterns of length 1, which requires one full database scan. This is how we started with in our preceding example.
2. For patterns of length 2, generate all the combinations of frequent 1-patterns, the so-called candidates, and test if they exceed the minimum support by doing another scan of D.
3. Importantly, we do not have to consider the combinations of infrequent patterns, since patterns containing infrequent patterns can not become frequent. This rationale is called the **apriori principle**.
4. For longer patterns, continue this procedure iteratively until there are no more patterns left to combine.

This algorithm, using a generate-and-test approach to pattern mining and utilizing the apriori principle to bound combinations, is called the apriori algorithm. There are many variations of this baseline algorithm, all of which share similar drawbacks in terms of scalability. For instance, multiple full database scans are necessary to carry out the iterations, which might already be prohibitively expensive for huge data sets. On top of that, generating candidates themselves is already expensive, but computing their combinations might simply be infeasible. In the next section, we will see how a parallel version of an algorithm called *FP-growth*, available in Spark, can overcome most of the problems just discussed.

The association rule mining problem

To advance our general introduction of concepts, let's next turn to *association rules*, as first introduced in *Mining Association Rules between Sets of Items in Large Databases*, available at `http://arbor.ee.ntu.edu.tw/~chyun/dmpaper/agrama93.pdf`. In contrast to solely counting the occurrences of items in our database, we now want to understand the rules or implications of patterns. What I mean is, given a pattern P_1 and another pattern P_2, we want to know whether P_2 is frequently present whenever P_1 can be found in D, and we denote this by writing $P_1 \Rightarrow P_2$. To make this more precise, we need a concept for rule frequency similar to that of support for patterns, namely *confidence*. For a rule $P_1 \Rightarrow P_2$, confidence is defined as follows:

$$conf(P_1 \Rightarrow P_2) = supp(P_1 \cup P_2) / supp(P_1)$$

This can be interpreted as the conditional support of P_2 given to P_1; that is, if it were to restrict D to all the transactions supporting P_1, the support of P_2 in this restricted database would be equal to $conf(P_1 \Rightarrow P_2)$. We call $P_1 \Rightarrow P_2$ a rule in D if it exceeds a minimum confidence threshold t, just as in the case of frequent patterns. Finding all the rules for a confidence threshold represents the formal answer to the second question, *association rule mining*. Moreover, in this situation, we call P_1 the *antecedent* and P_2 the *consequent* of the rule. In general, there is no restriction imposed on the structure of either the antecedent or the consequent. However, in what follows, we will assume that the consequent's length is 1, for simplicity.

In our running example, the pattern *{f, m}* occurs three times, while *{f, m, p}* is just present in two cases, which means that the rule *{f, m}* ⇒ *{p}* has confidence 2/3. If we set the minimum confidence threshold to $t = 0.6$, we can easily check that the following association rules with an antecedent and consequent of length 1 are valid for our case:

{a} ⇒ *{c}*, *{a}* ⇒ *{f}*, *{a}* ⇒ *{m}*, *{a}* ⇒ *{p}*

{c} ⇒ *{a}*, *{c}* ⇒ *{f}*, *{c}* ⇒ *{m}*, *{c}* ⇒ *{p}*

{f} ⇒ *{a}*, *{f}* ⇒ *{c}*, *{f}* ⇒ *{m}*

{m} ⇒ *{a}*, *{m}* ⇒ *{c}*, *{m}* ⇒ *{f}*, *{m}* ⇒ *{p}*

{p} ⇒ *{a}*, *{p}* ⇒ *{c}*, *{p}* ⇒ *{f}*, *{p}* ⇒ *{m}*

From the preceding definition of confidence, it should now be clear that it is relatively straightforward to compute the association rules once we have the support value of all the frequent patterns. In fact, as we will soon see, Spark's implementation of association rules is based on calculating frequent patterns upfront.

 At this point, it should be noted that while we will restrict ourselves to the measures of support and confidence, there are many other interesting criteria available that we can't discuss in this book; for instance, the concepts of *conviction, leverage,* or *lift*. For an in-depth comparison of the other measures, refer to `http://www.cse.msu.edu/~ptan/papers/IS.pdf`.

The sequential pattern mining problem

Let's move on to formalizing, the third and last pattern matching question we tackle in this chapter. Let's look at *sequences* in more detail. A sequence is different from the transactions we looked at before in that the order now matters. For a given item set *I*, a sequence *S* in *I* of length *l* is defined as follows:

$$S = <s_1, s_2, ..., s_l>$$

Here, each individual s_i is a concatenation of items, that is, $s_i = (a_{i1} ... a_{im})$, where a_{ij} is an item in *I*. Note that we do care about the order of sequence items s_i but not about the internal ordering of the individual a_{ij} in s_i. A sequence database *S* consists of pairs of sequence IDs and sequences, analogous to what we had before. An example of such a database can be found in the following table, in which the letters represent the same items as in our previous shopping cart example:

Sequence ID	Sequence
1	<a(abc)(ac)d(cf)>
2	<(ad)c(bc)(ae)>
3	<(ef)(ab)(df)cb>
4	<eg(af)cbc>

Table 2: A small sequence database with four short sequences.

In the example sequences, note the round brackets to group individual items into a sequence item. Also note that we drop these redundant braces if the sequence item consists of a single item. Importantly, the notion of a subsequence requires a little more carefulness than for unordered structures. We call $u = (u_1, ..., u_n)$ a subsequence of $s = (s_1, ..., s_l)$ and write $u < s$ if there are indices $1 \le i1 < i2 < ... < in \le m$ so that we have the following:

$$u_1 < s_{i1}, ..., u_n < s_{in}$$

Here, the $<$ signs in the last line mean that u_j is a subpattern of s_{ij}. Roughly speaking, u is a subsequence of s if all the elements of u are subpatterns of s in their given order. Equivalently, we call s a supersequence of u. In the preceding example, we see that $<a(ab)ac>$ and $a(cb)(ac)dc>$ are examples of subsequences of $<a(abc)(ac)d(cf)>$ and that $<(fa)c>$ is an example of a subsequence of $<eg(af)cbc>$.

With the help of the notion of supersequences, we can now define the *support* of a sequence s in a given sequence database S as follows:

$$supp_S(s) = supp(s) = |\{ s' \in S \mid s < s'\}| / |S|$$

Note that, structurally, this is the same definition as for plain unordered patterns, but the $<$ symbol means something else, that is, a subsequence. As before, we drop the database subscript in the notation of *support* if the information is clear from the context. Equipped with a notion of *support*, the definition of sequential patterns follows the previous definition completely analogously. Given a minimum support threshold t, a sequence s in S is said to be a *sequential pattern* if $supp(s)$ is greater than or equal to t. The formalization of the third question is called the *sequential pattern mining problem*, that is, find the full set of sequences that are sequential patterns in S for a given threshold t.

Even in our little example with just four sequences, it can already be challenging to manually inspect all the sequential patterns. To give just one example of a sequential pattern of *support 1.0*, a subsequence of length 2 of all the four sequences is $<ac>$. Finding all the sequential patterns is an interesting problem, and we will learn about the so-called *prefix span* algorithm that Spark employs to address the problem in the following section.

Pattern mining with Spark MLlib

After having motivated and introduced three pattern mining problems along with the necessary notation to properly talk about them, we will next discuss how each of these problems can be solved with an algorithm available in Spark MLlib. As is often the case, actually applying the algorithms themselves is fairly simple due to Spark MLlib's convenient `run` method available for most algorithms. What is more challenging is to understand the algorithms and the intricacies that come with them. To this end, we will explain the three pattern mining algorithms one by one, and study how they are implemented and how to use them on toy examples. Only after having done all this will we apply these algorithms to a real-life data set of click events retrieved from `http://MSNBC.com`.

The documentation for the pattern mining algorithms in Spark can be found at `https://spark.apache.org/docs/2.1.0/mllib-frequent-pattern-mining.html`. It provides a good entry point with examples for users who want to dive right in.

Frequent pattern mining with FP-growth

When we introduced the frequent pattern mining problem, we also quickly discussed a strategy to address it based on the apriori principle. The approach was based on scanning the whole transaction database again and again to expensively generate pattern candidates of growing length and checking their support. We indicated that this strategy may not be feasible for very large data.

The so called *FP-growth algorithm*, where **FP** stands for **frequent pattern**, provides an interesting solution to this data mining problem. The algorithm was originally described in *Mining Frequent Patterns without Candidate Generation*, available at `https://www.cs.sfu.ca/~jpei/publications/sigmod00.pdf`. We will start by explaining the basics of this algorithm and then move on to discussing its distributed version, *parallel FP-growth*, which has been introduced in *PFP: Parallel FP-Growth for Query Recommendation*, found at `https://static.googleusercontent.com/media/research.google.com/en//pubs/archive/34668.pdf`. While Spark's implementation is based on the latter paper, it is best to first understand the baseline algorithm and extend from there.

The core idea of FP-growth is to scan the transaction database D of interest precisely once in the beginning, find all the frequent patterns of length 1, and build a special tree structure called *FP-tree* from these patterns. Once this step is done, instead of working with D, we only do recursive computations on the usually much smaller FP-tree. This step is called the *FP-growth step* of the algorithm, since it recursively constructs trees from the subtrees of the original tree to identify patterns. We will call this procedure *fragment pattern growth*, which does not require us to generate candidates but is rather built on a *divide-and-conquer* strategy that heavily reduces the workload in each recursion step.

To be more precise, let's first define what an FP-tree is and what it looks like in an example. Recall the example database we used in the last section, shown in *Table 1*. Our item set consisted of the following 15 grocery items, represented by their first letter: $b, c, a, e, d, f, p, m, i, l, o, h, j, k, s$. We also discussed the frequent items; that is, patterns of length 1, for a minimum support threshold of $t = 0.6$, were given by $\{f, c, b, a, m, p\}$. In FP-growth, we first use the fact that the ordering of items does not matter for the frequent pattern mining problem; that is, we can choose the order in which to present the frequent items. We do so by ordering them by decreasing frequency. To summarize the situation, let's have a look at the following table:

Transaction ID	Transaction	Ordered frequent items
1	a, c, d, f, g, i, m, p	f, c, a, m, p
2	a, b, c, f, l, m, o	f, c, a, b, m
3	b, f, h, j, o	f, b
4	b, c, k, s, p	c, b, p
5	a, c, e, f, l, m, n, p	f, c, a, m, p

Table 3: Continuation of the example started with Table 1, augmenting the table by ordered frequent items.

As we can see, ordering frequent items like this already helps us to identify some structure. For instance, we see that the item set $\{f, c, a, m, p\}$ occurs twice and is slightly altered once as $\{f, c, a, b, m\}$. The key idea of FP-growth is to use this representation to build a tree from the ordered frequent items that reflect the structure and interdependencies of the items in the third column of *Table 3*. Every FP-tree has a so-called *root* node that is used as a base for connecting ordered frequent items as constructed. On the right of the following diagram, we see what is meant by this:

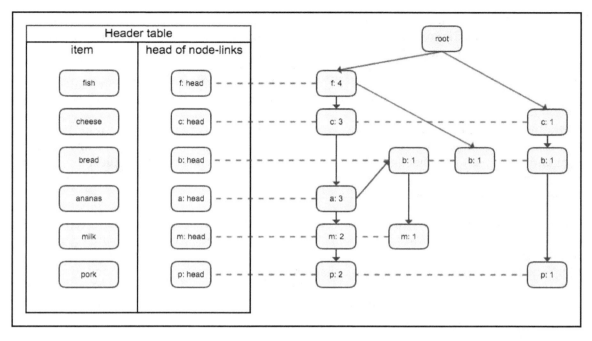

Figure 1: FP-tree and header table for our frequent pattern mining running example.

The left-hand side of *Figure 1* shows a header table that we will explain and formalize in just a bit, while the right-hand side shows the actual FP-tree. For each of the ordered frequent items in our example, there is a directed path starting from the root, thereby representing it. Each node of the tree keeps track of not only the frequent item itself but also of the number of paths traversed through this node. For instance, four of the five ordered frequent item sets start with the letter *f* and one with *c*. Thus, in the FP-tree, we see f: 4 and c: 1 at the top level. Another interpretation of this fact is that *f* is a *prefix* for four item sets and *c* for one. For another example of this sort of reasoning, let's turn our attention to the lower left of the tree, that is, to the leaf node p: 2. Two occurrences of *p* tells us that precisely two identical paths end here, which we already know: *{f, c, a, m, p}* is represented twice. This observation is interesting, as it already hints at a technique used in FP-growth--starting at the leaf nodes of the tree, or the suffixes of the item sets, we can trace back each frequent item set, and the union of all these distinct root node paths yields all the paths--an important idea for parallelization.

The header table you see on the left of *Figure 1* is a smart way of storing items. Note that by the construction of the tree, a node is not the same as a frequent item but, rather, items can and usually do occur multiple times, namely once for each distinct path they are part of. To keep track of items and how they relate, the header table is essentially a *linked list* of items, that is, each item occurrence is linked to the next by means of this table. We indicated the links for each frequent item by horizontal dashed lines in *Figure 1* for illustration purposes.

With this example in mind, let's now give a formal definition of an FP-tree. An FP-tree *T* is a tree that consists of a root node together with frequent item prefix subtrees starting at the root and a frequent item header table. Each node of the tree consists of a triple, namely the item name, its occurrence count, and a node link referring to the next node of the same name, or `null` if there is no such next node.

To quickly recap, to build *T*, we start by computing the frequent items for the given minimum support threshold *t*, and then, starting from the root, insert each path represented by the sorted frequent pattern list of a transaction into the tree. Now, what do we gain from this? The most important property to consider is that all the information needed to solve the frequent pattern mining problem is encoded in the FP-tree *T* because we effectively encode all co-occurrences of frequent items with repetition. Since *T* can also have at most as many nodes as the occurrences of frequent items, *T* is usually much smaller than our original database D. This means that we have mapped the mining problem to a problem on a smaller data set, which in itself reduces the computational complexity compared with the naive approach sketched earlier.

Next, we'll discuss how to grow patterns recursively from fragments obtained from the constructed FP tree. To do so, let's make the following observation. For any given frequent item *x*, we can obtain all the patterns involving *x* by following the node links for *x*, starting from the header table entry for *x*, by analyzing at the respective subtrees. To explain how exactly, we further study our example and, starting at the bottom of the header table, analyze patterns containing *p*. From our FP-tree *T*, it is clear that *p* occurs in two paths: *(f:4, c:3, a:3, m:3, p:2)* and *(c:1, b:1, p:1)*, following the node links for *p*. Now, in the first path, *p* occurs only twice, that is, there can be at most two total occurrences of the pattern *{f, c, a, m, p}* in the original database D. So, conditional on *p* being present, the paths involving *p* actually read as follows: *(f:2, c:2, a:2, m:2, p:2)* and *(c:1, b:1, p:1)*. In fact, since we know we want to analyze patterns, given *p*, we can shorten the notation a little and simply write *(f:2, c:2, a:2, m:2)* and *(c:1, b:1)*. This is what we call the **conditional pattern base for p**. Going one step further, we can construct a new FP-tree from this conditional database. Conditioning on three occurrences of *p*, this new tree does only consist of a single node, namely *(c:3)*. This means that we end up with *{c, p}* as a single pattern involving *p*, apart from *p* itself. To have a better means of talking about this situation, we introduce the following notation: the conditional FP-tree for *p* is denoted by *{(c:3)}* | *p*.

To gain more intuition, let's consider one more frequent item and discuss its conditional pattern base. Continuing bottom to top and analyzing *m*, we again see two paths that are relevant: *(f:4, c:3, a:3, m:2)* and *(f:4, c:3, a:3, b:1, m:1)*. Note that in the first path, we discard the *p:2* at the end, since we have already covered the case of *p*. Following the same logic of reducing all other counts to the count of the item in question and conditioning on *m*, we end up with the conditional pattern base *{(f:2, c:2, a:2), (f:1, c:1, a:1, b:1)}*. The conditional FP-tree in this situation is thus given by *{f:3, c:3, a:3}| m*. It is now easy to see that actually every possible combination of *m* with each of *f*, *c*, and *a* forms a frequent pattern. The full set of patterns, given *m*, is thus *{m}, {am}, {cm}, {fm}, {cam}, {fam}, {fcm}*, and *{fcam}*. By now, it should become clear as to how to continue, and we will not carry out this exercise in full but rather summarize the outcome of it in the following table:

Frequent pattern	Conditional pattern base	Conditional FP-tree
p	*{(f:2, c:2, a:2, m:2), (c:1, b:1)}*	*{(c:3)}| p*
m	*{(f :2, c:2, a:2), (f :1, c:1, a:1, b:1)}*	*{f:3, c:3, a:3}| m*
b	*{(f :1, c:1, a:1), (f :1), (c:1)}*	null
a	*{(f:3, c:3)}*	*{(f:3, c:3)}| a*
c	*{(f:3)}*	*{(f:3)}| c*
f	null	null

Table 4: The complete list of conditional FP-trees and conditional pattern bases for our running example.

As this derivation required a lot of attention to detail, let's take a step back and summarize the situation so far:

1. Starting from the original FP-tree *T*, we iterated through all the items using node links.
2. For each item *x*, we constructed its conditional pattern base and its conditional FP-tree. Doing so, we used the following two properties:
   - We discarded all the items following *x* in each potential pattern, that is, we only kept the *prefix* of *x*
   - We modified the item counts in the conditional pattern base to match the count of *x*
3. Modifying a path using the latter two properties, we called the transformed prefix path of *x*.

To finally state the FP-growth step of the algorithm, we need two more fundamental observations that we have already implicitly used in the example. Firstly, the support of an item in a conditional pattern base is the same as that of its representation in the original database. Secondly, starting from a frequent pattern x in the original database and an arbitrary set of items y, we know that xy is a frequent pattern if and only if y is. These two facts can easily be derived in general, but should be clearly demonstrated in the preceding example.

What this means is that we can completely focus on finding patterns in conditional pattern bases, as joining them with frequent patterns is again a pattern, and this way, we can find all the patterns. This mechanism of recursively growing patterns by computing conditional pattern bases is therefore called pattern growth, which is why FP-growth bears its name. With all this in mind, we can now summarize the FP-growth procedure in pseudocode, as follows:

```
def fpGrowth(tree: FPTree, i: Item):
    if (tree consists of a single path P){
        compute transformed prefix path P' of P
        return all combinations p in P' joined with i
    }
    else{
        for each item in tree {
            newI = i joined with item
            construct conditional pattern base and conditional FP-tree
newTree
            call fpGrowth(newTree, newI)
        }
    }
```

With this procedure, we can summarize our description of the complete FP-growth algorithm as follows:

1. Compute frequent items from D and compute the original FP-tree T from them (*FP-tree computation*).
2. Run `fpGrowth(T, null)` (*FP-growth computation*).

Having understood the base construction, we can now proceed to discuss a parallel extension of base FP-growth, that is, the basis of Spark's implementation. **Parallel FP-growth**, or **PFP** for short, is a natural evolution of FP-growth for parallel computing engines such as Spark. It addresses the following problems with the baseline algorithm:

- *Distributed storage:* For frequent pattern mining, our database D may not fit into memory, which can already render FP-growth in its original form unapplicable. Spark does help in this regard for obvious reasons.
- *Distributed computing:* With distributed storage in place, we will have to take care of parallelizing all the steps of the algorithm suitably as well and PFP does precisely this.
- *Adequate support values:* When dealing with finding frequent patterns, we usually do not want to set the minimum support threshold t too high so as to find interesting patterns in the long tail. However, a small t might prevent the FP-tree from fitting into memory for a sufficiently large D, which would force us to increase t. PFP successfully addresses this problem as well, as we will see.

The basic outline of PFP, with Spark for implementation in mind, is as follows:

- **Sharding**: Instead of storing our database D on a single machine, we distribute it to multiple partitions. Regardless of the particular storage layer, using Spark we can, for instance, create an RDD to load D.
- **Parallel frequent item count**: The first step of computing frequent items of D can be naturally performed as a map-reduce operation on an RDD.
- **Building groups of frequent items**: The set of frequent items is divided into a number of groups, each with a unique group ID.
- **Parallel FP-growth**: The FP-growth step is split into two steps to leverage parallelism:
    - **Map phase**: The output of a mapper is a pair comprising the group ID and the corresponding transaction.
    - **Reduce phase**: Reducers collect data according to the group ID and carry out FP-growth on these group-dependent transactions.
- **Aggregation**: The final step in the algorithm is the aggregation of results over group IDs.

In light of already having spent a lot of time with FP-growth on its own, instead of going into too many implementation details of PFP in Spark, let's instead see how to use the actual algorithm on the toy example that we have used throughout:

```
import org.apache.spark.mllib.fpm.FPGrowth
import org.apache.spark.rdd.RDD
```

```
val transactions: RDD[Array[String]] = sc.parallelize(Array(
  Array("a", "c", "d", "f", "g", "i", "m", "p"),
  Array("a", "b", "c", "f", "l", "m", "o"),
  Array("b", "f", "h", "j", "o"),
  Array("b", "c", "k", "s", "p"),
  Array("a", "c", "e", "f", "l", "m", "n", "p")
))

val fpGrowth = new FPGrowth()
  .setMinSupport(0.6)
  .setNumPartitions(5)
val model = fpGrowth.run(transactions)

model.freqItemsets.collect().foreach { itemset =>
  println(itemset.items.mkString("[", ",", "]") + ", " + itemset.freq)
}
```

The code is straightforward. We load the data into `transactions` and initialize
Spark's `FPGrowth` implementation with a minimum support value of *0.6* and *5* partitions.
This returns a model that we can `run` on the transactions constructed earlier. Doing so gives
us access to the patterns or frequent item sets for the specified minimum support, by calling
`freqItemsets`, which, printed in a formatted way, yields the following output of 18
patterns in total:

```
[m], 3
[m,c], 3
[m,c,f], 3
[m,a], 3
[m,a,c], 3
[m,a,c,f], 3
[m,a,f], 3
[m,f], 3
[f], 4
[c], 4
[c,f], 3
[p], 3
[p,c], 3
[a], 3
[a,c], 3
[a,c,f], 3
[a,f], 3
[b], 3
```

Recall that we have defined transactions as *sets*, and we often call them item sets. This means that within such an item set, a particular item can only occur once, and FPGrowth depends on this. If we were to replace, for instance, the third transaction in the preceding example by Array("b", "b", "h", "j", "o"), calling run on these transactions would throw an error message. We will see later on how to deal with such situations.

After having explained *association rules* and *prefix span* in a similar fashion to what we just did with FP-growth, we will turn to an application of these algorithms on a real-world data set.

Association rule mining

Recall from the association rule introduction that in computing association rules, we are about halfway there once we have frequent item sets, that is, patterns for the specified minimum threshold. In fact, Spark's implementation of association rules assumes that we provide an RDD of FreqItemsets[Item], which we have already seen an example of in the preceding call to model.freqItemsets. On top of that, computing association rules is not only available as a standalone algorithm but is also available through FPGrowth.

Before showing how to run the respective algorithm on our running example, let's quickly explain how association rules are implemented in Spark:

1. The algorithm is already provided with frequent item sets, so we don't have to compute them anymore.
2. For each pair of patterns, X and Y, compute the frequency of both items X and Y co-occurring and store $(X, (Y, supp(X \cup Y)))$. We call such pairs of patterns *candidate pairs*, where X acts as a potential antecedent and Y as a consequent.
3. Join all the patterns with the candidate pairs to obtain statements of the form, $(X, ((Y, supp(X \cup Y)), supp(X)))$.
4. We can then filter expressions of the form $(X, ((Y, supp(X \cup Y)), supp(X)))$ by the desired minimum confidence value to return all rules $X \Rightarrow Y$ with that level of confidence.

Assuming we didn't compute the patterns through FP-growth in the last section but, instead, were just given the full list of these item sets, we can create an RDD from a sequence of `FreqItemset` from scratch and then run a new instance of `AssociationRules` on it:

```
import org.apache.spark.mllib.fpm.AssociationRules
import org.apache.spark.mllib.fpm.FPGrowth.FreqItemset

val patterns: RDD[FreqItemset[String]] = sc.parallelize(Seq(
  new FreqItemset(Array("m"), 3L),
  new FreqItemset(Array("m", "c"), 3L),
  new FreqItemset(Array("m", "c", "f"), 3L),
  new FreqItemset(Array("m", "a"), 3L),
  new FreqItemset(Array("m", "a", "c"), 3L),
  new FreqItemset(Array("m", "a", "c", "f"), 3L),
  new FreqItemset(Array("m", "a", "f"), 3L),
  new FreqItemset(Array("m", "f"), 3L),
  new FreqItemset(Array("f"), 4L),
  new FreqItemset(Array("c"), 4L),
  new FreqItemset(Array("c", "f"), 3L),
  new FreqItemset(Array("p"), 3L),
  new FreqItemset(Array("p", "c"), 3L),
  new FreqItemset(Array("a"), 3L),
  new FreqItemset(Array("a", "c"), 3L),
  new FreqItemset(Array("a", "c", "f"), 3L),
  new FreqItemset(Array("a", "f"), 3L),
  new FreqItemset(Array("b"), 3L)
))

val associationRules = new AssociationRules().setMinConfidence(0.7)
val rules = associationRules.run(patterns)

rules.collect().foreach { rule =>
  println("[" + rule.antecedent.mkString(",") + "=>"
    + rule.consequent.mkString(",") + "]," + rule.confidence)
}
```

Note that after initializing the algorithm, we set the minimum confidence to `0.7` before collecting the results. Moreover, running `AssociationRules` returns an RDD of rules of the `Rule` type. These rule objects have accessors for `antecedent`, `consequent`, and `confidence`, which we use to collect the results that read as follows:

```
[m,a=>c],1.0
[m,a=>f],1.0
[m,a,c=>f],1.0
[m,a,f=>c],1.0
[a,f=>m],1.0
[a,f=>c],1.0
[m,c=>f],1.0
[m,c=>a],1.0
[a=>m],1.0
[a=>c],1.0
[a=>f],1.0
[a,c=>m],1.0
[a,c=>f],1.0
[m,f=>c],1.0
[m,f=>a],1.0
[m,c,f=>a],1.0
[c,f=>m],1.0
[c,f=>a],1.0
[a,c,f=>m],1.0
[m=>c],1.0
[m=>a],1.0
[m=>f],1.0
[f=>m],0.75
[f=>c],0.75
[f=>a],0.75
[p=>c],1.0
[c=>m],0.75
[c=>f],0.75
[c=>p],0.75
[c=>a],0.75
```

The reason we started this example from scratch is to convey the idea that association rules are indeed a standalone algorithm in Spark. Since the only built-in way to compute patterns in Spark is currently through FP-growth, and association rules depends on the concept of FreqItemset (imported from the FPGrowth submodule) anyway, this seems a bit unpractical. Using our results from the previous FP-growth example, we could well have written the following to achieve the same:

```
val patterns = model.freqItemsets
```

Interestingly, association rules can also be computed directly through the interface of `FPGrowth`. Continuing with the notation from the earlier example, we can simply write the following to end up with the same set of rules as before:

```
val rules = model.generateAssociationRules(confidence = 0.7)
```

In practical terms, while both the formulations can be useful, the latter one will certainly be more concise.

Sequential pattern mining with prefix span

Turning to sequential pattern matching, the *prefix span algorithm* is a little more complicated than association rules, so we need to take a step back and explain the basics first. Prefix span has first been described in `http://hanj.cs.illinois.edu/pdf/tkde04_spgjn.pdf` as a natural extension of the so-called *FreeSpan* algorithm. The algorithm itself represents a notable improvement over other approaches, such as **Generalized Sequential Patterns (GSP)**. The latter is based on the apriori principle and all the drawbacks we discussed earlier regarding many algorithms based on it carry over to sequential mining as well, that is, expensive candidate generation, multiple database scans, and so on.

Prefix span, in its basic formulation, uses the same fundamental idea as FP-growth, which is, projecting the original database to a usually smaller structure to analyze. While in FP-growth, we recursively built new FP-trees for each *suffix* of a branch in the original FP-tree, prefix span grows or spans new structures by considering *prefixes*, as the name suggests.

Let's first properly define the intuitive notions of prefix and suffix in the context of sequences. In what follows, we'll always assume that the items within a sequence item are alphabetically ordered, that is, if $s = <s_1, s_2, ..., s_i>$ is a sequence in S and each s_i is a concatenation of items, that is, $s_i = (a_{i1} ... a_{im})$, where a_{ij} are items in I, we assume that all a_{ij} are in the alphabetical order within s_i. In such a situation, an element $s' = <s'_1, s'_2, ..., s'm>$ is called a prefix of s if and only if the following three properties are satisfied:

- For all $i < m$, we have equality of sequence items, that is, $s'_i = s_i$
- $s'_m < s_m$, that is, the last item of s' is a subpattern of s_m
- If we subtract s'_m from s_m, that is, delete the subpattern s'_m from s_m, all the frequent items left in $s_m - s'_m$ have to come after all the elements in s'_m, in alphabetical order

While the first two points come fairly naturally, the last one might seem a little strange, so let's explain it in an example. Given a sequence, *<a(abc)>*, from a database D, in which *a*, *b*, and *c* are indeed frequent, then, *<aa>* and *<a(ab)>* are prefixes for *<a(abc)>*, but *<ab>* is not, because in the difference of the last sequence items, *<(abc)> - <b> = <(ac)>*, the letter *a* does not alphabetically come after *b* from *<ab>*. Essentially, the third property tells us that a prefix can only cut out parts at the beginning of the last sequence item it affects.

With the notion of the prefix defined, it is now easy to say what a suffix is. With the same notation as before, if *s'* is a prefix of *s*, then $s'' = <(s_m - s'_m), s_{m+1}, ..., s_l>$ is a suffix for this prefix, which we denote as *s'' = s / s'*. Furthermore, we will write *s = s's''* in a product notation. For instance, given that *<a(abc)>* is the original sequence and *<aa>* is the prefix, we denote the suffix for this prefix as follows:

$$<(\_bc)> = <a(abc)> / <aa>$$

Note that we use an underscore notation to denote the remainder of a sequence by a prefix.

Both the prefix and suffix notions are useful to split up or partition the original sequential pattern mining problem into smaller parts, as follows. Let $\{<p_1>, ..., <p_n>\}$ be the complete set of sequential patterns of length 1. Then, we can make the following observations:

- All the sequential patterns start with one of the p_i. This, in turn, means that we can partition all sequential patterns into *n* disjoint sets, namely those starting with p_i, for *i* between *1* and *n*.
- Applying this reasoning recursively, we end up with the following statement: if *s* is a given sequential pattern of length 1 and $\{s^1, ..., s^m\}$ is the complete list of length *l+1* sequential superpatterns of *s*, then all sequential patterns with the prefix *s* can be partitioned into *m* sets prefixed by s^i.

Both these statements are easy to arrive at but provide a powerful tool to subdivide the original problem set into disjointed smaller problems. Such a strategy is called *divide and conquer*. With this in mind, we can now proceed very similarly to what we did with conditioned databases in FP-growth, namely project databases with respect to a given prefix. Given a sequential pattern database S and a prefix *s*, the **s-projected database**, $S|_s$, is the set of all the suffixes for *s* in S.

We need one last definition to state and analyze the prefix span algorithm. If s is a sequential pattern in S and x is a pattern with a prefix s, then the *support count* of x in $S|_s$, denoted by $supp_{S|s}(x)$, is the number of sequences y in $S|_s$ so that $x < sy$; that is, we simply carry over the notion of support to s-projected databases. There are a few interesting properties we can derive from this definition that make our situation much easier. For instance, by definition, we see that for any sequence x with the prefix s, we have the following:

$$supp_s(x) = supp_{S|s}(x)$$

That is, it does not matter if we count the support in the original or projected database in this case. Moreover, if s' is a prefix of s, it is clear that $S|_s = (S|_{s'})|_{s'}$, meaning we can prefix consecutively without losing information. The last and most important statement from a computational complexity perspective is that a projected database cannot exceed its original size. This property should again be clear from the definitions, but it's immensely helpful to justify the recursive nature of prefix span.

Given all this information, we can now sketch the prefix span algorithm in pseudocode as follows. Note that we distinguish between an item `s'` being appended to the end of a sequential pattern `s` and the sequence `<s'>` generated from `s'` added to the end of `s`. To give an example, we could either add the letter *e* to *<a(abc)>* to form *<a(abce)>* or add *<e>* at the end to form *<a(abc)e>*:

```
def prefixSpan(s: Prefix, l: Length, S: ProjectedDatabase):
  S' = set of all s' in S|_s if {
    (s' appended to s is a sequential pattern) or
    (<s'> appended to s is a sequential pattern)
  }
  for s' in S' {
    s'' = s' appended to s
    output s''
    call prefixSpan(s'', l+1, S|_s'')
  }
}
call prefixSpan(<>, 0, S)
```

The prefix span algorithm, as outlined, finds all sequential patterns; that is, it represents a solution to the sequential pattern mining problem. We cannot outline the proof of this statement here, but we hopefully have provided you with enough intuition to see how and why it works.

Turning to Spark for an example, note that we did not discuss how to effectively parallelize the baseline algorithm. If you are interested in knowing about the implementation details, see `https://github.com/apache/spark/blob/v2.2.0/mllib/src/main/scala/org/apache/spark/mllib/fpm/PrefixSpan.scala`, as the parallel version is a little too involved would justify presenting it here. We will study the example first provided in *Table 2*, that is, the four sequences of *<a(abc)(ac)d(cf)>*, *<(ad)c(bc)(ae)>*, *<(ef)(ab)(df)cb>*, and *<eg(af)cbc>*. To encode the nested structure of sequences, we use arrays of arrays of strings and parallelize them to create an RDD from them. Initializing and running an instance of `PrefixSpan` works pretty much the same way as it did for the other two algorithms. The only thing noteworthy here is that, apart from setting the minimum support threshold to 0.7 via `setMinSupport`, we also specify the maximum length of the patterns to 5 through `setMaxPatternLength`. This last parameter is there to limit the recursion depth. Despite the clever implementation, the algorithm (and particularly, the computing database projections) can take a prohibitive amount of time:

```scala
import org.apache.spark.mllib.fpm.PrefixSpan

val sequences:RDD[Array[Array[String]]] = sc.parallelize(Seq(
  Array(Array("a"), Array("a", "b", "c"), Array("a", "c"), Array("d"),
Array("c", "f")),
 Array(Array("a", "d"), Array("c"), Array("b", "c"), Array("a", "e")),
 Array(Array("e", "f"), Array("a", "b"), Array("d", "f"), Array("c"),
Array("b")),
 Array(Array("e"), Array("g"), Array("a", "f"), Array("c"), Array("b"),
Array("c")) ))
val prefixSpan = new PrefixSpan()
  .setMinSupport(0.7)
  .setMaxPatternLength(5)
val model = prefixSpan.run(sequences)
model.freqSequences.collect().foreach {
  freqSequence => println(freqSequence.sequence.map(_.mkString("[", ", ",
"]")).mkString("[", ", ", "]") + ", " + freqSequence.freq) }
```

Running this code in your Spark shell should yield the following output of 14 sequential patterns:

```
[[e]], 3
[[d]], 3
[[b]], 4
[[c]], 4
[[f]], 3
[[a]], 4
[[d], [c]], 3
[[b], [c]], 3
[[c], [b]], 3
[[c], [c]], 3
[[a], [b]], 4
[[a], [c]], 4
[[a], [c], [b]], 3
[[a], [c], [c]], 3
```

Pattern mining on MSNBC clickstream data

Having spent a considerable amount of time explaining the basics of pattern mining, let's finally turn to a more realistic application. The data we will be discussing next comes from server logs from http://msnbc.com (and in parts from http://msn.com, when news-related), and represents a full day's worth of browsing activity in terms of page views of users of these sites. The data collected in September 1999 and has been made available for download at http://archive.ics.uci.edu/ml/machine-learning-databases/msnbc-mld/msnbc990928.seq.gz. Storing this file locally and unzipping it, the msnbc990928.seq file essentially consists of a header and space-separated rows of integers of varying length. The following are the first few lines of the file:

```
% Different categories found in input file:

frontpage news tech local opinion on-air misc weather msn-news health
living business msn-sports sports summary bbs travel

% Sequences:

1 1
2
3 2 2 4 2 2 2 3 3
5
1
6
1 1
```

```
6
6 7 7 7 6 6 8 8 8 8
```

Each row in this file is a *sequence* of encoded page visits of users within that day. Page visits have not been collected to the most granular level but rather grouped into 17 news-related categories, which are encoded as integers. The category names corresponding to these categories are listed in the preceding header and are mostly self-explanatory (with the exception of `bbs`, which stands for **bulletin board service**). The n-th item in this list corresponds to category n; for example, 1 stands for `frontpage`, while `travel` is encoded as 17. For instance, the fourth user in this file hit `opinion` once, while the third had nine page views in total, starting and ending with `tech`.

It is important to note that the page visits in each row have indeed been stored *chronologically*, that is, this really is sequential data with respect to page visit order. In total, data for 989,818 users has been collected; that is, the data set has precisely that number of sequences. Unfortunately, it is unknown how many URLs have been grouped to form each category, but we do know it ranges rather widely from 10 to 5,000. See the description available at `http://archive.ics.uci.edu/ml/machine-learning-databases/msnbc-mld/msnbc.data.html` for more information.

Just from the description of this data set, it should be clear that all the three pattern mining problems we have discussed so far can be applied to this data--we can search for sequential patterns in this sequential database and, neglecting the sequentiality, analyze both frequent patterns and association rules. To do so, let's first load the data using Spark. In what follows, we will assume that the header of the file has been removed and a Spark shell session has been created from the folder the sequence file is stored in:

```
val transactions: RDD[Array[Int]] = sc.textFile("./msnbc990928.seq") map {
line =>
  line.split(" ").map(_.toInt)
}
```

We load the sequence file into an RDD of integer-valued arrays first. Recall from earlier sections that one of the assumptions of transactions in frequent pattern mining was that the item sets are, in fact, sets and thus contain no duplicates. To apply FP-growth and association rule mining, we therefore have to delete duplicate entries, as follows:

```
val uniqueTransactions: RDD[Array[Int]] =
transactions.map(_.distinct).cache()
```

Note that not only did we restrict to distinct items for each transaction but we also cached the resulting RDD, which is recommended for all the three pattern mining algorithms. This allows us to run FP-growth on this data, for which we have to find a suitable minimum support threshold *t*. So far, in the toy examples, we have chosen *t* to be rather large (between 0.6 and 0.8). It is not realistic to expect *any* patterns to have such large support values in larger databases. Although we only have to deal with 17 categories, browsing behaviors can vary drastically from user to user. Instead, we choose a support value of just 5 % to gain some insights:

```
val fpGrowth = new FPGrowth().setMinSupport(0.05)
val model = fpGrowth.run(uniqueTransactions)
val count = uniqueTransactions.count()

model.freqItemsets.collect().foreach { itemset =>
    println(itemset.items.mkString("[", ",", "]") + ", " + itemset.freq /
count.toDouble )
}
```

The output of this computation shows that for *t=0.05* we only recover 14 frequent patterns, as follows:

```
[9], 0.09111978161641837
[2], 0.17708912143444552
[2,1], 0.07547246059376572
[4], 0.1229710916552336
[13], 0.0777395440373887
[10], 0.05112657074330836
[12], 0.11333699730657555
[1], 0.3164026113891645
[11], 0.05818948533972912
[14], 0.12036354158037134
[8], 0.09659856660517388
[6], 0.21933426145008475
[7], 0.08134222655073962
[3], 0.12320244731859796
```

Not only are there, maybe, less patterns than you may have expected, but among those, all but one have a length of *1*. Less surprising is the fact that the *front page* is hit most often, with 31%, followed by the categories, *on-air* and *news*. Both the *front page* and *news* sites have been visited by only 7% of users on that day and no other pair of site categories was visited by more than 5% of the user base. Categories 5, 15, 16, and 17 don't even make the list. If we repeat the experiment with a *t* value of 1% instead, the number of patterns increases to a total of 74.

Let's see how many length-3 patterns are among them:

```
model.freqItemsets.collect().foreach { itemset =>
  if (itemset.items.length >= 3)
    println(itemset.items.mkString("[", ",", "]") + ", " + itemset.freq /
count.toDouble )
}
```

Running this on an `FPGrowth` instance with a minimum support value of *t=0.01* will yield the following result:

```
[2,6,1], 0.015261391488132162
[4,2,1], 0.016736410127922506
[10,2,1], 0.01219820209371824
[12,2,1], 0.015683691345277615
[11,2,1], 0.013232735715050646
[14,2,1], 0.012118389441291228
[7,2,1], 0.013082202990852864
[7,4,2], 0.010486776356865606
[7,4,1], 0.014752206971382617
[7,6,1], 0.011334406931375263
[3,2,1], 0.014854245932080443
```

As one could have guessed, the most frequent length-1 patterns are also predominant among the 3-patterns. Within these 11 patterns, 10 concern the *front page,* and nine the *news.* Interestingly, the category *misc,* while only visited 7% of the time, according to the earlier analysis, shows up in a total of four 3-patterns. If we had more information about the underlying user groups, it would be interesting to follow up on this pattern. Speculatively, users that have an interest in a lot of *miscellaneous* topics will end up in this mixed category, along with some other categories.

Following this up with an analysis of association rules is technically easy; we just run the following lines to get all the rules with confidence 0.4 from the existing FP-growth `model`:

```
val rules = model.generateAssociationRules(confidence = 0.4)
rules.collect().foreach { rule =>
  println("[" + rule.antecedent.mkString(",") + "]=>"
    + rule.consequent.mkString(",") + "]," + (100 * rule.confidence).round
/ 100.0)
}
```

Note how we can conveniently access the antecedent, consequent, and confidence of the respective rules. The output of this is as follows; this time with the confidence rounded to two decimals:

```
[2,6=>1],0.59
[3,2=>1],0.58
[7=>6],0.41
[7=>1],0.45
[14,2=>1],0.63
[4,1=>2],0.42
[3,1=>2],0.44
[11,2=>1],0.75
[5=>1],0.49
[4,2=>1],0.6
[7,1=>4],0.4
[7,2=>1],0.65
[7,2=>4],0.52
[11=>1],0.57
[10=>1],0.52
[12,2=>1],0.66
[15=>6],0.48
[11,1=>2],0.4
[7,4=>1],0.54
[10,1=>2],0.46
[2=>1],0.43
[10,2=>1],0.68
```

Again, naturally, the most frequent length-1 patterns show up in many of the rules, most notably, *frontpage* as a consequent. Throughout this example, we chose the support and confidence values so that the outputs are short and counts easy to validate manually, but let's do some automated calculations on rule sets, regardless:

```
rules.count
val frontPageConseqRules = rules.filter(_.consequent.head == 1)
frontPageConseqRules.count
frontPageConseqRules.filter(_.antecedent.contains(2)).count
```

Executing these statements, we see that about two-thirds of the rules have *front page* as the consequent, that is, 14 of 22 rules in total, and among these, nine contain *news* in their antecedent.

Moving on to the sequence mining problem for this data set, we need to transform our original `transactions` to an RDD of the `Array[Array[Int]]` type first, since nested arrays are the way to encode sequences for prefix span in Spark, as we have seen before. While somewhat obvious, it is still important to point out that with sequences, we don't have to discard the additional information of repeating items, as we just did for FP-growth.

In fact, we even gain more structure by imposing sequentiality on individual records. To do the transformation just indicated, we simply do the following:

```
val sequences: RDD[Array[Array[Int]]] =
transactions.map(_.map(Array(_))).cache()
```

Again, we cache the result to improve the performance of the algorithm, this time, `prefixspan`. Running the algorithm itself is done as before:

```
val prefixSpan = new
PrefixSpan().setMinSupport(0.005).setMaxPatternLength(15)
val psModel = prefixSpan.run(sequences)
```

We set the minimum support value very low at 0.5%, to get a slightly bigger result set this time. Note that we also search for patterns no longer than 15 sequence items. Let's analyze the distribution over a frequent sequence length by running the following:

```
psModel.freqSequences.map(fs => (fs.sequence.length, 1))
  .reduceByKey(_ + _)
  .sortByKey()
  .collect()
  .foreach(fs => println(s"${fs._1}: ${fs._2}"))
```

In this chain of operations, we first map each sequence to a key-value pair consisting of its length and a count of 1. We then proceed with a reduce operation that sums up the values by key, that is, we count how often this length occurs. The rest is just sorting and formatting, which yields the following result:

```
1:  16
2:  132
3:  193
4:  184
5:  137
6:  99
7:  41
8:  17
9:  8
10: 6
11: 4
12: 3
13: 3
14: 1
```

As we can see, the longest sequence has a length of 14, which, in particular, means that our maximum value of 15 did not restrict the search space and we found all the sequential patterns for the chosen support threshold of t=0.005. Interestingly, most of the frequent sequential visits of users have a length between two and six touch points on http://msnbc.com.

To complete this example, let's see what the most frequent pattern of each length is and what the longest sequential pattern actually looks like. Answering the second question will also give us the first, since there is only one length-14 pattern. Computing this can be done as follows:

```
psModel.freqSequences
    .map(fs => (fs.sequence.length, fs))
    .groupByKey()
    .map(group => group._2.reduce((f1, f2) => if (f1.freq > f2.freq) f1 else
f2))
    .map(_.sequence.map(_.mkString("[", ", ", "]")).mkString("[", ", ", "]"))
    .collect.foreach(println)
```

Since this is one of the more complicated RDD operations we've considered so far, let's discuss all the steps involved. We first map each frequent sequence to a pair consisting of its length and the sequence itself. This may seem a bit strange at first, but it allows us to group all the sequences by length, which we do in the next step. Each group consists of its key and an iterator over frequent sequences. We map each group to its iterator and reduce the sequences by only keeping the one with the largest frequency. To then properly display the result of this operation, we make use of mkString twice to create a string from the otherwise not readable nested arrays (when printed). The result of the preceding chain is as follows:

```
[[1], [1], [1], [1], [1], [1]]
[[1], [1], [1]]
[[1], [1], [1], [1], [1], [1], [1], [1], [1], [1], [1], [1]]
[[1], [1], [1], [1], [1], [1], [1], [1], [1]]
[[1], [1], [1], [1], [1], [1], [1], [1], [1], [1], [1], [1], [1]]
[[1], [1], [1], [1]]
[[1]]
[[1], [1], [1], [1], [1], [1], [1]]
[[1], [1], [1], [1], [1], [1], [1], [1], [1], [1]]
[[1], [1], [1], [1], [1], [1], [1], [1], [1], [1], [1]]
[[1], [1], [1], [1], [1], [1], [1], [1], [1], [1], [1], [1], [1], [1]]
[[1], [1], [1], [1], [1], [1], [1], [1]]
[[1], [1], [1], [1], [1]]
[[1], [1]]
```

We discussed earlier that *front page* was the most frequent item by far, which makes a lot of sense intuitively, since it is the natural entry point to a website. However, it is a bit of a surprise that the most frequent sequences of all lengths, for the chosen threshold, consist of *front page* hits only. Apparently many users spend a lot of time, and clicks, in and around the front page, which might be a first indication of it's advertising value, as compared to the pages of the other categories. As we indicated in the introduction of this chapter, analyzing data like this, especially if enriched with other data sources, can be of a tremendous value for owners of the respective websites, and we hope to have shown how frequent pattern mining techniques can serve their part in doing so.

Deploying a pattern mining application

The example developed in the last section was an interesting playground to apply the algorithms we have carefully laid out throughout the chapter, but we have to recognize the fact that *we were just handed the data*. At the time of writing this book, it was often part of the culture in building data products to draw a line in the sand between *data science* and *data engineering* at pretty much exactly this point, that is, between real-time data collection and aggregation, and (often offline) analysis of data, followed up by feeding back reports of the insights gained into the production system. While this approach has its value, there are certain drawbacks to it as well. By not taking the full picture into account, we might, for instance, not exactly know the details of how the data has been collected. Missing information like this can lead to false assumptions and eventually wrong conclusions. While specialization is both useful and necessary to a certain degree, at the very least, practitioners should strive to get a basic understanding of applications *end-to-end*.

When we introduced the MSNBC data set in the last section, we said that it had been retrieved from the server logs of the website. We drastically simplified what this entails, so let us have a closer look:

- *High availability and fault tolerance:* Click events on a website need to be tracked without downtime at any point throughout the day. Some businesses, especially when it comes to any sort of payment transactions, for example, in online shops, can not afford to lose certain events.
- *High throughput of live data and scalability:* We need a system that can store and process such events in real time and can cope with a certain load without slowing down. For instance, the roughly *one million* unique users in the MSNBC data set mean that, on average, there is activity of about 11 users per second. There are many more events to keep track of, especially keeping in mind that the only thing we have measured were page views.

- *Streaming data and batching thereof:* In principle, the first two points could be addressed by writing events to a sufficiently sophisticated log. However, we haven't even touched the topic of aggregating data yet and we preferably need an online processing system to do so. First, each event has to be attributed to a user, which will have to be equipped with some sort of ID. Next, we will have to think about the concept of a user session. While the user data has been aggregated on a daily level in the MSNBC data set, this is not granular enough for many purposes. It makes sense to analyze users' behavior for the time period they are actually active. For this reason, it is customary to consider *windows* of activities and aggregate clicks and other events as per such windows.
- *Analytics on streaming data:* Assuming we had a system like we just described and access to aggregated user session data in real time, what could we hope to achieve? We would need an analytics platform that allows us to apply algorithms and gain insights from this data.

Spark's proposal to address these problems is its **Spark Streaming** module, which we will briefly introduce next. Using Spark Streaming, we will build an application that can at least *mock* generating and aggregating events in order to then apply the pattern mining algorithms we studied to *streams of events*.

The Spark Streaming module

There is not enough time to give an in-depth introduction to Spark Streaming here, but we can, at the very least, touch on some of the key notions, provide some examples, and give some guidance to more advanced topics.

Spark Streaming is Spark's module for stream data processing, and it is indeed equipped with all the properties we explained in the preceding list: it is a highly fault-tolerant, scalable, and high-throughput system for processing and analyzing streams of live data. Its API is a natural extension of Spark itself and many of the tools available for RDDs and DataFrames carry over to Spark Streaming.

The core abstraction of Spark Streaming applications is the notion of *DStream*, which stands for *discretized stream.* To explain the nomenclature, we often think of data streams as a continuous flow of events, which is, of course, an idealization, since all we can ever measure are discrete events. Regardless, this continuous flow of data will hit our system, and for us to process it further, we *discretize* it into disjoint batches of data. This stream of discrete data batches is realized as DStream in Spark Streaming and is internally implemented as a *sequence of RDDs*.

The following diagram gives a high-level overview of the data flow and transformation with Spark Streaming:

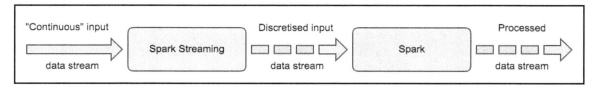

Figure 2: Input data is fed into Spark Streaming. which discretises this stream as a so called DStream. These sequences of RDDs can then be further transformed and processed by Spark and any module thereof.

As the diagram shows, the data enters Spark Streaming through an input data stream. This data can be produced and ingested from many different sources, which we will discuss further later on. We speak of systems generating events that Spark Streaming can process as *sources*. Input DStreams take data from sources and do so via *receivers* for these sources. Once an input DStream has been created, it can be processed through a rich API that allows for many interesting transformations. It serves as a good mental model to think of DStreams as sequences or collections of RDDs, which we can operate on through an interface that is very close to that of RDDs in the Spark core. For instance, operations such as map-reduce, and filter are available for DStreams as well and simply carry over the respective functionality from the individual RDDs to sequences of RDDs. We will discuss all of this in more detail, but let's first turn to a basic example.

As the first example to get started with Spark Streaming, let's consider the following scenario. Assume that we have already loaded the MSNBC data set from earlier and have computed the prefix span model (psModel) from it. This model was fit with data from a single day of user activity, say, yesterday's data. Today, new events of user activity come in. We will create a simple Spark Streaming application with a basic source that generates user data in precisely the schema we had for the MSNBC data; that is, we are given space-separated strings containing numbers between 1 and 17. Our application will then pick up these events and create DStream from them. We can then apply our prefix span model to the data of DStream to find out if the new sequences fed into the system are indeed frequent sequences according to psModel.

To start with a Spark Streaming application in the first place, we need to create a so-called StreamingContext API, which, by convention, will be instantiated as ssc. Assuming that we start an application from scratch, we create the following context:

```
import org.apache.spark.streaming.{Seconds, StreamingContext}
import org.apache.spark.{SparkConf, SparkContext}

val conf = new SparkConf()
  .setAppName("MSNBC data first streaming example")
```

```
  .setMaster("local[2]")
val sc = new SparkContext(conf)
val ssc = new StreamingContext(sc, batchDuration = Seconds(10))
```

If you work with the Spark shell, all but the first and last lines are not necessary, since, in such a case, you will be provided with a Spark context (sc) already. We include the creation of the latter regardless, since we aim at a self-contained application. The creation of a new StreamingContext API takes two arguments, namely a SparkContext and an argument called batchDuration, which we set to 10 seconds. The batch duration is the value that tells us *how to discretize* data for a DStream, by specifying for how long the streaming data should be collected to form a batch within the DStream, that is, one of the RDDs in the sequence. Another detail we want to draw your attention to is that the Spark master is set to two cores by setting local[2]. Since we assume you are working locally, it is important to assign at least two cores to the application. The reason is that one thread will be used to receive input data, while the other will then be free to process it. Should you have more receivers in more advanced applications, you need to reserve one core for each.

Next, we essentially repeat parts of the prefix span model for the sake of completeness of this application. As before, the sequences are loaded from a local text file. Note that this time, we assume the file is in the resources folder of your project, but you can choose to store it anywhere you want:

```
val transactions: RDD[Array[Int]] =
sc.textFile("src/main/resources/msnbc990928.seq") map { line =>
  line.split(" ").map(_.toInt)
}
val trainSequences = transactions.map(_.map(Array(_))).cache()
val prefixSpan = new
PrefixSpan().setMinSupport(0.005).setMaxPatternLength(15)
val psModel = prefixSpan.run(trainSequences)
val freqSequences = psModel.freqSequences.map(_.sequence).collect()
```

In the last step of the preceding computation, we collect all the frequent sequences on the master and store them as freqSequences. The reason we do this is that we want to compare this data against the incoming data to see if the sequences of the new data are frequent with respect to the current model (psModel). Unfortunately, unlike many of the algorithms from MLlib, none of the three available pattern mining models in Spark are built to take new data once trained, so we have to do this comparison on our own, using freqSequences.

Next, we can finally create a DStream object of the String type. To this end, we call socketTextStream on our streaming context, which will allow us to receive data from a server, running on port 8000 of localhost, listening on a TCP socket:

```
val rawSequences: DStream[String] = ssc.socketTextStream("localhost", 8000)
```

What we call rawSequences is the data received through that connection, discretized into 10-second intervals. Before we discuss *how to actually send data*, let's first continue with the example of processing it once we have received it. Recall that the input data will have the same format as before, so we need to preprocess it in exactly the same way, as follows:

```
val sequences: DStream[Array[Array[Int]]] = rawSequences
 .map(line => line.split(" ").map(_.toInt))
 .map(_.map(Array(_)))
```

The two map operations we use here are structurally the same as before on the original MSNBC data, but keep in mind that this time, map has a different context, since we are working with DStreams instead of RDDs. Having defined sequences, a sequence of RDDs of the Array[Array[Int]] type, we can use it to match against freqSequences. We do so by iterating over each RDD in sequences and then again over each array contained in these RDDs. Next, we count how often the respective array is found in freqSequences, and if it is found, we print that the sequence corresponding to array is indeed frequent:

```
print(">>> Analyzing new batch of data")
sequences.foreachRDD(
 rdd => rdd.foreach(
   array => {
     println(">>> Sequence: ")
     println(array.map(_.mkString("[", ", ", "]")).mkString("[", ", ",
"]"))
     freqSequences.count(_.deep == array.deep) match {
       case count if count > 0 => println("is frequent!")
       case _ => println("is not frequent.")
     }
   }
 )
)
print(">>> done")
```

Note that in the preceding code, we need to compare deep copies of arrays, since nested arrays can't be compared on the nose. To be more precise, one can check them for equality, but the result will always be false.

Having done the transformation, the only thing we are left with on the receiving side of the application is to actually tell it to start listening to the incoming data:

```
ssc.start()
ssc.awaitTermination()
```

Through the streaming context, `ssc`, we tell the application to start and await its termination. Note that in our specific context and for most other applications of this fashion, we rarely want to terminate the program at all. By design, the application is intended as a *long-running job*, since, in principle, we want it to listen to and analyze new data indefinitely. Naturally, there will be cases of maintenance, but we may also want to regularly update (re-train) `psModel` with the newly acquired data.

We have already seen a few operations on DStreams and we recommend you to refer to the latest Spark Streaming documentation (`http://spark.apache.org/docs/latest/streaming-programming-guide.html`) for more details. Essentially, many of the (functional) programming functionalities available on basic Scala collections that we also know from RDDs carry over seamlessly to DStreams as well. To name a few, these are `filter`, `flatMap`, `map`, `reduce`, and `reduceByKey`. Other SQL-like functionalities, such as cogroup, `count`, `countByValue`, `join`, or `union`, are also at your disposal. We will see some of the more advanced functionalities later on in a second example.

Now that we have covered the receiving end, let's briefly discuss how to create a data source for our app. One of the simplest ways to send input data from a command line over a TCP socket is to use *Netcat*, which is available for most operating systems, often preinstalled. To start Netcat locally on port 8000, run the following command in a terminal separate from your Spark application or shell:

```
nc -lk 8000
```

Assuming you already started the Spark Streaming application for receiving data from before, we can now type new sequences into the Netcat terminal window and confirm each by hitting *Enter*. For instance, type the following four sequences *within 10 seconds*:

You will see the following output:

```
>>> Analysing new batch of data
>>> Sequence:
[[1]]
is frequent!
>>> Sequence:
[[2]]
is frequent!
>>> Sequence:
[[23]]
is not frequent.
>>> Sequence:
[[4], [5]]
is not frequent.
>>> done
```

If you are either really slow at typing or so unlucky that you start typing when the 10-second window is almost over, the output might be split into more parts. Looking at the actual output, you will see that the often discussed categories *front page* and *news*, represented by categories 1 and 2, are frequent. Also, since 23 is not a sequence item contained in the original data set, it can't be frequent. Lastly, the sequence <4, 5> is apparently also not frequent, which is something we didn't know before.

Choosing Netcat for this example is a natural choice for the time and space given in this chapter, but you will never see it used for this purpose in serious production environments. In general, Spark Streaming has two types of sources available: basic and advanced. Basic sources can also be queues of RDDs and other custom sources apart from file streams, which the preceding example represents. On the side of advanced sources, Spark Streaming has a lot of interesting connectors to offer: Kafka, Kinesis, Flume, and advanced custom sources. This wide variety of advanced sources makes it attractive to incorporate Spark Streaming as a production component, integrating well with the other infrastructure components.

Taking a few steps back and considering what we have achieved by discussing this example, you may be inclined to say that apart from introducing Spark Streaming itself and working with data producers and receivers, the application itself did not solve many of our aforementioned concerns. This criticism is valid, and in a second example, we want to address the following remaining issues with our approach:

- Input data for our DStreams had the same structure as our offline data, that is, it was already pre-aggregated with respect to users, which is not very realistic
- Apart from the two calls to map and one to foreachRDD, we didn't see much in terms of functionality and added value in operating with DStreams
- We did not do any analytics on data streams but only checked them against a list of precomputed patterns

To resolve these issues, let's slightly redefine our example setting. This time, let's assume that one event is represented by one user clicking on one site, where each such site falls under one of the categories 1-17, as before. Now, we cannot possibly simulate a complete production environment, so we make the simplifying assumption that each unique user has already been equipped with an ID. Given this information, let's say events come in as key-value pairs consisting of a user ID and a category of this click event.

With this setup, we have to think about how to aggregate these events to generate sequences from them. For this purpose, we need to collect data points for each user ID in a given window. In the original data set, this window was obviously one full day, but depending on the application, it may make sense to choose a much smaller window. If we think about the scenario of a user browsing his favorite online shop, the click and other events that go back a few hours will unlikely influence his or her current desire to buy something. For this reason, a reasonable assumption made in online marketing and related fields is to limit the window of interest to about 20-30 minutes, a so-called *user session*. In order for us to see results much quicker, we will use an even smaller window of 20 seconds for our application. We call this the **window length**.

Now that we know how far back we want to analyze the data from a given point in time, we also have to define *how often* we want to carry out the aggregation step, which we will call the *sliding interval*. One natural choice would be to set both to the same amount of time, leading to disjoint windows of aggregation, that is, every 20 seconds. However, it might also be interesting to choose a shorter sliding window of 10 seconds, which would lead to aggregation data that overlaps 10 seconds each. The following diagram illustrates the concepts we just discussed:

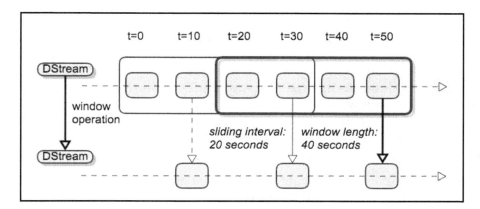

Figure 3: Visualisation of a window operation transforming a DStream to another. In this example the batch duration of the Spark Streaming application has been set to 10 seconds. The window length for the transformation operating on batches of data is 40 seconds and we carry out the window operation every 20 seconds, leading to an overlap of 20 seconds each and a resulting DStream that is batched in 20-second blocks.

To turn this knowledge into a concrete example, we assume that the event data has the form *key:value,* that is, one such event could be `137: 2`, meaning that the user with ID `137` clicked on a page with the category *news.* To process these events, we have to modify our preprocessing like this:

```
val rawEvents: DStream[String] = ssc.socketTextStream("localhost", 9999)
val events: DStream[(Int, String)] = rawEvents.map(line => line.split(":
"))
  .map(kv => (kv(0).toInt, kv(1)))
```

With these key-value pairs, we can now aim to do the aggregation necessary to group events by the user ID. As outlined earlier, we do this by aggregating on a given window of 20 seconds with a sliding interval of 10 seconds:

```
val duration = Seconds(20)
val slide = Seconds(10)

val rawSequencesWithIds: DStream[(Int, String)] = events
  .reduceByKeyAndWindow((v1: String, v2: String) => v1 + " " + v2,
duration, slide)
val rawSequences = rawSequencesWithIds.map(_.2)
// remainder as in previous example
```

In the preceding code, we are using a more advanced operation on DStreams, namely `reduceByKeyAndWindow`, in which we specify an aggregation function on values of key-value pairs, as well as a window duration and sliding interval. In the last step of the computation, we strip the user IDs so that the structure of `rawSequences` is identical to the previous example. This means that we have successfully converted our example to work on unprocessed events, and it will still check against frequent sequences of our baseline model. We will not show more examples of how the output of this application looks, but we encourage you to play around with this application and see how the aggregation works on key-value pairs.

To wrap up this example, and the chapter, let's look at one more interesting way of aggregating event data. Let's say we want to dynamically count how often a certain ID occurs in the event stream, that is, how many page clicks a user generates. We already have our `events` DStream defined previously, so we could approach the count as follows:

```
val countIds = events.map(e => (e._1, 1))
val counts: DStream[(Int, Int)] = countIds.reduceByKey(_ + _)
```

In a way, this works as we intended; it counts events for IDs. However, note that what is returned is again a DStream, that is, we do not actually aggregate *across streaming windows* but just within the sequences of RDDs. To aggregate across the full stream of events, we need to keep track of count states since from the start. Spark Streaming offers a method on DStreams for precisely this purpose, namely `updateStateByKey`. It can be used by providing `updateFunction`, which takes the current state and new values as input and returns an updated state. Let's see how it works in practice for our event count:

```
def updateFunction(newValues: Seq[Int], runningCount: Option[Int]):
Option[Int] = {
  Some(runningCount.getOrElse(0) + newValues.sum)
}
val runningCounts = countIds.updateStateByKey[Int](updateFunction _)
```

We first define our update function itself. Note that the signature of `updateStateByKey` requires us to return an `Option`, but in essence, we just compute the running sum of state and incoming values. Next, we provide `updateStateByKey` with an `Int` type signature and the previously created `updateFunction` method. Doing so, we get precisely the aggregation we wanted in the first place.

Summarizing, we introduced event aggregation, two more complex operations on DStreams (`reduceByKeyAndWindow` and `updateStateByKey`), and counted events in a stream with this example. While the example is still simplistic in what it does, we hope to have provided the reader with a good entry point for more advanced applications. For instance, one could extend this example to calculate moving averages over the event stream or change it towards computing frequent patterns on a per-window basis.

Summary

In this chapter, we introduced a new class of algorithms, that is, frequent pattern mining applications, and showed you how to deploy them in a real-world scenario. We first discussed the very basics of pattern mining and the problems that can be addressed using these techniques. In particular, we saw how to implement the three available algorithms in Spark, *FP-growth, association rules*, and *prefix span*. As a running example for the applications we used clickstream data provided by MSNBC, which also helped us to compare the algorithms qualitatively.

Next, we introduced the basic terminology and entry points of Spark Streaming and considered a few real-world scenarios. We discussed how to deploy and evaluate one of the frequent pattern mining algorithms with a streaming context first. After that, we addressed the problem of aggregating user session data from raw streaming data. To this end, we had to find a solution to mock providing click data as streaming events.

7
Graph Analytics with GraphX

In our interconnected world, graphs are omnipresent. The **World Wide Web (WWW)** is just one example of a complex structure that we can consider a graph, in which web pages represent entities that are connected by incoming and outgoing links between them. In Facebook's social graph, many millions of users form a network, connecting friends around the globe. Many other important structures that we see and can collect data for today come equipped with a natural graph structure; that is, they can, at a very basic level, be understood as a collection of *vertices* that are connected to each other in a certain way by what we call *edges*. Stated in this generality, this observation reflects how ubiquitous graphs are. What makes it valuable is that the graphs are well-studied structures and that there are many algorithms available that allow us to gain important insights about what these graphs represent.

Spark's GraphX library is a natural entry point to study graphs at scale. Leveraging RDDs from the Spark core to encode vertices and edges, we can do graph analytics on vast amounts of data with GraphX. To give an overview, you will learn about the following topics in this chapter:

- Basic graph properties and important graph operations
- How GraphX represents property graphs and how to work with them
- Loading graph data in various ways and generating synthetic graph data to experiment with
- Essential graph properties by using GraphX's core engine
- Visualizing graphs with an open source tool called Gephi
- Implementing efficient graph-parallel algorithms using two of GraphX's key APIs.

- Using GraphFrames, an extension of DataFrames to graphs, and studying graphs using an elegant query language
- Running important graph algorithms available in GraphX on a social graph, consisting of retweets and a graph of actors appearing in movies together

Basic graph theory

Before diving into Spark GraphX and its applications, we will first define graphs on a basic level and explain what properties they may come with and what structures are worth studying in our context. Along the way of introducing these properties, we will give more concrete examples of graphs that we consider in everyday life.

Graphs

To formalize the notion of a graph briefly sketched in the introduction, on a purely mathematical level, a graph $G = (V, E)$ can be described as a pair of *vertices* V and *edges* E, as follows:

$$V = \{v_1, ..., v_n\}$$

$$E = \{e_1, ..., e_m\}$$

We call the element v_i in V a vertex and e_i in E an edge, where each edge connecting two vertices v_1 and v_2 is, in fact, just a pair of vertices, that is, $e_i = (v_1, v_2)$. Let's construct a simple graph consisting of five vertices and six edges, as specified by the following graph data:

$$V = \{v_1, v_2, v_3, v_4, v_5\}$$

$$E = \{e_1 = (v_1, v_2), e_2 = (v_1, v_3), e_3 = (v_2, v_3),$$

$$e_4 = (v_3, v_4), e_5 = (v_4, v_1), e_6 = (v_4, v_5)\}$$

This is what the graph will look like:

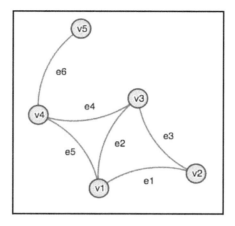

Figure 1: A simple undirected graph with five vertices and six edges

Note that in the realization of the graph in *Figure 1*, the relative position of nodes to each other, the length of the edges, and other visual properties are inessential to the graph. In fact, we could have displayed the graph in any other way by means of deforming it. The graph definition entirely determines its *topology*.

Directed and undirected graphs

In a pair of vertices that make up an edge *e*, by convention, we call the first vertex the *source* and the second one the *target*. The natural interpretation here is that the connection represented by edge *e* has a *direction*; it flows from the source to the target. Note that in *Figure 1*, the graph displayed is undirected; that is, we did not distinguish between the source and target.

Using the exact same definition, we can create a directed version of our graph, as shown in the following image. Note that the graph looks slightly different in the way it is presented, but the connections of vertices and edges remain unchanged:

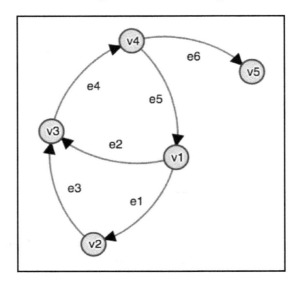

Figure 2: A directed graph with the same topology as the previous one. In fact, forgetting edge directions would yield the same graph as in Figure 1

Each directed graph naturally has an associated undirected graph, realized by simply forgetting all the edge directions. From a practical perspective, most implementations of graphs inherently build on directed edges and suppress the additional information of direction whenever needed. To give an example, think of the preceding graph as a group of five people connected by the relationship, *friendship*. We may argue that friendship is a symmetric property in that if you are a friend of mine, I am also a friend of yours. With this interpretation, directionality is not a very useful concept in this example, so we are, in fact, better off to treat this as an undirected graph example. In contrast, if we were to run a social network that allows users to actively send friend requests to other users, a directed graph might be better to encode this information.

Order and degree

For any graph, directed or not, we can read off some basic properties that are of interest later in the chapter. We call the number of vertices |V| the *order* of the graph and the number of edges |E| its *degree*, sometimes also referred to as its *valency*. The degree of a vertex is the number of edges that have this vertex as either source or target. In the case of directed graphs and a given vertex v, we can additionally distinguish between *in-degree*, that is, the sum of all the edges pointing towards v, and *out-degree*, that is, the sum of all the edges starting at v. To give an example of this, the undirected graph in *Figure 1* has order 5 and degree 6, same as the directed graph shown in *Figure 2*. In the latter, vertex v1 has out-degree 2 and in-degree 1, while v5 has out-degree 0 and in-degree 1.

In the last two examples, we annotated the vertices and edges with their respective identifiers, as specified by the definition $G = (V, E)$. For most graph visualizations that follow, we will assume that the identity of vertices and edges is implicitly known and will instead represent them by labeling our graphs with additional information. The reason we make this explicit distinction between identifiers and labels is that GraphX identifiers can't be strings, as we will see in the next section. An example of a labeled graph with relationships of a group of people is shown in the following diagram:

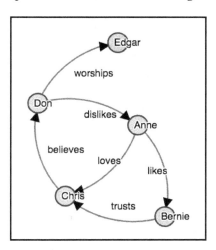

Figure 3: A directed labelled graph showing a group of people and their relationships

Directed acyclic graphs

The next notion we want to discuss is that of acyclicity. A *cyclic graph* is one in which there is at least one vertex for which there is a path through the graph, connecting this vertex to itself. We call such a path a *cycle*. In an undirected graph, any chain creating a cycle will do, while in a directed graph, we only speak of cycles if we can reach the starting vertex by means of following the directed edges. For example, consider some of the graphs we have seen before. In *Figure 2*, there is precisely one cycle formed by *{e2, e4, e5}*, while in its undirected version, shown in *Figure 1*, there are precisely two cycles, namely *{e2, e4, e5}* and *{e1, e2, e3}*.

There are a few special cases of cyclic graphs that are worth mentioning here. Firstly, if a vertex is connected to itself by a single edge, we will say the graph has a *loop*. Secondly, a directed graph that does not contain any two-loops, that is, without pairs of vertices joined by edges in both directions, is called an *oriented graph*. Thirdly, a graph with three-loops is said to contain *triangles*. The notion of triangles is an important one, as it is often used to assess the connectivity of a graph, which we will discuss later on. The following diagram shows an artificial example with different types of loops:

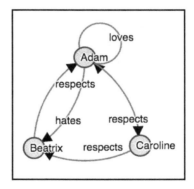

Figure 4: A toy graph illustrating loops or self-edges, two-loops and triangles.

In general, studying n-loops in a graph for any natural number *n* can tell you a lot about a graph, but triangles are the most common. As directed cycles are not only more expensive to compute but also rarer than their undirected versions, we will often look for undirected triangles only in a graph; that is, we'll forget its directed structure.

An important class of graphs found repeatedly in many applications is that of **Directed Acyclic Graphs** (**DAGs**). We already know what a DAG is from the last paragraph, namely a directed graph without cycles, but since DAGs are so ubiquitous, we should spend a little more time on them.

One instance of a DAG that we have implicitly used throughout all the chapters leading up to this one is Spark's job execution graph. Remember that any Spark job consists of stages executed in a certain order. Stages consist of tasks executed on each partition, some of which may be independent, while others depend on each other. We can thus interpret the execution of a Spark job as a directed graph consisting of stages (or tasks) as vertices, in which an edge represents the output of one computation being required for the next. The prototypical example might be that of a reduce stage that needs the output of a preceding map stage. Naturally, this execution graph does not contain any cycles, as this would mean we are to feed the output of some operators into the graph ad infinitum, preventing our program to eventually halt. Thus, this execution graph can be represented, and is in fact implemented in the Spark scheduler, as DAG:

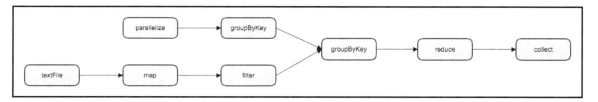

Figure 5: Visualizing a chain of operations carried out on RDDs with Spark. The execution graph is by definition a DAG.

Connected components

Another important property of graphs is that of *connectivity*. A graph is said to be *connected* if there is a path of edges connecting any two vertices we choose, regardless of the edge directions. So, for directed graphs, we completely neglect the directions for this definition. What can be a stricter definition of connectivity used for directed graphs? A graph is said to be *strongly connected* if any two vertices are connected by a directed chain of edges. Note that strong connectivity is a very strong assumption to impose on a directed graph. In particular, any strongly connected graph is cyclic. These definitions allow us to define the closely related concept of (strongly) connected components. Every graph can be decomposed into connected components. If it is connected, there is precisely one such component. If it is not, there are at least two. Formally defined, a connected component is the largest subgraph of a given graph that is still connected. The same rationale holds for strongly connected components. Connectivity is an important measure, as it allows us to cluster the vertices of a graph into groups that naturally belong together.

For instance, one might be interested in the number of connected components in a social graph indicating friendship. In a small graph, there may be many separate components. However, the larger the graph, one might suspect that it is more likely to have just a single connected component, following the commonly accepted rationale that everyone is connected to each other by around six connections.

We will see how to compute connected components with GraphX in the next section; for now, let's just inspect one simple example. In the following diagram, we see a directed graph with twelve vertices:

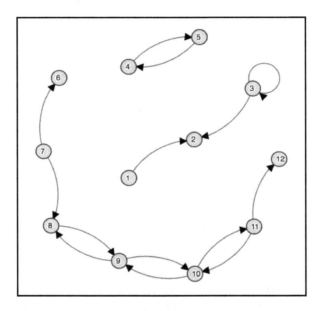

Figure 6: Connected and strongly connected components can easily be read off in small graphs, but this becomes increasingly difficult for larger graphs.

We can immediately see that it has three connected components, namely the three sets of vertices *{1, 2, 3}, {4, 5}*, and *{6, 7, 8, 9, 10, 11, 12}*. As for strongly connected components, that requires a little more effort than a quick visual inspection. We can see that *{4, 5}* forms a strongly connected component, and so does *{8, 9, 10, 11}*. All the other six vertices form their own strongly connected components, that is, they are isolated. This example goes on to show that for a massive graph with millions of vertices, with the right visualization tool, we may be lucky to find roughly connected components, but strongly connected components are a little more complicated to compute, and this is just one use case where Spark GraphX comes in handy.

Trees

With the definition of connected components in our hands, we can turn to another interesting class of graphs, namely trees. A *tree* is a connected graph in which there is precisely one path connecting any given vertex to another. A graph consisting of a disjointed group of trees is called a forest. In the following diagram, we see a schematic *decision tree* ran on the well known Iris dataset. Note that this is for illustration purposes only, that is, to show how the output of this algorithm can be seen as a graph:

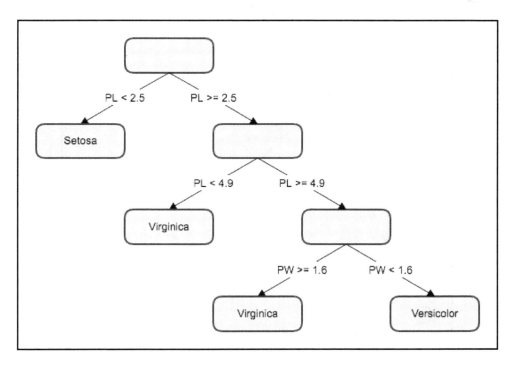

Figure 7: A simple decision tree ran on Iris, classifying into the three categories Setosa, Virginica and Versicolor by means of two features, namely petal length (PL) and petal width (PW)

Multigraphs

Generally, a graph without loops or multiple edges is called *simple*. Most graphs we will encounter in the applications of this chapter do not share this property. Very often, graphs constructed from real-world data will have multiple edges between vertices. In literature, graphs with multiple edges are referred to as multi-graphs or pseudo graphs. Throughout the chapter, we will stick with the multigraph notion and will follow the convention that such a multigraph can include loops as well. Since Spark supports multigraphs (including loops), this notion will be very useful in the applications. In the following diagram, we see a complex multigraph with multiple connected components:

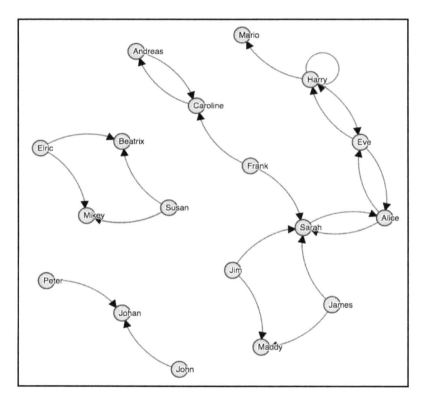

Figure 8: A slightly more involved social multigraph with loops and multiple edges.

Property graphs

Before we move on to introduce GraphX as a graph processing engine, let's look at an extension of graphs as we have seen them before. We have already considered labeled graphs as a convenient way to name vertices and edges. In general, the graph data we will consider in the applications will have more information attached to both vertices and edges, and we need a way to model this additional information within our graph. To this end, we can utilize the notion of *property graphs*.

From the basic definition of a graph as a pair of vertices and edges, it is not directly possible to attach additional information to the two structures. Historically, one way to circumvent this is to blow up the graph and create more vertices corresponding to properties, connected to the original vertices by new edges that encode the relationship to the new vertices. For instance, in our previous examples of friend graphs, if we also want to encode the home addresses in our graph, each vertex representing a person must be connected to a vertex representing their address with the edge between them *lives at*. It does not take a lot of imagination to realize that this approach creates a lot of complexity, especially if the vertex properties interrelate. Representing properties in a graph by subject-predicate-object *triples* has been formalized in the so-called **Resource Description Framework** (**RDF**), and the result of this is called an RDF-model. RDFs are a subject on their own and allow for a little more flexibility than we presented. In any case, it is good to be familiar with the concept and understand its limitations.

In a *property graph*, in contrast, we can augment both vertices and edges with essentially arbitrary additional structure. As with anything, gaining flexibility in this generality usually comes as a trade-off. In our case, basic graphs as implemented in many graph databases allow for the powerful optimization of queries, while with property graphs, we should be careful when it comes to performance. We will touch this topic in more detail in the next section, when we show how Spark GraphX implements property graphs.

Throughout the rest of the chapter, we'll use the following convention for property graphs. The additional data attached to vertices is called *vertex data* and the one for edges is called *edge data*. To give an example of a little more involved vertex and edge data, see the following diagram for an extension of our idea of extending a friend graph. This example also displays what we mean by a *triplet*, that is, an edge with its adjacent vertices and all their properties:

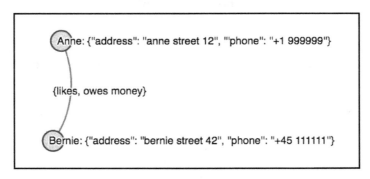

Figure 9: A property graph showing friends augmented by address data, connected by more than one relation. Property data is encoded in JSON format.

Note that in the preceding example, we kept it simple on purpose, but in a more realistic scenario, we would have the need for nested data structures--for example, to answer how much money is owed and when it is due.

An interesting special case of a property graph in our context is that of a *weighted graph*, in which edges, vertices, or both have weights, for example, integers or floating point numbers attached to them. A prototypical example for this is a graph consisting of a set of cities as vertices ,with the edges connecting them carrying the distance between locations. A few classical questions arise in this scenario. One example would be to find the shortest path between two given cities. A related issue is the *traveling salesman problem*, in which a hypothetical salesman is asked to visit every city using the shortest route possible.

As a closing remark for this section, it is important to know that in literature, there is a widely used synonymous notion for vertices, namely nodes. We will not use this term here, since in the context of Spark, it might easily be confused with compute nodes on which workers execute tasks. Instead, we will stick to vertices throughout the chapter. Also, whenever we speak of a graph, we generally assume that it is a *finite graph*, that is, the number of vertices and edges is finite, which, in practice, hardly counts as restriction.

GraphX distributed graph processing engine

Along with Spark MLlib for machine learning, which we have already encountered a few times in this book, and others like Spark Streaming, which we will cover in Chapter 8, *Lending Club Loan Prediction*, Spark GraphX is one of the core components of the Spark ecosphere. GraphX is tailored for processing large graphs in an efficient way by building on top of RDDs.

Using the nomenclature developed in the last section, a graph in GraphX is a finite multigraph with loops, where by *graph*, we actually mean the property graph extension discussed earlier. Next, we will see how graphs are built internally in GraphX.

For the examples used, we recommend firing up `spark-shell` locally, which will automatically provide dependencies for GraphX. To test whether this works properly in your setup, try importing the full GraphX core module using Scala's wildcard operator, as follows:

```
import org.apache.spark.graphx._
```

On your screen, you should see the following prompt:

```
scala> import org.apache.spark.graphx._
import org.apache.spark.graphx._
```

If you would rather follow the examples by building a package using sbt, you should include the following `libraryDependencies` in your `build.sbt`:

```
"org.apache.spark" %% "spark-graphx" % "2.1.1"
```

Doing so should allow you to import GraphX, as shown previously, to create an app of your choice that you can call with spark-submit instead.

Graph representation in GraphX

Recall that a property graph is, for us, a directed multigraph with loops that have custom data objects for both vertices and edges. The central entry point of GraphX is the `Graph` API, which has the following signature:

```
class Graph[VD, ED] {
  val vertices: VertexRDD[VD]
  val edges: EdgeRDD[ED]
}
```

So, internally, a graph in GraphX is represented by one RDD encoding for vertices and one for edges. Here, VD is the vertex data type, and ED is the edge data type of our property graph. We will discuss both VertexRDD and EdgeRDD in more detail, as they are so essential for what follows.

In Spark GraphX, vertices have unique identifiers of the Long type, which are called VertexId. A VertexRDD[VD] is, in fact, just an extension of RDD[(VertexId, VD)], but optimized and with an extensive list of utility functionality that we will talk about at length. Thus, vertices in GraphX, simply put, are RDDs with identifiers and vertex data, which goes hand in hand with the intuition developed earlier.

To explain the concept of EdgeRDD, let's quickly explain what Edge is in GraphX. In a simplified form, Edge is defined by the following signature:

```
case class Edge[ED] (
  var srcId: VertexId,
  var dstId: VertexId,
  var attr: ED
)
```

So, an edge is completely determined by a source vertex ID, given by srcId, a target or destination vertex ID, provided as dstId, and an attribute object, attr, of the ED data type. Similar to the preceding vertex RDDs, we can understand EdgeRDD[ED] as an extension of RDD[Edge[ED]]. Thus, edges in GraphX are given by an RDD of edges of the ED type, which again lines up with what we discussed so far.

We now know that as of Spark 2.1, graphs in GraphX are essentially pairs of vertex and edge RDDs. This is important information, as it allows us, in principle, to apply the full functionality and power of RDDs from Spark core to these graphs. As a word of warning, though, graphs come with a lot of functionality that is optimized for the purpose of graph processing. Whenever you find yourself using basic RDD functionality, see if you can find a specific graph equivalent, which will likely be more performant.

To give a concrete example, let's construct a graph from scratch, using what we just learned. We assume that you have a Spark context available as sc. We will create a graph with people connected to each other, namely the one from *Figure 3* of the previous section, that is, a labelled graph. In the GraphX language we just acquired, to create such a graph, we need both vertex and edge data types to be of the String type. We do this by using parallelize to create vertices as follows:

```
import org.apache.spark.rdd.RDD
val vertices: RDD[(VertexId, String)] = sc.parallelize(
  Array((1L, "Anne"),
```

```
    (2L, "Bernie"),
    (3L, "Chris"),
    (4L, "Don"),
    (5L, "Edgar")))
```

In the same way, we can create edges; note the use of `Edge` in the following definition:

```
val edges: RDD[Edge[String]] = sc.parallelize(
  Array(Edge(1L, 2L, "likes"),
    Edge(2L, 3L, "trusts"),
    Edge(3L, 4L, "believes"),
    Edge(4L, 5L, "worships"),
    Edge(1L, 3L, "loves"),
    Edge(4L, 1L, "dislikes")))
```

Having these two RDDs ready is already sufficient to create `Graph`, which is as simple as the following line:

```
val friendGraph: Graph[String, String] = Graph(vertices, edges)
```

Note that we explicitly write out the types for all variables, which is just for clarity. We could just leave them out and rely on the Scala compiler to infer them for us. Furthermore, as indicated by the preceding signature, we can access vertices with `friendGraph.vertices` and edges with `friendGraph.edges`. Just to give a first glimpse of what is possible, we can now collect all the vertices and print them as follows:

```
friendGraph.vertices.collect.foreach(println)
```

The following is the output:

```
(4,Don)
(1,Anne)
(5,Edgar)
(2,Bernie)
(3,Chris)
```

Note that this does not use any GraphX-specific functionality, just what we already know from RDDs. As another example, let's count all the edges for which the source ID is larger than the target ID. This could be done as follows:

```
friendGraph.edges.map( e => e.srcId > e.dstId ).filter(_ == true).count
```

This gives back the expected answer, that is, 1, but has a drawback. Once we call .edges on the graph, we completely lose all the graph structure that we previously had. Assuming that we want to further process a graph with transformed edges, this is not the way to go. In such a case, it is better to use the built-in Graph functionality instead, like the following mapEdges method:

```
val mappedEdgeGraph: Graph[String, Boolean] =
    friendGraph.mapEdges( e => e.srcId > e.dstId )
```

Note that the return value in this case is again a graph, but the edge data type is now Boolean, as expected. We will see many more examples of graph processing possibilities in just a bit. Having seen this example, let's take a step back and discuss why Spark GraphX implements graphs as it does. One reason is that we can effectively leverage both *data parallelism* and *graph parallelism*. In the previous chapters, we already encountered how RDDs and data frames in Spark exploit data parallelism by distributing data across partitions by keeping data in memory on each node. So, if we are only concerned about vertices or edges on their own and don't want to study their relationship, working with the vertex and edge RDDs will be very efficient.

In contrast, by graph parallelism we mean operations carried out in parallel *relative to notions of the graph*. For instance, a graph-parallel task will be to sum the weights of all the inbound edges for each vertex. To carry out this task, we need to work with both the vertex and edge data, which involves multiple RDDs. Doing this efficiently needs a suitable internal representation. GraphX tries to strike a balance between both the paradigms, which few other alternative programs offer.

Graph properties and operations

Having seen yet another artificial example, let's turn to a more interesting example next, which we will use to investigate some of the core properties that we have studied in the previous section. The data we will be considering in this chapter can be found at http://networkrepository.com/, an open network data repository with a vast amount of interesting data. First, we will load a relatively small data set retrieved from Twitter, which can be downloaded from http://networkrepository.com/rt-occupywallstnyc.php. Download the zip file available on this page, that is, store **rt_occupywallstnyc.zip** and unpack it to access the file, **rt_occupywallstnyc.edges**. The file is in the CSV format with commas as separators. Each row represents a retweet of a tweet concerning the *occupy Wall Street* movement in New York City. The first two columns show Twitter user IDs and the third represents an ID for the retweet; that is, the user in the second column retweeted a tweet from the respective user in the first.

The first ten items look as follows:

```
3212,221,1347929725
3212,3301,1347923714
3212,1801,1347714310
3212,1491,1347924000
3212,1483,1347923691
3212,1872,1347939690
1486,1783,1346181381
2382,3350,1346675417
2382,1783,1342925318
2159,349,1347911999
```

For instance, we can see that the tweets from user 3,212 have been retweeted at least six times, but since we don't know if the file is ordered in any way and that contains roughly 3.6k vertices, we should utilize GraphX to answer such questions for us.

To build a graph, we will proceed by first creating an RDD of edges from this file, that is, RDD[Edge[Long]], by using basic Spark functionality:

```
val edges: RDD[Edge[Long]] =
  sc.textFile("./rt_occupywallstnyc.edges").map { line =>
    val fields = line.split(",")
    Edge(fields(0).toLong, fields(1).toLong, fields(2).toLong)
  }
```

Recall that IDs in GraphX are of the Long type, which is why we cast all the values to Long after loading the text file and splitting each line by comma; that is, our edge data type in this case is Long. Here, we assume that the file in question resides in the same folder that we started spark-shell in; adapt it to your needs, if necessary. Having such an edge RDD, we can now use the fromEdges method of the Graph companion object as follows:

```
val rtGraph: Graph[String, Long] = Graph.fromEdges(edges, defaultValue =
"")
```

It may not come as a surprise that we need to supply edges to this method, but the defaultValue keyword deserves some explanation. Note that so far, we only have knowledge of edges, and while the vertex IDs are implicitly available as sources and targets of edges, we still have not settled on a vertex data type VD needed for any GraphX graph. The defaultValue allows you to create a default vertex data value, which comes with a type. In our case, we chose an empty string, which explains the signature of rtGraph.

With this first real-world data graph loaded, let's check for some basic properties. Using the notation from earlier, the *order* and *degree* of the graph can be computed as follows:

```
val order = rtGraph.numVertices
val degree = rtGraph.numEdges
```

The preceding code will yield 3,609 and 3,936, respectively. As for the degree of individual vertices, GraphX provides the `degrees` method on Graphs that returns a graph of integer vertex data type, which is used to store degrees. Let's compute the average degree of our retweet graph:

```
val avgDegree = rtGraph.degrees.map(_._2).reduce(_ + _) / order.toDouble
```

The result of this operation should be roughly `2.18`, which means that each vertex has about two edges connected to it on average. The notation used in this concise operation may seem a bit dense, mostly due to the many wildcards used, so let's dissect it a little. To explain this, we first call degrees, as discussed. Afterwards, we extract the degrees only by mapping to the second item of the pair; that is, we forget the vertex IDs. This leaves us with an RDD of integer values, which we can sum up by reducing by addition. The last step is casting `order.toDouble` to make sure we get floating division and then dividing by this total. The next code listing shows the same four steps expanded in more detail:

```
val vertexDegrees: VertexRDD[Int] = rtGraph.degrees
val degrees: RDD[Int] = vertexDegrees.map(v => v._2)
val sumDegrees: Int = degrees.reduce((v1, v2) => v1 + v2 )
val avgDegreeAlt = sumDegrees / order.toDouble
```

Next, we compute in-degree and out-degree of this directed graph by simply calling `inDegrees` and `outDegrees`, respectively. To make things more interesting, let's compute the maximum in-degree, as well as the minimum out-degree, over all the vertices present in the graph and return its ID as well. We tackle the maximum in-degree first:

```
val maxInDegree: (Long, Int) = rtGraph.inDegrees.reduce(
  (v1,v2) => if (v1._2 > v2._2) v1 else v2
)
```

Carrying out this computation, you should see that the vertex with ID `1783` has in-degree 401, meaning that the user with this ID retweeted 401 different tweets. So, an interesting follow-up question to ask is, "From how many different users has this user retweeted?" Again, we can answer this in a very quick manner by counting the distinct sources of this target in all the edges:

```
rtGraph.edges.filter(e => e.dstId == 1783).map(_.srcId).distinct()
```

Executing this command should prompt 34, so on average, user `1783` retweeted about 12 tweets from any given user that he retweeted from at all in this data set. This in turn means that we found a meaningful example of a multigraph--there are pairs of vertices in this graph with many different connections between each other. Answering the question of minimum out-degree is now straightforward:

```
val minOutDegree: (Long, Int) = rtGraph.outDegrees.reduce(
  (v1,v2) => if (v1._2 < v2._2) v1 else v2
)
```

The answer is `1` in this case, which means that in this data set, each tweet has been retweeted at least once.

Recall that a *triplet* of a property graph consists of an edge and its data, as well as both of the joining vertices and their respective data. In Spark GraphX, this concept is implemented in a class called `EdgeTriplet`, in which we can retrieve the edge data as `attr` and vertex data and IDs naturally through `srcAttr`, `dstAttr`, `srcId`, and `dstId`. To get triplets for our retweet graph, we can simply call the following:

```
val triplets: RDD[EdgeTriplet[String, Long]] = rtGraph.triplets
```

Triplets often prove practical, as we can directly retrieve the corresponding edge and vertex data, which would otherwise live in separate RDDs in the graph. For instance, we can quickly transform the generated triplets to give us somewhat readable data for each retweet by executing the following:

```
val tweetStrings = triplets.map(
  t => t.dstId + " retweeted " + t.attr + " from " + t.srcId
)
tweetStrings.take(5)
```

The preceding code results in the following output:

```
scala>   tweetStrings.take(5).foreach(println)
17/06/20 11:24:48 WARN Executor: 1 block locks were not released by TID = 22:
[rdd_3_0]
1783 retweeted 1343119747 from 26
1783 retweeted 1346025855 from 41
1783 retweeted 1345453950 from 57
877 retweeted 1347395797 from 84
1783 retweeted 1347883683 from 90
```

When we discussed the `friendGraph` example earlier, we took note that `mapEdges` was, in certain regards, superior to first calling `edges` and then `map` them. The same holds true for vertices and triplets as well. Let's say we want to change the vertex data of our graph to simply be the vertex IDs instead of the previously chosen default value. This can be most quickly and efficiently achieved by mapping the vertices as follows:

```
val vertexIdData: Graph[Long, Long] = rtGraph.mapVertices( (id, _) => id)
```

Similarly, instead of retrieving triplets first, we can start equally well from our initial graph and directly transform triplets using `mapTriplets`, returning a Graph object with modified edge data. To achieve the same effect as with the preceding `tweetStrings` but keeping the graph structure intact, we can run the following:

```
val mappedTripletsGraph = rtGraph.mapTriplets(
  t => t.dstId + " retweeted " + t.attr + " from " + t.srcId
)
```

As a last example of basic graph processing functionality, we will now look at the subgraphs of a given graph and how to join graphs with each other. Consider the task of extracting information of all the Twitter users in our graph that have been retweeted at least 10 times. We have already seen how to obtain out-degree from `rtGraph.outDegrees`. To make this information accessible in our original graph, we need to join this information to it. For this purpose, GraphX has the functionality provided by `outerJoinVertices` in place. To do so, we need to provide a `VertexRDD` of vertex data type, `U`, to join with and a function that determines how to aggregate the vertex data. If we call the RDD to join `other`, this looks as follows on paper:

```
def outerJoinVertices[U, VD2](other: RDD[(VertexId, U)])
  (mapFunc: (VertexId, VD, Option[U]) => VD2): Graph[VD2, ED]
```

Note that since we carry out an outer join, not all IDs in the original graph may have a corresponding value in `other`, which is why we see the `Option` type in the respective map function. Doing this for our concrete example at hand works as follows:

```
val outDegreeGraph: Graph[Long, Long] =
  rtGraph.outerJoinVertices[Int, Long](rtGraph.outDegrees)(
    mapFunc = (id, origData, outDeg) => outDeg.getOrElse(0).toLong
  )
```

We join with our original graph with the out-degree, `VertexRDD`, and as the map function, we simply discard the original vertex data and replace it with out-degree. If there is no out-degree available, we simply set it to 0 by using `getOrElse` to resolve the `Option`.

Next, we want to retrieve the subgraph of this graph, in which each vertex has at least 10 retweets. A subgraph of a graph consists of a subset of the original vertices and edges. Formally, we define a subgraph to be the result of a *predicate* on edges, vertices, or both. By this, we mean an expression evaluated on the vertices or edges that returns either true or false. The signature of the subgraph method on graphs is defined as follows:

```
def subgraph(
  epred: EdgeTriplet[VD,ED] => Boolean = (x => true),
  vpred: (VertexId, VD) => Boolean = ((v, d) => true)): Graph[VD, ED]
```

Note that since the default functions are provided, we can choose to provide only one of either `vpred` or `epred`. In our concrete example, we want to restrict to vertices with a degree of at least `10`, which can be done as follows:

```
val tenOrMoreRetweets = outDegreeGraph.subgraph(
  vpred = (id, deg) => deg >= 10
)
tenOrMoreRetweets.vertices.count
tenOrMoreRetweets.edges.count
```

The resulting graph has a mere `10` vertices and `5` edges, but it's interesting to see that these influencers seem to connect to each other in about as much as the average.

To close this section, an interesting technique to know is that of *masking*. Assume that we now want to know the subgraph of vertices with less than 10 retweets, which is somewhat the opposite of the preceding `tenOrMoreRetweets`. Of course, this can be done by a subgraph definition, but we can also mask the original graph by `tenOrMoreRetweets`, as follows:

```
val lessThanTenRetweets = rtGraph.mask(tenOrMoreRetweets)
```

If we wanted, we could reconstruct `rtGraph` by joining `tenOrMoreRetweets` to `lessThanTenRetweets`.

Building and loading graphs

In the last section, we made a lot of leeway in graph analytics and discussed an interesting retweet graph. Before we dive into more complicated operations, let's take a step back and consider other options to construct graphs with GraphX. Having completed this interlude, we will have a quick look into visualization tools and then turn to the more involved applications.

In fact, we have already seen two ways to create GraphX graphs, one was to construct the vertex and edge RDDs explicitly, ourselves, to construct a graph from it; the other one was to use `Graph.fromEdges`. Another very handy possibility is to load a so-called *edge list file*. An example of this format is the following:

```
1 3
5 3
4 2
3 2
1 5
```

So, an edge list file is a text file with pairs of IDs per row, separated by a space. Assuming that we store the preceding data as `edge_list.txt` in the current working directory, we can load a graph object in one line from it, using the `GraphLoader` interface:

```
import org.apache.spark.graphx.GraphLoader
val edgeListGraph = GraphLoader.edgeListFile(sc, "./edge_list.txt")
```

This represents a very convenient entry point, given that we have data provided in the right format. Additional vertex and edge data has to be joined to the resulting graph after loading the edge list file, though. Another similar approach to constructing a graph from the preceding data is to use the `fromEdgeTuples` method provided by the `Graph` object, which can be utilised as shown in the following code snippet:

```
val rawEdges: RDD[(VertexId, VertexId)] =
sc.textFile("./edge_list.txt").map {
  line =>
    val field = line.split(" ")
    (field(0).toLong, field(1).toLong)
}
val edgeTupleGraph = Graph.fromEdgeTuples(
  rawEdges=rawEdges, defaultValue="")
```

The difference from the previous construction is that we create a raw-edge RDD, containing pairs of vertex IDs, which, together with a default value for vertex data, feeds into the construction of the graph.

With this last example, we have essentially seen every single way currently supported in GraphX to load a graph from the given data. There is, however, also the possibility of *generating* random and deterministic graphs, which is very helpful for tests, quick sanity checks, and demonstrations. To this end, we import the following class:

```
import org.apache.spark.graphx.util.GraphGenerators
```

This class has a lot of functionality to offer. The two deterministic graph construction methods help build *star* and *grid* graphs. A star graph consists of a single central vertex and several vertices connecting only to the central one by means of one single edge. Here is how to create a star graph with ten vertices connecting to the central vertex:

```
val starGraph = GraphGenerators.starGraph(sc, 11)
```

The following image is a graphical representation of a star graph:

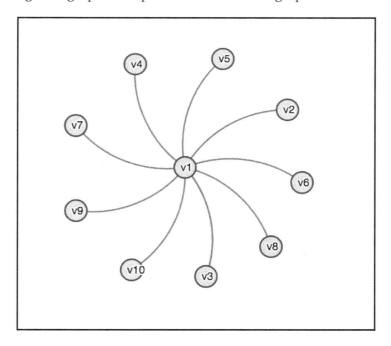

Figure 10: A star graph with ten vertices surrounding a central one.

The other deterministic method for graph creation builds a grid, meaning that the vertices are organised in a matrix, and each vertex connects to its direct neighbours both vertically and horizontally. In a grid graph with *n* rows and *m* columns, there are precisely *n(m-1)* + *m(n-1)* edges--the first term is for all the vertical connections and the second one is for all the horizontal grid connections. This is how to build a 5 times 5 grid with 40 edges in GraphX:

```
val gridGraph = GraphGenerators.gridGraph(sc, 5, 5)
```

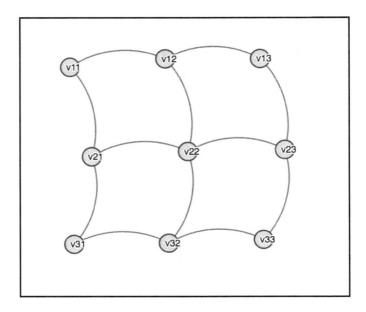

Figure 11: A quadratic 3 by 3 grid graph with twelve vertices.

As far as random graphs are concerned, we will cover one creation method that approximately reflects many real-world graphs structurally, namely *log normal graphs*. Many structures found in real life follow a *power law*, in which the measure of an entity is given by the power of another. A concrete example for this would be the Pareto-principle, often called 80/20 principle, which implies that 80% of the wealth is possessed by 20% of the people, that is, most wealth is attributed to a few. A variant of this, called *Zipf's law*, applies to our scenario, namely a few vertices have very high degree, while most have very little connections. In the context of a social graph, very few people tend to have a lot of followers, while the majority have very little. This leads to a distribution of vertex degrees that follows a *log-normal distribution*. The star graph in *Figure 10* is an extreme variant of this behavior, in which all the edges are centered around one vertex.

Creating a log normal graph with 20 vertices in graphX is simply done as follows:

```
val logNormalGraph  = GraphGenerators.logNormalGraph(
  sc, numVertices = 20, mu=1, sigma = 3
)
```

In the preceding code snippet, we also impose a mean of one out-degree per vertex and a standard deviation of three. Let's see if we can confirm the log-normal distribution on vertex out-degree:

```
logNormalGraph.outDegrees.map(_._2).collect().sorted
```

This will produce a Scala array that should look as follows.

```
Array[Int] = Array(1, 1, 2, 2, 3, 4, 6, 7, 9, 10, 11, 12, 13, 15)
```

Note that you might get different results, since the graph is randomly generated. Next, let's see how to visualize some of the graphs that we have constructed so far.

Visualizing graphs with Gephi

GraphX does not come with a built-in graph visualization tool, so for us to tackle visualizing massive graphs, we have to consider other options. There are many general-purpose visualization libraries out there, as well as a few specialized graph visualization tools. In this chapter, we choose *Gephi* for essentially two reasons:

- It is a free open source tool that is available for all the major platforms
- We can utilise a simple exchange format, GEXF, to persist GraphX graphs, and can load them into the Gephi GUI to specify the visualization with it

While the first point should be universally considered a plus, not everyone is a fan of the GUIs and it's certainly more in the spirit of most developers to define visualizations programatically. Note that this is in fact also possible with Gephi, but more on this later. The reason we chose the mentioned approach is to keep the book self-contained and the coding parts about Spark only, by still using powerful visualizations provided by Gephi.

Gephi

To get started, download Gephi from `https://gephi.org/` and install it locally on your machine. At the time of writing this book, the stable version is 0.9.1, which we will use throughout. Upon opening the Gephi application, you will be prompted a welcome message and can choose from a few examples to explore. We will use `Les Miserables.gexf` to familiarize ourselves with the tool. We will discuss the GEXF file format in more detail later; for now, let's just focus on the application. The underlying graph data of this example consists of vertices representing characters of the piece, *Les Miserables*, and edges denoting the association of characters, *weighted* by an assessment of the importance of the connection.

Gephi is a very rich tool and we can only discuss a few basics here. Once you open the preceding file you should already see a preview of the example graph. Gephi has three main views:

- **Overview**: This is the view in which we can manipulate all the visual attributes of the graph and get a preview. For our purposes, this is the most important view, and we will discuss it in more detail.
- **Data Laboratory**: This view shows raw graph data in a table format, split into *Nodes* and *Edges*, which can also be extended and modified as needed.
- **Preview**: The preview view is used to see the result, that is, the graph visualization, as it can also be exported to various formats, such as SVG, PDF, and PNG.

If it is not already active, select **Overview** to proceed. In the main menu of the application, filed under *Window*, you can choose various tabs. Make sure to have **Graph**, **Preview Settings**, **Appearance**, **Layout**, and **Statistics** open, as indicated in the following image:

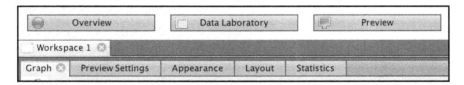

Figure 12: Gephi's three main views and the essential tabs used in the Overview view

The **Graph** tab, in which you should already see a visual representation of the sample *les miserables* graph, can be used for final touch-ups and visual inspection. For instance, the *Rectangle selection* on the left of the respective window allows you to select subgraphs by selecting vertices, whereas with *Drag*, you can move around vertices to your aesthetic needs.

In **Preview settings**, potentially the most interesting tab for us, we can configure most of the visual aspects of the graph. **Presets** allow you to change the general style of the graph, such as curved versus straight edges. We will keep the **Default** setting as is. You may have noticed that the graph preview has no vertex or edge labels, so it's impossible to see what each vertex stands for. We can change this by selecting **Show Labels** in the **Node Labels** category and then deselecting the **Proportional size** checkbox so that all the labels have the same size. If you now go to the **Preview** view, the graph you see should look as shown in the following image:

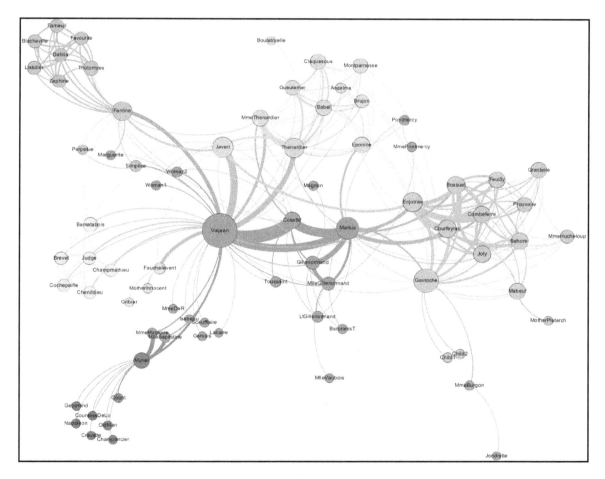

Figure 13: Les miserables example graph, slightly modified with Gephi. Vertices are characters of the piece and edges represent importance of connection by means of edge thickness. Vertex size is determined by degree and vertices are additionally grouped by colour to indicate family membership, the latter of which can't be seen in print.

Note that the preceding graph comes with visual attributes that we did not specifically set. The vertex size is proportional to the vertex degree, the edge thickness is determined by the weight, and the graph is color-coded to show which family the individual characters belong to. To understand how this is done, we discuss the *Appearance* tab next, which also distinguishes between *Nodes* and *Edges*. In the top-right corner of this tab, there are four options to choose from, and we select **Size**, which is depicted by an icon showing several circles. Having done so, we can first select **Nodes** in the top-left corner and then *Ranking* right below it. In the drop-down menu, we can choose an attribute to determine the node size by, which, in the preceding example, is *degree*. Similarly, the other two attributes discussed previously can be configured.

Moving on, the next tab we discuss is *Layout*, in which we can select methods to automatically arrange the graph. Interesting layouts to play with are the two available *Force Atlas* schemes, which simulate vertices gravitating toward each other with configurable vertex attraction and repulsion properties. In *Figure 13*, no layout was chosen, but it can be interesting to explore them a little. Whatever layout you choose, activate them by hitting the **Run** button.

Using the *Statistics* tab, we can explore graph properties from within Gephi, such as connected components and PageRank. Since we will discuss how to do this with GraphX, which is also much more performant, we will just leave it at that, although you are encouraged to experiment with the functionality in this tab, as it can help build intuition quickly.

Having configured the attributes to our needs, we can now switch to the **Preview** view to see if the resulting graph is what we expect it to be. Assuming that everything worked out, the **SVG/PDF/PNG** button of the **Preview settings** tab can be used to export our final infographic to be used in your product, be it reports, further analyses, or other use cases.

Creating GEXF files from GraphX graphs

To connect the graph visualization capabilities of Gephi with Spark GraphX graphs, we need to address a way to communicate between the two. The canonical candidate for doing so is Gephi's **Graph Exchange XML Format (GEXF)**, a description of which can be found at https://gephi.org/gexf/format/. A very simple example of how graphs are described in this format is displayed in the following code listing:

```
<?xml version="1.0" encoding="UTF-8"?>
<gexf xmlns="http://www.gexf.net/1.2draft" version="1.2">
    <meta lastmodifieddate="2009-03-20">
        <creator>Gexf.net</creator>
        <description>A hello world! file</description>
    </meta>
```

```
    <graph mode="static" defaultedgetype="directed">
        <nodes>
            <node id="0" label="Hello" />
            <node id="1" label="Word" />
        </nodes>
        <edges>
            <edge id="0" source="0" target="1" />
        </edges>
    </graph>
</gexf>
```

Apart from the header and the meta data of the XML, the graph encoding itself is self-explanatory. It is useful to know that the preceding XML is just the bare minimum required for graph descriptions, and in fact, GEXF can be used to encode other properties, such as edge weights or even visual attributes that are automatically picked up by Gephi.

To connect with GraphX, let's write a little helper function that takes a `Graph` version and returns a `String` version of the preceding XML format:

```
def toGexf[VD, ED](g: Graph[VD, ED]): String = {
  val header =
    """<?xml version="1.0" encoding="UTF-8"?>
      |<gexf xmlns="http://www.gexf.net/1.2draft" version="1.2">
      |  <meta>
      |    <description>A gephi graph in GEXF format</description>
      |  </meta>
      |    <graph mode="static" defaultedgetype="directed">
    """.stripMargin

  val vertices = "<nodes>\n" + g.vertices.map(
    v => s"""<node id=\"${v._1}\" label=\"${v._2}\"/>\n"""
  ).collect.mkString + "</nodes>\n"

  val edges = "<edges>\n" + g.edges.map(
    e => s"""<edge source=\"${e.srcId}\" target=\"${e.dstId}\"
label=\"${e.attr}\"/>\n"""
  ).collect.mkString + "</edges>\n"

  val footer = "</graph>\n</gexf>"

  header + vertices + edges + footer
}
```

While the code might seem a bit cryptic at first sight, very little is happening. We define the header and the footer for the XML. We need to map the edge and vertex properties to the <nodes> and <edges> XML tags. To this end, we use Scala's convenient ${} notation to ingest variables directly into strings. For a change, let's use this toGexf function in a complete Scala app, which uses our simple friend graph from earlier. Note that for this to work, it is assumed that toGexf is available to GephiApp. So, either store it in the same object or in another file to import it from there. If you want to continue using spark-shell, just pasting the imports and the body of the main method, excluding the creation of conf and sc, should work without problems:

```scala
import java.io.PrintWriter
import org.apache.spark._
import org.apache.spark.graphx._
import org.apache.spark.rdd.RDD

object GephiApp {
  def main(args: Array[String]) {

    val conf = new SparkConf()
      .setAppName("Gephi Test Writer")
      .setMaster("local[4]")
    val sc = new SparkContext(conf)

    val vertices: RDD[(VertexId, String)] = sc.parallelize(
      Array((1L, "Anne"),
        (2L, "Bernie"),
        (3L, "Chris"),
        (4L, "Don"),
        (5L, "Edgar")))

    val edges: RDD[Edge[String]] = sc.parallelize(
      Array(Edge(1L, 2L, "likes"),
        Edge(2L, 3L, "trusts"),
        Edge(3L, 4L, "believes"),
        Edge(4L, 5L, "worships"),
        Edge(1L, 3L, "loves"),
        Edge(4L, 1L, "dislikes")))

    val graph: Graph[String, String] = Graph(vertices, edges)

    val pw = new PrintWriter("./graph.gexf")
    pw.write(toGexf(graph))
    pw.close()
  }
}
```

This app stores our friend graph as `graph.gexf`, which we can use to import into Gephi. To do so, go to **File**, then click on **Open** to select this file and import the graph. The following diagram shows the result of this procedure by tweaking the visual attributes using the tabs and methods described earlier:

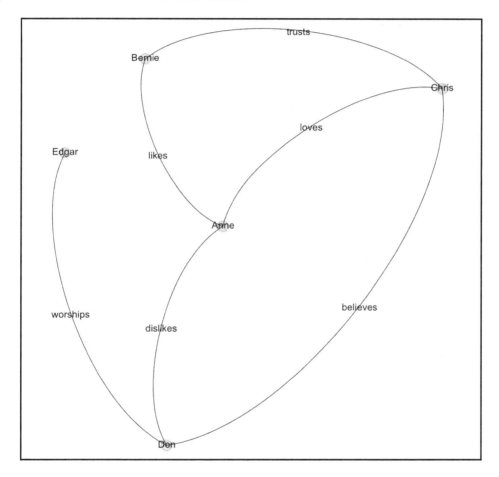

Figure 14: Our example friend graph displayed using Gephi

 As noted earlier, it is indeed possible to define visual attributes programmatically, using *Gephi Toolkit*, a Java library you can import into your project. There are other language wrappers available, but this is the supported library, available as a single JAR. It's far beyond the scope of this book to discuss the toolkit, but if you are interested, you can refer to `https://gephi.org/toolkit/`, which serves as a good entry point.

Advanced graph processing

After a quick interlude into graph generation and visualization, let's turn towards more challenging applications and more advanced techniques for graph analytics. To recap, what we have done so far in terms of graph processing is just using the basic properties of the underlying edge and vertex RDDs of a GraphX graph, as well as a few transformations, including `mapVertices`, `mapEdges`, and `mapTriplets`. As we have seen, these techniques are already quite useful, but by themselves not powerful enough to implement graph-parallel algorithms with. For this purpose, GraphX graph has two strong candidates, which we will discuss next. Most of the built-in GraphX algorithms, including triangle counting, PageRank and so on, are implemented using either one or the other.

Aggregating messages

First, we discuss the `aggregateMessages` method that GraphX graphs come with. The basic idea is to pass messages along edges in parallel across the whole graph, aggregate these messages suitably and store the result for further processing. Let's have a closer look at how `aggregateMessages` is defined:

```
def aggregateMessages[Msg: ClassTag](
  sendMsg: EdgeContext[VD, ED, Msg] => Unit,
  mergeMsg: (Msg, Msg) => Msg,
  tripletFields: TripletFields = TripletFields.All
): VertexRDD[Msg]
```

As you can see, to implement an `aggregateMessages` algorithm we need to specify a message type `Msg` and provide three functions, which we will explain next. You may notice that there are two additional types that we haven't encountered before, namely `EdgeContext` and `TripletFields`. Simply put, an edge context is an extension of `EdgeTriplets` that we have already seen, that is, an edge plus all information about adjacent vertices, with the only difference being that we can additionally send information to the source and target vertex defined as follows:

```
def sendToSrc(msg: A): Unit
def sendToDst(msg: A): Unit
```

`TripletFields` allows one to restrict the `EdgeContext` fields used in the computation, which defaults to all available fields. In fact, in what follows we will simply use this default for `tripletFields` and focus on `sendMsg` and `mergeMsg` only. As indicated in the introduction to this topic, `sendMsg` is used to pass messages along edges, `mergeMsg` aggregates them and we store the result of this operation in a vertex RDD of `Msg` type. To make this more concrete, consider the following example, an alternative way to compute in-degree for all vertices for our little friend graph from earlier:

```
val inDegVertexRdd: VertexRDD[Int] = friendGraph.aggregateMessages[Int](
  sendMsg = ec => ec.sendToDst(1),
  mergeMsg = (msg1, msg2) => msg1+msg2
)
assert(inDegVertexRdd.collect.deep == friendGraph.inDegrees.collect.deep)
```

In this example, sending a message is defined by taking an edge context and using its `sendToDst` method to send an integer message to each target vertex, namely the number one. What this means is that for each edge in parallel we send a one to each vertex this edge points to. This way vertices get send messages that we need to merge. The `mergeMsg` here should be understood the same way as `reduce` for RDDs in general, that is, we specify how two messages are merged and this recipe is used to collapse all messages into one. In the example at hand we just sum up all messages, which by definition yields the in-degree for each vertex. We confirm this by asserting equality of the arrays we get from collecting both `inDegVertexRdd` and `friendGraph.inDegrees` on master.

Note that the return value of `aggregateMessages` is a vertex RDD, not a graph. So, using this mechanism iteratively, we need to generate a new graph object in each iteration, which is not ideal. Since Spark is especially strong with iterative algorithms due to keeping partition data in memory and the fact that a lot of interesting graph algorithms are in fact iterative, we next discuss the slightly more complicated, but extremely powerful, Pregel API.

Pregel

Pregel is a system internally developed by Google, the companion paper of which is very accessible and available for download at http://www.dcs.bbk.ac.uk/~dell/teaching/cc/paper/sigmod10/p135-malewicz.pdf. It represents an efficient, iterative graph-parallel compute model that allows one to implement a large class of graph algorithms. GraphX's implementation of Pregel differs slightly from the preceding paper, but we can't go into any details of this.

In flavor, GraphX's `Pregel` implementation is very close to `aggregateMessages`, but has a few key differences. Traits that are shared by both approaches are the send and merge message mechanics. On top of that, with Pregel we can define a so-called *vertex program* `vprog` that is executed before sending, to transform vertex data. Also, we start with a shared initial message on each vertex and can specify for how many iterations we want to execute the *vprog-send-merge* cycle, that is, iterations are part of the specification.

The `apply` method of the Pregel implementation is sketched. Note that it takes two sets of inputs, namely a quadruple consisting of the graph itself, an initial message, the maximum iterations to be executed and a field called `activeDirection`. The last argument deserves some more attention. A detail of the Pregel specification we have not talked about yet is that *we only send new messages from vertices that have received messages in the previous iteration*. The active direction defaults to `Either`, but can also be both, `In` or `Out`. This behavior naturally lets algorithms converge in many cases and it also explains why the third argument is called `maxIterations` - we might stop earlier than specified:

```
object Pregel {
  def apply[VD: ClassTag, ED: ClassTag, A: ClassTag]
    (graph: Graph[VD, ED],
     initialMsg: A,
     maxIterations: Int = Int.MaxValue,
     activeDirection: EdgeDirection = EdgeDirection.Either)
    (vprog: (VertexId, VD, A) => VD,
     sendMsg: EdgeTriplet[VD, ED] => Iterator[(VertexId, A)],
     mergeMsg: (A, A) => A)
  : Graph[VD, ED]
}
```

The second set of arguments to Pregel is the triple we already sketched, namely the vertex program, as well as sending and merging messages functions. The only noteworthy difference from before is the signature of `sendMsg`, which returns an *iterator over vertex ID and message pairs*. This does not change much for us, but interestingly, the signature of `sendMsg` in `aggregateMessage` has been such an iterator until Spark 1.6 and was changed to what we discussed previously in the update to Spark 2.0. Very likely, the signature of Pregel will be changed accordingly as well, but as of 2.1.1 it remains as described.

To illustrate the possibilities of the Pregel API let's sketch an implementation of an algorithm that computes connected components. This is a slight modification of the implementation currently available in GraphX. We define the `ConnectedComponents` object with a single following method, namely `run`, which takes any graph and a maximum number of iterations. The core idea of the algorithm is easy enough to explain. For each edge, whenever its source has a smaller ID than its target, send the source ID to the target and vice versa. To aggregate these messages, simply take the minimum of all broadcasted values and iterate this procedure long enough so that it runs out of updates. At this point, every vertex that is connected to another bears the same ID as vertex data, namely the smallest ID available in the original graph:

```scala
import org.apache.spark.graphx._
import scala.reflect.ClassTag

object ConnectedComponents extends Serializable {

  def run[VD: ClassTag, ED: ClassTag](graph: Graph[VD, ED],
                                      maxIterations: Int)
  : Graph[VertexId, ED] = {

    val idGraph: Graph[VertexId, ED] = graph.mapVertices((id, _) => id)

    def vprog(id: VertexId, attr: VertexId, msg: VertexId): VertexId = {
      math.min(attr, msg)
    }

    def sendMsg(edge: EdgeTriplet[VertexId, ED]): Iterator[(VertexId,
VertexId)] = {
        if (edge.srcAttr < edge.dstAttr) {
          Iterator((edge.dstId, edge.srcAttr))
        } else if (edge.srcAttr > edge.dstAttr) {
          Iterator((edge.srcId, edge.dstAttr))
        } else {
          Iterator.empty
        }
    }

    def mergeMsg(v1: VertexId, v2: VertexId): VertexId = math.min(v1, v2)

    Pregel(
      graph = idGraph,
      initialMsg = Long.MaxValue,
      maxIterations,
      EdgeDirection.Either)(
      vprog,
      sendMsg,
```

```
    mergeMsg)
  }
}
```

Going step by step, the algorithm does as follows. We first forget all previously available vertex data by defining `idGraph`. Next, we define the vertex program to emit the minimum of the current vertex data attribute and the current message. This way we can store the minimum vertex ID as vertex data. The `sendMsg` method propagates the smaller ID for each edge to either source or target, as described before and `mergeMsg` again just takes the minimum over IDs. Having these three key methods defined, we can simply run `Pregel` on the `idGraph` with `maxIterations` as specified. Note that we do not care about which direction the messages flow, so we use `EdgeDirection.Either`. Also, we start with the maximum available Long value as our initial message, which works since we take the minimum over vertex IDs everywhere.

Having defined this allows us to find connected components on the retweet graph `rtGraph` from earlier as follows, choosing five iterations as maximum:

```
val ccGraph = ConnectedComponents.run(rtGraph, 5)
cc.vertices.map(_._2).distinct.count
```

Counting distinct vertex data items of the resulting graph gives us the number of connected components (in this case it is just one component), that is, all tweets in the data set are connected if we forget directionality. It is interesting to note that we do in fact need five iterations for the algorithm to converge. Running it with fewer iterations, that is, 1, 2, 3 or 4, yields 1771, 172, 56 and 4 connected components. Since there has to be at least one connected component, we know that further increasing iterations would not change the outcome. However, in general we would rather not specify the number of iterations, unless time or computing power are an issue. By wrapping the preceding run method as follows, we can run this algorithm on graphs only, without explicitly providing iterations:

```
def run[VD: ClassTag, ED: ClassTag](graph: Graph[VD, ED])
: Graph[VertexId, ED] = {
  run(graph, Int.MaxValue)
}
```

Simply add this as an additional method to the `ConnectedComponents` object. For the retweet graph, we can now simply write instead. Having seen both `aggregateMessages` and Pregel, the reader should now be adequately equipped to develop their own graph algorithms:

```
val ccGraph = ConnectedComponents.run(rtGraph)
```

GraphFrames

Note that so far, to compute any interesting indicators on a given graph, we had to use the compute model of the graph, an extension of what we know from RDDs. With Spark's DataFrame or Dataset concept in mind, the reader may wonder if there is any possibility to use an SQL-like language to do run queries against a graph for analytics. Query languages often provide a convenient way to get results quickly.

This is indeed possible with GraphFrames. The library was developed by Databricks and serves as natural extension of GraphX graphs to Spark DataFrames. Unfortunately, GraphFrames are not part of Spark GraphX, but instead available as Spark package. To load GraphFrames upon starting spark-submit, simply run

```
spark-shell --packages graphframes:graphframes:0.5.0-spark2.1-s_2.11
```

and suitably adapt preceding version numbers for both your preferred Spark and Scala versions. Converting a GraphX Graph to a `GraphFrame` and vice versa is as easy as it gets; in the following we convert our friend graph from earlier to a `GraphFrame` and then back:

```
import org.graphframes._

val friendGraphFrame = GraphFrame.fromGraphX(friendGraph)
val graph = friendGraphFrame.toGraphX
```

As indicated before, one added benefit of GraphFrames is that you can use Spark SQL with them, as they are built on top of DataFrames. This also means that GraphFrames are much faster than Graphs, since the Spark core team has brought a lot of speed gains to DataFrames through their catalyst and tungsten frameworks. Hopefully we see GraphFrames added to Spark GraphX in one of the next releases.

Instead of looking at a Spark SQL example, which should be familiar enough from previous chapters, we consider another query language available for GraphFrames, that has a very intuitive compute model. GraphFrames has borrowed the *Cypher* SQL dialect from the graph database *neo4j*, which can be used for very expressive queries. Continuing with the `friendGraphFrame`, we can very easily find all length two paths for which either end in the vertex "Chris" or pass through the edge "trusts" first by using one concise command:

```
friendGraphFrame.find("(v1)-[e1]->(v2); (v2)-[e2]->(v3)").filter(
  "e1.attr = 'trusts' OR v3.attr = 'Chris'"
).collect.foreach(println)
```

Note how we can specify the graph structure in a manner that lets you think in terms of the actual graph, that is, we have two edges *e1* and *e2*, that are connected to each other by a common vertex *v2*. The result of this operation is listed in the following screenshot, which indeed gives back the three paths that suffice the preceding condition:

```
[[4,Don],[4,1,dislikes],[1,Anne],[1,3,loves],[3,Chris]]
[[1,Anne],[1,2,likes],[2,Bernie],[2,3,trusts],[3,Chris]]
[[2,Bernie],[2,3,trusts],[3,Chris],[3,4,believes],[4,Don]]
```

Unfortunately, we can not discuss GraphFrames here in more detail, but the interested reader is referred to the documentation available at `https://graphframes.github.io/` for more details. Instead, we will now turn to the algorithms available in GraphX and apply them to a massive graph of actor data.

Graph algorithms and applications

For this application section, in which we will discuss triangle counting, (strongly) connected components, PageRank and other algorithms available in GraphX, we will load another interesting graph dataset from `http://networkrepository.com/`. This time please download data from `http://networkrepository.com/ca-hollywood-2009.php`, which consists of an undirected graph whose vertices represent actors occurring in movies. Each line of the file contains two vertex IDs representing an edge, meaning that these actors appeared together in a movie.

The dataset consists of about 1.1 million vertices and has 56.3 million edges. Although the file size, even after unzipping, is not particularly large, a graph of this size is a real challenge for a graph processing engine. Since we assume you work with Spark's standalone mode locally, this graph will likely not fit into your computer's memory and will crash the Spark application. To prevent this, let's restrict the data a little, which also gives us the chance to clean up the file header. We assume you have unpacked `ca-hollywood-2009.mtx` and stored it in your current working directory. We use unix tools *tail* and *head* to delete the first two lines and then restrict to the first million edges:

```
tail -n+3 ca-hollywood-2009.mtx | head -1000000 > ca-hollywood-2009.txt
```

If these tools should not be available to you, any other will do, including manually modifying the file. From the structure described previously we can simply use `edgeListFile` functionality to load the graph into Spark and confirm that it indeed has a million edges:

```
val actorGraph = GraphLoader.edgeListFile(sc, "./ca-hollywood-2009.txt")
actorGraph.edges.count()
```

Next, let's see what we can do with GraphX to analyze this graph.

Clustering

Given a graph, a natural question to ask is if there are any subgraphs to it that naturally belong together, that is, that cluster the graph in some way. This question can be addressed in many ways, one of which we have already implemented ourselves, namely by studying connected components. Instead of using our own implementation, let's use GraphX's built-in version this time. To do so, we can simply call `connectedComponents` directly on the graph itself:

```
val actorComponents = actorGraph.connectedComponents().cache
actorComponents.vertices.map(_._2).distinct().count
```

As in our own implementation, the vertex data of the graph contains cluster IDs, which correspond to the minimum available vertex ID within the cluster. This allows us to directly count connected components, by collecting distinct cluster IDs. The answer for our restricted cluster graph is 173. Computing components, we cache the graph so we can further use it for other computations. For instance, we might ask how large the connected components are, for example by computing the maximum and the minimum cluster size in terms of vertices. We can do this by using the cluster ID as key and reducing each group by counting its items:

```
val clusterSizes =actorComponents.vertices.map(
  v => (v._2, 1)).reduceByKey(_ + _)
clusterSizes.map(_._2).max
clusterSizes.map(_._2).min
```

It turns out the largest cluster spans a respectable group of 193,518 actors, while the smallest consists of a mere three actors. Next, let's ignore the fact that the graph in question does not actually have directionality, since appearing in a movie together is symmetric, and act as if the edge pairs were directed. We don't have to impose anything here, since an edge in Spark GraphX always has a source and a target. This allows us to study *strongly* connected components as well. We can call this algorithm similarly to that for connected components, but in this case we have to specify a number of iterations as well. The reason for this is that it's much more computationally demanding to "trace" directed edges in the same way we did for connected components and convergence is slower.

Let's settle for just one iteration to carry out the computation, since it is very expensive:

```
val strongComponents = actorGraph.stronglyConnectedComponents(numIter = 1)
strongComponents.vertices.map(_._2).distinct().count
```

This computation might take a few minutes to complete. In case you have problems running even this example on your machine, consider further restricting `actorGraph`.

Next, let's compute triangles for the actor graph, yet another way to cluster it. To do so, we need to slightly prepare the graph, namely we have to *canonicalize* the edges and specify a *graph partition strategy*. To canonicalize a graph means to get rid of loops and duplicate edges and make sure that the source ID is always smaller than the target ID for all the edges:

```
val canonicalGraph = actorGraph.mapEdges(
  e => 1).removeSelfEdges().convertToCanonicalEdges()
```

Graph partition strategies, like RDD partitions we have already encountered, are concerned with the question of how to distribute a graph across the cluster efficiently. Of course, what efficiently means depends in large part on what we do with our graph. Roughly speaking, there are two basic partition strategies, namely *vertex cut* and *edge cut*. Vertex cut strategy means enforce split edges in a disjointed manner by cutting vertices, that is, vertices are repeated across partitions, if necessary. Edge cut strategy does the opposite in that vertices are unique throughout the cluster, but we may duplicate edges. GraphX has four partition strategies that are all based on vertex cut. We will not discuss them here in detail, but rather just use `RandomVertexCut`, which hashes vertex IDs so that all same-direction edges between vertices are located on the same partition.

 Note that when creating a graph without specifying a partition strategy, the graph is distributed by simply adopting the structure of the underlying EdgeRDD that has been provided for construction. Depending on your use-case, this might not be ideal, for instance because edge partitions might be strongly imbalanced.

To partition `canonicalGraph` and continue with triangle counting, we now partition our graph using said strategy as follows:

```
val partitionedGraph =
canonicalGraph.partitionBy(PartitionStrategy.RandomVertexCut)
```

Computing triangles is conceptually simple. We first collect all neighboring vertices for each vertex and then compute the intersection of these sets for each edge. The logic is, if both source and target vertex sets contain the same third vertex, the three form a triangle. As a last step, we send the *count of the intersection set* to both source and target, thereby counting each triangle twice and we simply divide by two to get a triangle count per vertex. Doing the triangle count now boils down to running:

```
import org.apache.spark.graphx.lib.TriangleCount
val triangles = TriangleCount.runPreCanonicalized(partitionedGraph)
```

In fact, instead of canonicalising `actorGraph` explicitly, we could simply have gotten away with just imposing `triangleCount` directly on the initial graph, that is, by computing the following:

```
actorGraph.triangleCount()
```

Equivalently, we can also import `TriangleCount` and call it on our actor graph as follows:

```
import org.apache.spark.graphx.lib.TriangleCount
TriangleCount.run(actorGraph)
```

Note, however, that these last two equivalent operations will in fact canonicalize the graph in question the same way we did, and canonicalisation is a computationally very expensive operation. So, whenever you see the chance to already load your graph in canonical form, the first approach shown will be more efficient.

Vertex importance

In a graph of friends connected to each other, an interesting question to ask is who the most influential person in the group is. Is it the person with the most connections, that is, the vertex with the highest degree? For directed graphs, in-degree might be a good first guess. Or is it rather the person who knows a selected few people who themselves have a lot of connections? There are certainly many ways to describe how important or authoritative a vertex is and the concrete answer will depend on the problem domain a lot, as well as on what additional data we are given with the graph. Moreover, in the example we have given, for a specific person in the graph another person might be the most influential for their own, very subjective reasons.

Still, seeking for vertex importance in a given graph is a challenging problem, and one historically important example of such an algorithm is *PageRank*, which was described back in 1998 in the seminal paper "The Anatomy of a Large-Scale Hypertextual Web Search Engine" available at `http://ilpubs.stanford.edu:8090/361/1/1998-8.pdf`. In it, Sergey Brin and Larry Page laid the foundations of what ran their search engine Google when the company had just started out. While PageRank had a significant impact on finding relevant search results in the vast graph of web pages connected by links, the algorithm has since been replaced by other approaches within Google over the years. However, PageRank remains a prime example of how to rank web pages, or graphs in general, to gain a deeper understanding of it. GraphX provides an implementation of PageRank, which we will have a look at after describing the algorithm itself.

PageRank is an iterative algorithm for directed graphs that is initialized by setting the same value to each vertex, namely *1/N* where *N* denotes the order of the graph, that is, the number of vertices. It then repeats the same procedure of updating vertex values, that is, their PageRank, until we choose to stop or certain convergence criteria is fulfilled. More specifically, in each iteration a vertex sends its *current PageRank divided by its out-degree* to all vertices it has an outbound connection to, that is, it distributes its current PageRank evenly over all outbound edges. Vertices then sum up all the values they receive to set their new PageRank. If overall PageRanks did not change much in the last iteration, stop the procedure. This is the very basic formulation of the algorithm and we will further specify the stopping criterion when discussing the GraphX implementation.

However, we also need to slightly extend the baseline algorithm by introducing a *damping factor d*. The damping factor was invented to prevent so called *rank sinks*. Imagine a strongly connected component that has only incoming edges from the rest of the graph, then by preceding prescription this component will accumulate more and more PageRank through incoming edges in each iteration, but never "release" any of it through outbound connections. This scenario is called a rank sink and to get rid of it we need to introduce more *rank sources* through damping. What PageRank does is simulate the idealistic idea of a completely random user following links probabilistically with likelihood given by the link target's PageRank. The idea of damping changes this by introducing a chance of probability d the user follows their current path, and with likelihood (*1-d*), gets bored and continues reading a completely different page.

In our rank sink example above the user would leave the strongly connected component and end up somewhere else in the graph, thereby increasing relevance, that is, PageRank, of other parts of the graph. To wrap up this explanation, the PageRank update rule with damping can be written as follows:

$$PR(v) = (1 - d) + d \cdot \sum_{w \to v} \frac{PR(w)}{out(w)}$$

that is, to update PageRank *PR* for vertex *v*, we sum over the PageRank of all inbound vertices *w* divided by their respective out-degree *out(w)*.

Spark GraphX has two implementations for PageRank, one called static, the other dynamic. In the static version, we simply carry out the preceding update rule for a fixed amount of iterations `numIter` specified upfront. In the dynamic version, we specify a *tolerance* `tol` for convergence, namely that a vertex drops out of the computation if its PageRank did not change at least by `tol` in the last iteration, which means it will neither emit new PageRanks nor update its own anymore. Let's compute PageRank in both static and dynamic versions for the tiny `friendGraph`. The static version with 10 iterations is called as follows:

```
friendGraph.staticPageRank(numIter = 10).vertices.collect.foreach(println)
```

After running the algorithm, we simply collect all vertices on master and print them, which yields the following:

```
(1,0.42988729103845036)
(2,0.3308390977362031)
(3,0.6102873825386869)
(4,0.6650182732476072)
(5,0.42988729103845036)
```

It's interesting to see how PageRanks change with varying numbers of iterations; see the following table for details:

numIter / vertex	Anne	Bernie	Chris	Don	Edgar
1	0.213	0.213	0.341	0.277	0.213
2	0.267	0.240	0.422	0.440	0.267
3	0.337	0.263	0.468	0.509	0.337
4	0.366	0.293	0.517	0.548	0.366
5	0.383	0.305	0.554	0.589	0.383
10	0.429	0.330	0.610	0.665	0.429
20	0.438	0.336	0.622	0.678	0.438
100	0.438	0.336	0.622	0.678	0.483

While the general tendency of which vertex is more important than the other, that is, the relative ranking of the vertices is already established after only two iterations, note that it takes about 20 iterations for the PageRanks to stabilize even for this tiny graph. So, if you are only interested in ranking vertices roughly or it is simply too expensive to run the dynamic version, the static algorithm can come in handy. To compute the dynamic version, we specify the tolerance `tol` to be `0.0001` and the so called `resetProb` to `0.15`. The latter is nothing but *1-d*, that is, the probability to leave the current path and pop up at a random vertex in the graph. In fact, `0.15` is the default value for `resetProb` and reflects the suggestion of the original paper:

```
friendGraph.pageRank(tol = 0.0001, resetProb = 0.15)
```

Running this yields the following PageRank values, displayed in *Figure 15*. The numbers should look familiar, as they are the same as from the static version with 20 or more iterations:

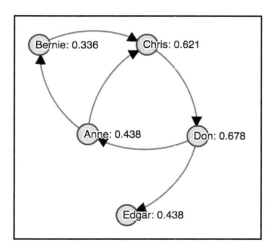

Figure 15: PageRanks computed for our toy friend graph, using the dynamic GraphX implementation.

For a more interesting example, let's turn to the actor graph once more. With the same tolerance as in the preceding example, we can quickly find the vertex ID with the highest PageRank:

```
val actorPrGraph: Graph[Double, Double] = actorGraph.pageRank(0.0001)
actorPrGraph.vertices.reduce((v1, v2) => {
  if (v1._2 > v2._2) v1 else v2
})
```

This returns ID 33024 with a PageRank of 7.82. To highlight how PageRank differs from the naive idea of simply taking in-degree as shot at vertex importance, consider the following analysis:

```
actorPrGraph.inDegrees.filter(v => v._1 == 33024L).collect.foreach(println)
```

Restricting to the vertex ID in question and checking its in-degree results in 62 incoming edges. Let's see what the top ten highest in-degrees in the graph are:

```
actorPrGraph.inDegrees.map(_._2).collect().sorted.takeRight(10)
```

This results in `Array(704, 733, 746, 756, 762, 793, 819, 842, 982, 1007)`, which means the vertex with the highest PageRank does not even come close to having among the highest in-degrees. In fact, there is a total of 2167 vertices that have at least 62 inbound edges, as can be seen by running:

```
actorPrGraph.inDegrees.map(_._2).filter(_ >= 62).count
```

So, while this still means the vertex is in the top 2% of all vertices in terms of in-degree, we see that PageRank yields a completely different answer from other approaches.

GraphX in context

Having seen a lot of applications of graph analytics throughout the chapter, a natural question to follow up with is how GraphX fits into other parts of the Spark ecosphere and how we can use it for machine learning applications in conjunction with systems like MLlib, which we have seen earlier.

The quick answer is that while the concept of graphs is limited to Spark GraphX only, due to the underlying vertex and edge RDDs of a graph, we can seamlessly talk to any other module of Spark. In fact, we have used many core RDD operations throughout the chapter, but it does not stop there. MLlib does make use of GraphX functionality in a few selected places, like *Latent Dirichlet Analysis* or *Power Iteration Clustering*, which are unfortunately beyond the scope of this chapter to explain. Instead, we focused on explaining the basics of GraphX from first principles. However, the reader is encouraged to apply what we have learnt in this chapter, together with the ones before, and experiment with the preceding algorithms. For sake of completeness, there is one machine learning algorithm completely implemented in GraphX, namely *SVD++*, which you can read more about at `http://public.research.att.com/~volinsky/netflix/kdd08koren.pdf`, and which is a graph-based recommender algorithm.

Summary

In this chapter, we have seen how to put large-scale graph analytics in practice using Spark GraphX. Modeling entity relationships as graphs with vertices and edges is a powerful paradigm to assess many interesting problems.

In GraphX, graphs are finite, directed property graphs, potentially with multiple edges and loops. GraphX does graph analytics on highly optimized versions of vertex and edge RDDs, which allows you to leverage both data and graph-parallel applications. We have seen how such graphs can be read by either loading them from `edgeListFile` or constructing them individually from other RDDs. On top of that, we have seen how easy it is to create both random and deterministic graph data for quick experiments. Using just the rich built-in functionality of the `Graph` model, we have shown how to investigate a graph for core properties. To visualize more complex graphs, we introduced *Gephi* and an interface to it, which allows one to gain intuition about the graph structure at hand.

Among the many other possibilities that Spark GraphX has to offer, we introduced two powerful graph analytics tools, namely `aggregateMessages` and the `Pregel` API. Most of GraphX's built-in algorithms are written using one of these options. We have seen how to write our own algorithms using each of these APIs. We also gave a brief overview of the GraphFrames package, which builds on top of DataFrames, comes equipped with an elegant query language that is not available in plain GraphX, and can come in handy for analytics purposes.

In terms of practical applications, we have seen an interesting retweet graph, as well as a Hollywood movie actor graph in action. We carefully explained and applied Google's PageRank algorithm, studied (strongly) connected components of graphs, and counted triangles thereof as a means of doing clustering. We finished by discussing the relationship between Spark MLlib and GraphX for advanced machine learning applications.

8
Lending Club Loan Prediction

We are almost at the end of the book, but the last chapter is going to utilize all the tricks and knowledge we covered in the previous chapters. We showed you how to utilize the power of Spark for data manipulation and transformation, and we showed you the different methods for data modeling, including linear models, tree models, and model ensembles. Essentially, this chapter will be the *kitchen sink* of chapters, whereby we will deal with many problems all at once, ranging from data ingestion, manipulation, preprocessing, outlier handling, and modeling, all the way to model deployment.

One of our main goals is to provide a realistic picture of a data scientists' daily life--start with almost raw data, explore the data, build a few models, compare them, find the best model, and deploy into production--if only it were this easy all the time! In this final chapter, we will borrow a real-life scenario from Lending Club, a company that provides peer-to-peer loans. We will apply all the skills you learned to see if we can build a model that determines the riskiness of a loan. Furthermore, we will compare the results with actual Lending Club data to evaluate our process.

Motivation

The Lending Club goal is to minimize the investment risk of providing bad loans, the loans with a high probability of defaulting or being delayed, but also to avoid rejecting good loans and hence losing profits. Here, the main criterion is driven by accepted risk - how much risk Lending Club can accept to be still profitable.

Furthermore, for prospective loans, Lending Club needs to provide an appropriate interest rate reflecting risk and generating income or provide loan adjustments. Therefore, it follows that if a given loan has a high interest rate, we can possibly infer that there is more inherent risk than a loan with a lower interest rate.

In our book, we can benefit from the Lending Club experience since they provide historical tracking of not only good loans but also bad loans. Furthermore, all historical data is available, including final loan statuses representing a unique opportunity to fit into the role of a Lending Club data scientist and try to match or even beat their prediction models.

We can even go one step further-we can imagine an "autopilot mode". For each submitted loan,we can define the investment strategy (that is, how much risk we want to accept). The autopilot will accept/reject the loan and propose a machine-generated interest rate and compute expected return. The only condition is if you make some money using our models, we expect a cut of the profits!

Goal

The overall goal is to create a machine learning application that will be able to train models respecting given investment strategy and deploy these models as a callable service, processing incoming loan applications. The service will be able to decide about a given loan application and compute an interest rate. We can define our intentions with a top-down approach starting from business requirements. Remember, a good data scientist has a firm understanding of the question(s) being asked, which is dependent on understanding the business requirement(s), which are as follows:

- We need to define what the investment strategy means and how it optimizes/influences our machine learning model creation and evaluation. Then, we will take the model's findings and apply them to our portfolio of loans to best optimize our profits based on specified investment strategy.
- We need to define a computation of expected return based on the investment strategy, and the application should provide the expected return of a lender. This is an important loan attribute for investors since it directly connects the loan application, investment strategy (that is, risk), and possible profit. We should keep this fact in mind, since in real life, the modeling pipelines are used by users who are not experts in data science or statistics and who are more interested in more high-level interpretation of modeling outputs.

- Furthermore, we need means to design and realize a loan prediction pipeline, which consists of the following:
  - A model that is based on loan application data and investment strategy decides about the loan status-if the loan should be accepted or rejected.
    - The model needs to be robust enough to reject all bad loans (that is, loans that would lead to an investment loss), but on the other hand, do not miss any good loans (that is, do not miss any investment opportunity).
    - The model should be interpretable-it should provide an explanation as to why a loan was rejected. Interestingly, there is a lot of research regarding this subject; the interpretability of models with key stakeholders who want something more tangible than just *the model said so.*

For those interested in further reading regarding model interpretability, Zachary Lipton (UCSD) has an outstanding paper titled *The Mythos of Model Interpretability,* `https://arxiv.org/abs/1606.03490` which directly addresses this topic. This is an especially useful paper for those data scientists who are constantly in the hot seat of explaining all their magic!

  - There is another model that recommends the interest rate for accepted loans. Based on the specified loan application, the model should decide the best interest rate-not too high lose a borrower, but not too low to miss a profit.
  - Finally, we need to decide how to deploy this complex, multi-faceted machine learning pipeline. Much like our previous chapter, which combines multiple models in a single pipeline, we will take all the inputs we have in our dataset-which we will see are very different types-and perform processing, feature extraction, model prediction, and recommendations based on our investment strategy: a tall order but one that we will accomplish in this chapter!

Data

Lending Club provides all available loan applications and their results publicly. The data for years 2007-2012 and 2013-2014 can be directly downloaded from https://www.lendingclub.com/info/download-data.action.

Download the **DECLINED LOAN DATA,** as shown in the following screenshot:

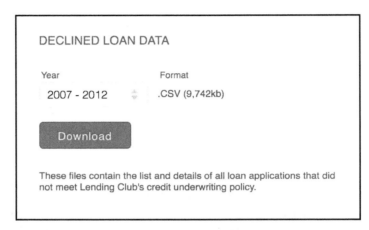

The downloaded files contain filesLoanStats3a.CSV and LoanStats3b.CSV.

The file we have contains approximately 230 k rows that are split into two sections:

- Loans that meet the credit policy: 168 k
- Loans that do not meet the credit policy: 62 k (note the imbalanced dataset)

As always, it is advisable to look at the data by viewing a sample row or perhaps the first 10 rows; given the size of the dataset we have here, we can use Excel see at what a row looks like:

id	member_id	loan_amnt	funded_amn	funded_amn	term	int_rate	installment	grade	sub_grade	emp_title	emp_length	home_owne	annual_inc	verification_	issue_d	loan_status	pymnt_plan
1077501	1296599	5000	5000	4975	36 months	10.65%	162.87	B	B2		10+ years	RENT	24000	Verified	Dec-11	Fully Paid	n
1077430	1314167	2500	2500	2500	60 months	15.27%	59.83	C	C4	Ryder	< 1 year	RENT	30000	Source Verifi	Dec-11	Charged Off	n

 Be careful since the downloaded file can contain a first line with a Lending Club download system comment. The best way is to remove it manually before loading into Spark.

Data dictionary

The Lending Club download page also provides a data dictionary that contains explanations of individual columns. Specifically, the dataset contains 115 columns with specific meanings, collecting data about borrowers, including their bank history, credit history, and their loan application. Furthermore, for accepted loans, data includes payment progress or the final state of the loan-if it was fully paid or defaulted. One reason why it's crucial to study the data dictionary is to prevent using a column that can possibly pre-hint at the result you are trying to predict and thereby result in a model that is inaccurate. The message is clear but very important: study and know your data!

Preparation of the environment

In this Chapter, instead of using Spark shell, we will build two standalone Spark applications using Scala API: one for model preparation and the second for model deployment. In the case of Spark, the Spark application is a normal Scala application with a main method that serves as an entry point for execution. For example, here is a skeleton of application for model training:

```scala
object Chapter8 extends App {

val spark = SparkSession.builder()
    .master("local[*]")
    .appName("Chapter8")
    .getOrCreate()

val sc = spark.sparkContext
sc.setLogLevel("WARN")
script(spark, sc, spark.sqlContext)


def script(spark: SparkSession, sc: SparkContext, sqlContext: SQLContext):
Unit = {
    // ...code of application
}
}
```

Moreover, we will try to extract parts, which can be shared between both applications, into a library. This will allow us to follow the DRY (do-not-repeat-yourself) principle:

```scala
object Chapter8Library {
    // ...code of library
  }
```

Data load

As usual, the first step involves the loading of data into memory. At this point, we can decide to use Spark or H2O data-loading capabilities. Since data is stored in the CSV file format, we will use the H2O parser to give us a quick visual insight into the data:

```
val DATASET_DIR = s"${sys.env.get("DATADIR").getOrElse("data")}"
val DATASETS = Array("LoanStats3a.CSV", "LoanStats3b.CSV")
import java.net.URI

import water.fvec.H2OFrame
val loanDataHf = new H2OFrame(DATASETS.map(name =>
URI.create(s"${DATASET_DIR}/${name}")):_*)
```

The loaded dataset can be directly explored in the H2O Flow UI. We can directly verify the number of rows, columns, and size of data stored in memory:

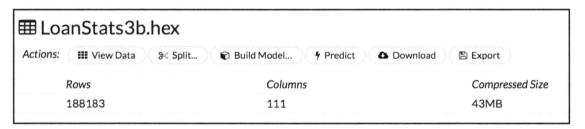

Exploration – data analysis

Now, it is time to explore the data. There are many questions that we can ask, such as the following:

- What target features would we like to model supporting our goals?
- What are the useful training features for each target feature?
- Which features are not good for modeling since they leak information about target features (see the previous section)?
- Which features are not useful (for example, constant features, or features containing lot of missing values)?
- How to clean up data? What to do with missing values? Can we engineer new features?

Basic clean up

During data exploration, we will execute basic data clean up. In our case, we can utilize the power of booth tools together: we use the H2O Flow UI to explore the data, find suspicious parts of the data, and transform them directly with H2O, or, even better, with Spark.

Useless columns

The first step is to remove columns that contain unique values per line. Typical examples of this are user IDs or transaction IDs. In our case, we will identify them manually based on data description:

```
import com.packtpub.mmlwspark.utils.Tabulizer.table
val idColumns = Seq("id", "member_id")
println(s"Columns with Ids: ${table(idColumns, 4, None)}")
```

The output is as follows:

```
Columns with Ids:
+--+---------+
|id|member_id|
+--+---------+
```

The next step is to identify useless columns, such as the following:

- Constant columns
- Bad columns (containing only missing values)

The following code will help us do so:

```
val constantColumns = loanDataHf.names().indices
    .filter(idx => loanDataHf.vec(idx).isConst || loanDataHf.vec(idx).isBad)
    .map(idx => loanDataHf.name(idx))
println(s"Constant and bad columns: ${table(constantColumns, 4, None)}")
```

The output is as follows:

```
Constant and bad columns:
+-------------------------+-------------------------+------------------+-----------+
|              policy_code|         application_type|annual_inc_joint|   dti_joint|
|verification_status_joint|              open_acc_6m|      open_il_6m|open_il_12m|
|              open_il_24m|         mths_since_rcnt_il|    total_bal_il|    il_util|
|              open_rv_12m|              open_rv_24m|      max_bal_bc|   all_util|
|                   inq_fi|              total_cu_tl|    inq_last_12m|         -|
+-------------------------+-------------------------+------------------+-----------+
```

String columns

Now, it is time to explore different type of columns within our dataset. The easy step is to look at columns containing strings-these columns are like ID columns since they hold unique values:

```scala
val stringColumns = loanDataHf.names().indices
    .filter(idx => loanDataHf.vec(idx).isString)
    .map(idx => loanDataHf.name(idx))
println(s"String columns:${table(stringColumns, 4, None)}")
```

The output is shown in the following screenshot:

```
String columns:
+---+
|url|
+---+
```

The question is whether the `url` feature contains any useful information that we can extract. We can explore data directly in H2O Flow and look at some samples of data in the feature column in the following screenshot:

```
url
https://lendingclub.com/browse/loanDetail.action?
loan_id=10159611

https://lendingclub.com/browse/loanDetail.action?
loan_id=10129477



https://lendingclub.com/browse/loanDetail.action?
loan_id=10149342
```

We can see directly that the `url` feature contains only pointers to the Lending Club site using the application ID that we already dropped. Hence, we can decide to drop it.

Loan progress columns

Our target goal is to make a prediction of inherent risk based on loan application data, but some of the columns contain information about loan payment progress or they were assigned by Lending Club itself. In this example, for simplicity, we will drop them and focus only on columns that are part of the loan-application process. It is important to mention that in real-life scenarios, even these columns could carry interesting information (for example, payment progress) usable for prediction. However, we wanted to build our model based on the initial application of the loan and not when a loan has already been a) accepted and b) there is historical payment history that would not be known at the time of receiving the application. Based on the data dictionary, we detected the following columns:

```
val loanProgressColumns = Seq("funded_amnt", "funded_amnt_inv", "grade",
"initial_list_status",
"issue_d", "last_credit_pull_d", "last_pymnt_amnt", "last_pymnt_d",
"next_pymnt_d", "out_prncp", "out_prncp_inv", "pymnt_plan",
"recoveries", "sub_grade", "total_pymnt", "total_pymnt_inv",
"total_rec_int", "total_rec_late_fee", "total_rec_prncp")
```

Now, we can directly record all the columns that we need to remove since they do not bring any value for modelling:

```
val columnsToRemove = (idColumns ++ constantColumns ++ stringColumns ++
loanProgressColumns)
```

Categorical columns

In the next step, we will explore categorical columns. The H2O parser marks a column as a categorical column only if it contains a limited set of string values. This is the main difference from columns that are marked as string columns. They contain more than 90 percent of unique values (see, for example, the `url` column that we explored in the previous paragraph). Let's collect a list of all the categorical columns in our dataset and also the sparsity of individual features:

```
val categoricalColumns = loanDataHf.names().indices
  .filter(idx => loanDataHf.vec(idx).isCategorical)
  .map(idx => (loanDataHf.name(idx), loanDataHf.vec(idx).cardinality()))
  .sortBy(-_._2)

println(s"Categorical columns:${table(tblize(categoricalColumns, true,
2))}")
```

The output is as follows:

```
Categorical columns:
+-------------------------------+------+
|                     emp_title|138269|
|                          desc|109621|
|                         title| 62199|
|                     revol_util| 1171|
|                      zip_code|  863|
|                      int_rate|  477|
|               mo_sin_old_il_acct|  424|
|     mths_since_last_major_derog|  136|
|          mths_since_last_delinq|  133|
|  mths_since_recent_revol_delinq|  132|
|         mths_since_last_record|  124|
|       mths_since_recent_bc_dlq|  113|
|                     addr_state|   50|
|                     sub_grade|   35|
|          mths_since_recent_inq|   26|
|                       purpose|   14|
|                    emp_length|   12|
|                   loan_status|    9|
```

Now, we can explore individual columns. For example, the **"purpose"** column contains 13 categories, and the main purpose of it is debt consolidation:

```
cs   grid inspect "domain", getColumnSummary "LoanStats3b.hex", "purpose"

     label               count                  percent
     debt_consolidation  111451    59.22479713895517
     credit_card          43170    22.940435639776176
     home_improvement     10297     5.471801384822221
     other                 8896     4.727313306728026
     major_purchase        3659     1.9443839241589305
     small_business        2745     1.4586864913408757
     car                   1951     1.0367567739912744
     medical               1519     0.8071929983048416
     wedding               1331      0.707290244070931
     house                 1093     0.5808176083918314
     moving                1038     0.5515907388021235
     vacation               909    0.48304044467353585
     renewable_energy       122    0.06483051072626114
```

This column seems valid, but now, we should focus on suspicious columns, that is, first high-cardinality columns: emp_title, title, desc. There are several observations:

- The highest value for each column is an empty "value". That can mean a missing value. However, for these types of column (that is, columns representing a set of values) a dedicated level for a missing value makes very good sense. It just represents another possible state, "missing". Hence, we can keep it as it is.
- The "title" column overlaps with the purpose column and can be dropped.
- The emp_title and desc columns are purely textual descriptions. In this case, we will not treat them as categorical, but apply NLP techniques to extract important information later.

Now, we will focus on columns starting with "mths_", As the name of the column suggests, the column should contain numeric values, but our parser decided that the columns are categorical. That could be caused by inconsistencies in collected data. For example, when we explore the domain of the **"mths_since_last_major_derog"** column, we can easily spot a reason:

```
grid inspect "domain", getColumnSummary "LoanStats3b.hex", "mths_since_last_major_derog"
```

label	count	percent
	155665	82.72001190330688
38	570	0.3028966484751545
40	561	0.2981140698150205
42	558	0.29651987692830917
43	558	0.29651987692830917

The most common value in the column is an empty value (that is, the same deficiency that we already explored earlier). In this case, we need to decide how to replace this value to transform a column to a numeric column: should it be replaced by the missing value?

If we want to experiment with different strategies, we can define a flexible transformation for this kind of column. In this situation, we will leave the H2O API and switch to Spark and define our own Spark UDF. Hence, as in the previous chapters, we will define a function. In this case, a function which for a given replacement value and a string, produces a float value representing given string or returns the specified value if string is empty. Then, the function is wrapped into the Spark UDF:

```
import org.apache.spark.sql.functions._
val toNumericMnths = (replacementValue: Float) => (mnths: String) => {
if (mnths != null && !mnths.trim.isEmpty) mnths.trim.toFloat else
replacementValue
}
val toNumericMnthsUdf = udf(toNumericMnths(0.0f))
```

 A good practice is to keep our code flexible enough to allow for experimenting, but do not make it over complicated. In this case, we simply keep an open door for cases that we expect to be explored in more detail.

There are two more columns that need our attention: `int_rate` and `revol_util`. Both should be numeric columns expressing percentages; however, if we explore them, we can easily see a problem--instead of a numeric value, the column contains the "%" sign. Hence, we have two more candidates for column transformations:

```
cs   grid inspect "domain", getColumnSummary "LoanStats3b.hex", "revol_util"

     label   count          percent
     0%         624   0.3315921204359586
     61.5%      342   0.1817379890850927
     64.6%      340   0.18067519382728514
```

However, we will not process the data directly but define the Spark UDF transformation, which will transform the string-based rate into a numeric rate. However, in definition of our UDF, we will simply use information provided by H2O, which is confirming that the list of categories in both columns contains only data suffixed by the percent sign:

```
import org.apache.spark.sql.functions._
val toNumericRate = (rate: String) => {
val num = if (rate != null) rate.stripSuffix("%").trim else ""
if (!num.isEmpty) num.toFloat else Float.NaN
}
val toNumericRateUdf = udf(toNumericRate)
```

The defined UDF will be applied later with the rest of the Spark transformations. Furthermore, we need to realize that these transformations need to be applied during training as well as scoring time. Hence, we will put them into our shared library.

Text columns

In the previous section, we identified the `emp_title` and `desc` columns as targets for text transformation. Our theory is that these columns can carry useful information that could help distinguish between good and bad loans.

Missing data

The last step in our data-exploration journey is to explore missing values. We already observed that some columns contain a value that represents a missing value; however, in this section, we will focus on pure missing values. First, we need to collect them:

```
val naColumns = loanDataHf.names().indices
    .filter(idx => loanDataHf.vec(idx).naCnt() >0)
    .map(idx =>
            (loanDataHf.name(idx),
              loanDataHf.vec(idx).naCnt(),
    f"${100*loanDataHf.vec(idx).naCnt()/loanDataHf.numRows().toFloat}%2.1f%%")
    ).sortBy(-_._2)
println(s"Columns with NAs (#${naColumns.length}):${table(naColumns)}")
```

The list contains 111 columns with the number of missing values varying from 0.2 percent to 86 percent:

```
Columns with NAs (#111):
+------------------------------+------+------+
|                  next_pymnt_d|198807|86.2%|
|                pct_tl_nvr_dlq| 70434|30.5%|
|                  avg_cur_bal | 70287|30.5%|
|           mo_sin_old_rev_tl_op| 70282|30.5%|
|          mo_sin_rcnt_rev_tl_op| 70282|30.5%|
|                 tot_coll_amt | 70281|30.5%|
|                  tot_cur_bal | 70281|30.5%|
|               total_rev_hi_lim| 70281|30.5%|
|                 mo_sin_rcnt_tl| 70281|30.5%|
|          num_accts_ever_120_pd| 70281|30.5%|
|                num_actv_bc_tl | 70281|30.5%|
|               num_actv_rev_tl | 70281|30.5%|
|                    num_bc_tl  | 70281|30.5%|
|                    num_il_tl  | 70281|30.5%|
|                num_op_rev_tl  | 70281|30.5%|
|                  num_rev_accts| 70281|30.5%|
|             num_rev_tl_bal_gt_0| 70281|30.5%|
|                 num_tl_30dpd  | 70281|30.5%|
|             num_tl_90g_dpd_24m| 70281|30.5%|
|            num_tl_op_past_12m | 70281|30.5%|
|                 tot_hi_cred_lim| 70281|30.5%|
|         total_il_high_credit_limit| 70281|30.5%|
|                  num_bc_sats  | 58595|25.4%|
|                    num_sats   | 58595|25.4%|
```

There are plenty of columns with five missing values, which can be caused by wrong data collection, and we can easily filter them out if they are represented in a pattern. For more "polluted columns" (for example, where there are many missing values), we need to figure out the right strategy per column based on the column semantics described in the data dictionary.

In all these cases, H2O Flow UI allows us to easily and quickly explore basic properties of data or even execute basic data cleanup. However, for more advanced data manipulations, Spark is the right tool to utilize because of a provided library of pre-cooked transformations and native SQL support.

Whew! As we can see, the data clean up, while being fairly laborious, is an extremely important task for the data scientist and one that will-hopefully-yield good answers to well thought out questions. This process must be carefully considered before each and every new problem that is looking to be solved. As the old ad age goes, *"Garbage in, garbage out"* - if the inputs are not right, our model will suffer the consequences.

At this point, it is possible to compose all the identified transformations together into shared library functions:

```
def basicDataCleanup(loanDf: DataFrame, colsToDrop: Seq[String] = Seq()) =
{
    (
        (if (loanDf.columns.contains("int_rate"))
            loanDf.withColumn("int_rate", toNumericRateUdf(col("int_rate")))
else
loanDf)
            .withColumn("revol_util", toNumericRateUdf(col("revol_util")))
            .withColumn("mo_sin_old_il_acct",
toNumericMnthsUdf(col("mo_sin_old_il_acct")))
            .withColumn("mths_since_last_delinq",
toNumericMnthsUdf(col("mths_since_last_delinq")))
            .withColumn("mths_since_last_record",
toNumericMnthsUdf(col("mths_since_last_record")))
            .withColumn("mths_since_last_major_derog",
toNumericMnthsUdf(col("mths_since_last_major_derog")))
            .withColumn("mths_since_recent_bc",
toNumericMnthsUdf(col("mths_since_recent_bc")))
            .withColumn("mths_since_recent_bc_dlq",
toNumericMnthsUdf(col("mths_since_recent_bc_dlq")))
            .withColumn("mths_since_recent_inq",
toNumericMnthsUdf(col("mths_since_recent_inq")))
            .withColumn("mths_since_recent_revol_delinq",
toNumericMnthsUdf(col("mths_since_recent_revol_delinq")))
    ).drop(colsToDrop.toArray :_*)
}
```

The method takes a Spark DataFrame as an input and applies all identified cleanup transformations. Now, it is time to build some models!

Prediction targets

After performing our data cleanup, it's time to examine our prediction targets. Our ideal modeling pipeline includes two models: one that controls acceptance of the loan and one that estimates interest rate. Already you should be thinking that the first model is a binary classification problem (accept or reject the loan) while the second model is a regression problem, where the outcome is a numeric value.

Loan status model

The first model needs to distinguish between bad and good loans. The dataset already provides the `loan_status` column, which is the best feature representation of our modeling target. Let's look at the column in more detail.

The loan status is represented by a categorical feature that has seven levels:

- Fully paid: borrower paid the loan and all interest
- Current: the loan is actively paid in accordance with a plan
- In grace period: late payment 1-15 days
- Late (16-30 days): late payment
- Late (31-120 days): late payment
- Charged off: a loan is 150 days past the due date
- Default: a loan was lost

For the first modeling goal, we need to distinguish between good and bad loans. Good loans could be the loans that were fully paid. The rest of the loans could be considered as bad loans with the exception of current loans that need more attention (for example, survival analysis) or we could simply remove all rows that contain the "Current" status. For transformation of the `loan_status` feature into a binary feature, we will define a Spark UDF:

```
val toBinaryLoanStatus = (status: String) => status.trim.toLowerCase()
match {
case "fully paid" =>"good loan"
case _ =>"bad loan"
}
val toBinaryLoanStatusUdf = udf(toBinaryLoanStatus)
```

We can explore the distribution of individual categories in more detail. In the following screenshot,we can also see that the ratio between good and bad loans is highly unbalanced. We need to keep this fact during the training and evaluation of the model, since we would like to optimize the recall probability of detection of the bad loan:

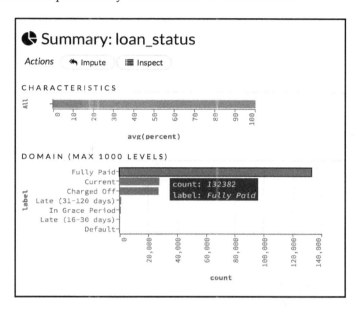

Properties of the loan_status column.

Base model

At this point, we have prepared the target prediction column and cleaned up the input data, and we can now build a base model. The base model gives us basic intuition about data. For this purpose, we will use all columns except columns detected as being useless. We will also skip handling of missing values, since we will use H2O and the RandomForest algorithm, which can handle missing values. However, the first step is to prepare a dataset with the help of defined Spark transformations:

```
import com.packtpub.mmlwspark.chapter8.Chapter8Library._
val loanDataDf = h2oContext.asDataFrame(loanDataHf)(sqlContext)
val loanStatusBaseModelDf = basicDataCleanup(
    loanDataDf
      .where("loan_status is not null")
      .withColumn("loan_status", toBinaryLoanStatusUdf($"loan_status")),
    colsToDrop = Seq("title") ++ columnsToRemove)
```

We will simply drop all known columns that are correlated with our target prediction column, all high categorical columns that carry a text description (except `title` and `desc`, which we will use later), and apply all basic the cleanup transformation we identified in the sections earlier.

The next step involves splitting data into two parts. As usual, we will keep the majority of data for training and rest for model validation and transforming into a form that is accepted by H2O model builders:

```
val loanStatusDfSplits = loanStatusBaseModelDf.randomSplit(Array(0.7, 0.3),
seed = 42)

val trainLSBaseModelHf = toHf(loanStatusDfSplits(0).drop("emp_title",
"desc"), "trainLSBaseModelHf")(h2oContext)
val validLSBaseModelHf = toHf(loanStatusDfSplits(1).drop("emp_title",
"desc"), "validLSBaseModelHf")(h2oContext)
def toHf(df: DataFrame, name: String)(h2oContext: H2OContext): H2OFrame = {
val hf = h2oContext.asH2OFrame(df, name)
val allStringColumns = hf.names().filter(name => hf.vec(name).isString)
    hf.colToEnum(allStringColumns)
    hf
  }
```

With the cleanup data, we can easily build a model. We will blindly use the RandomForest algorithm since it gives us direct insight into data and importance of individual features. We say "blindly" because as you recall from Chapter 2, *Detecting Dark Matter - The Higgs-Boson Particle*, a RandomForest model can take inputs of many different types and build many different trees using different features, which gives us confidence to use this algorithm as our out-of-the-box model, given how well it performs when including all our features. Thus, the model also defines a baseline that we would like to improve by engineering new features.

We will use default settings. RandomForest brings out-of-the-box validation schema based on out-of-bag samples, so we can skip cross-validation for now. However, we will increase the number of constructed trees, but limit the model builder execution by a `Logloss`-based stopping criterion. Furthermore, we know that the prediction target is imbalanced where the number of good loans is much higher than bad loans, so we will ask for upsampling minority class by enabling the `balance_classes` option:

```
import _root_.hex.tree.drf.DRFModel.DRFParameters
import _root_.hex.tree.drf.{DRF, DRFModel}
import _root_.hex.ScoreKeeper.StoppingMetric
import com.packtpub.mmlwspark.utils.Utils.let
```

```
val loanStatusBaseModelParams = let(new DRFParameters) { p =>
    p._response_column = "loan_status"
p._train = trainLSBaseModelHf._key
p._ignored_columns = Array("int_rate")
    p._stopping_metric = StoppingMetric.logloss
p._stopping_rounds = 1
p._stopping_tolerance = 0.1
p._ntrees = 100
p._balance_classes = true
p._score_tree_interval = 20
}
val loanStatusBaseModel1 = new DRF(loanStatusBaseModelParams,
water.Key.make[DRFModel]("loanStatusBaseModel1"))
    .trainModel()
    .get()
```

When the model is built, we can explore its quality, as we did in the previous chapters, but our first look will be at the importance of the features:

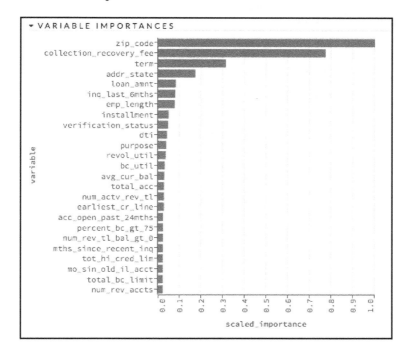

The most surprising fact is that the **zip_code** and **collection_recovery_fee** features have a much higher importance than the rest of the columns. This is suspicious and could indicate direct correlation between the column and the target variable.

We can revisit the data dictionary, which describes the **zip_code** column as "the first three numbers of the zip code provided by the borrower in the loan application" and the second column as "post-charge off collection fee". The latter one indicates a direct connection to the response column since "good loans" will have a value equal to zero. We can also validate this fact by exploring the data. In the case of **zip_code**, there is no obvious connection to the response column.

We will therefore do one more model run, but in this case, we will try to ignore both the zip_code and collection_recovery_fee columns:

```
loanStatusBaseModelParams._ignored_columns = Array("int_rate",
"collection_recovery_fee", "zip_code")
val loanStatusBaseModel2 = new DRF(loanStatusBaseModelParams,
water.Key.make[DRFModel]("loanStatusBaseModel2"))
    .trainModel()
    .get()
```

After the model is built, we can explore the variable importance graph again and see a more meaningful distribution of the importance between the variables. Based on the graph, we can decide to use only top 10 input features to simplify the model's complexity and decrease modeling time. It is important to say that we still need to consider the removed columns as relevant input features:

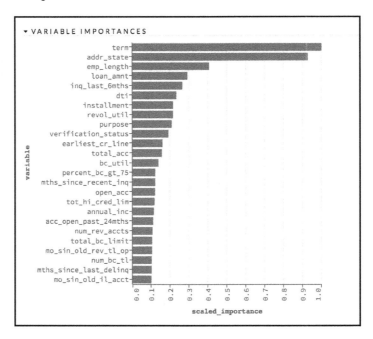

Base model performance

Now, we can look at the model performance of the created model. We need to keep in mind that in our case, the following applies:

- The performance of the model is reported on out-of-bag samples, not on unseen data.
- We used fixed parameters as the best guess; however, it would be beneficial to perform a random parameter search to see how the input parameters influence the model's performance.

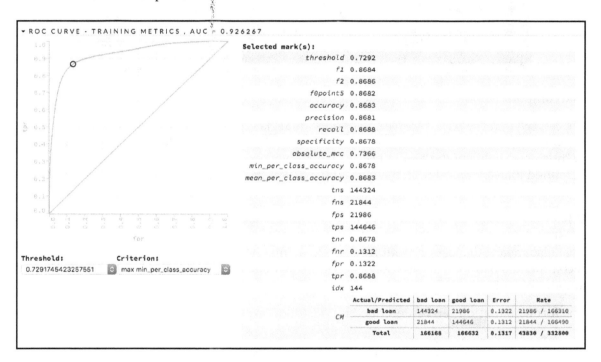

We can see that the AUC measured on out-of-bag sample of data is quite high. Even individual class errors are for a selected threshold, which minimizes individual classes accuracy, low. However, let's explore the performance of the model on the unseen data. We will use the prepared part of the data for validation:

```
import _root_.hex.ModelMetrics
val lsBaseModelPredHf = loanStatusBaseModel2.score(validLSBaseModelHf)
println(ModelMetrics.getFromDKV(loanStatusBaseModel2, validLSBaseModelHf))
```

The output is as follows:

```
Model Metrics Type: Binomial
 Description: N/A
 model id: loanStatusBaseModel2
 frame id: validLSBaseModelHf
 MSE: 0.17421468
 RMSE: 0.41739032
 AUC: 0.730328
 logloss: 0.5278169
 mean_per_class_error: 0.365515
 default threshold: 0.6057690978050232
 CM: Confusion Matrix (Row labels: Actual class; Column labels: Predicted class):
           bad loan  good loan   Error           Rate
 bad loan      6628      12678  0.6567   12,678 / 19,306
 good loan     3697      46032  0.0743    3,697 / 49,729
   Totals     10325      58710  0.2372   16,375 / 69,035
```

The computed model metrics can be explored visually in the Flow UI as well.

We can see that the AUC is lower, and individual class errors are higher, but are still reasonably good. However, all the measured statistical properties do not give us any notion of "business" value of the model-how much money was lent, how much money was lost for defaulted loans, and so on. In the next step, we will try to design ad-hoc evaluation metrics for the model.

What does it mean by the statement that the model made a wrong prediction? It can consider a good loan application as bad, which will result in the rejection of the application. That also means the loss of profit from the loan interest. Alternatively, the model can recommend a bad loan application as good, which will cause the loss of the full or partial amount of lent money. Let's look at both situations in more detail.

The former situation can be described by the following function:

```scala
def profitMoneyLoss = (predThreshold: Double) =>
    (act: String, predGoodLoanProb: Double, loanAmount: Int, intRate:
Double, term: String) => {
val termInMonths = term.trim match {
case "36 months" =>36
case "60 months" =>60
}
val intRatePerMonth = intRate / 12 / 100
if (predGoodLoanProb < predThreshold && act == "good loan") {
        termInMonths*loanAmount*intRatePerMonth / (1 -
Math.pow(1+intRatePerMonth, -termInMonths)) - loanAmount
    } else 0.0
}
```

The function returns the amount of money lost if a model predicted a bad loan, but the actual data indicated that the loan was good. The returned amount considers the predicted interest rate and term. The important variables are predGoodLoanProb, which holds the model's predicted probability of considering the actual loan as a good loan, and predThreshold, which allows us to set up a bar when the probability of predicting a good loan is good enough for us.

In a similar way, we will describe the latter situation:

```
val loanMoneyLoss = (act: String, predGoodLoanProb: Double, predThreshold:
Double, loanAmount: Int) => {
if (predGoodLoanProb > predThreshold /* good loan predicted */
&& act == "bad loan" /* actual is bad loan */) loanAmount else 0
}
```

It is good to realize that we are just following the confusion matrix definition for false positives and false negatives and applying our domain knowledge of input data to define ad-hoc model evaluation metrics.

Now, it is time to utilize both functions and define totalLoss-how much money we can lose on accepting bad loans and missing good loans if we follow our model's recommendations:

```
import org.apache.spark.sql.Row
def totalLoss(actPredDf: DataFrame, threshold: Double): (Double, Double,
Long, Double, Long, Double) = {

val profitMoneyLossUdf = udf(profitMoneyLoss(threshold))
val loanMoneyLossUdf = udf(loanMoneyLoss(threshold))

val lostMoneyDf = actPredDf
    .where("loan_status is not null and loan_amnt is not null")
    .withColumn("profitMoneyLoss", profitMoneyLossUdf($"loan_status",
$"good loan", $"loan_amnt", $"int_rate", $"term"))
    .withColumn("loanMoneyLoss", loanMoneyLossUdf($"loan_status", $"good
loan", $"loan_amnt"))

  lostMoneyDf
    .agg("profitMoneyLoss" ->"sum", "loanMoneyLoss" ->"sum")
    .collect.apply(0) match {
case Row(profitMoneyLossSum: Double, loanMoneyLossSum: Double) =>
      (threshold,
        profitMoneyLossSum, lostMoneyDf.where("profitMoneyLoss >
0").count,
        loanMoneyLossSum, lostMoneyDf.where("loanMoneyLoss > 0").count,
```

```
            profitMoneyLossSum + loanMoneyLossSum
        )
    }
}
```

The `totalLoss` function is defined for a Spark DataFrame and a threshold. The Spark DataFrame holds actual validation data and prediction composed of three columns: actual prediction for default threshold, the probability of a good loan, and the probability of a bad loan. The threshold helps us define the right bar for the good loan probability; that is, if the good loan probability is higher than threshold, we can consider that the model recommends to accept the loan.

If we run the function for different thresholds, including one that minimizes individual class errors, we will get the following table:

```
import _root_.hex.AUC2.ThresholdCriterion
val predVActHf: Frame = lsBaseModel2PredHf.add(validLSBaseModelHf)
 water.DKV.put(predVActHf)
val predVActDf = h2oContext.asDataFrame(predVActHf)(sqlContext)
val DEFAULT_THRESHOLDS = Array(0.4, 0.45, 0.5, 0.55, 0.6, 0.65, 0.7, 0.75,
0.8, 0.85, 0.9, 0.95)

println(
table(Array("Threshold", "Profit Loss", "Count", "Loan loss", "Count",
"Total loss"),
        (DEFAULT_THRESHOLDS :+
ThresholdCriterion.min_per_class_accuracy.max_criterion(lsBaseModel2PredMod
elMetrics.auc_obj()))
        .map(threshold =>totalLoss(predVActDf, threshold)),
Map(1 ->"%,.2f", 3 ->"%,.2f", 5 ->"%,.2f")))
```

The output is as follows:

```
+-----------------+----------------+-----+---------------+-----+--------------+
|       Threshold|    Profit Loss|Count|     Loan loss|Count|    Total loss|
+-----------------+----------------+-----+---------------+-----+--------------+
|             0.4|   7,650,192.46|  679|266,770,025.00|17383|274,420,217.46|
|            0.45|  14,680,715.31| 1345|244,860,275.00|16287|259,540,990.31|
|             0.5|  23,080,809.55| 2109|219,695,475.00|15037|242,776,284.55|
|            0.55|  31,431,709.19| 2891|193,740,850.00|13788|225,172,559.19|
|             0.6|  39,323,940.36| 3648|172,997,075.00|12763|212,321,015.36|
|            0.65|  47,554,045.80| 4453|156,048,425.00|11916|203,602,470.80|
|             0.7|  55,335,760.25| 5460|140,604,175.00|11040|195,939,935.25|
|            0.75|  67,478,722.66| 7994|121,433,725.00| 9690|188,912,447.66|
|             0.8|  91,174,983.19|14610| 89,563,100.00| 7254|180,738,083.19|
|            0.85| 126,258,672.73|26481| 45,659,950.00| 3732|171,918,622.73|
|             0.9| 161,805,504.11|41048| 10,482,500.00|  854|172,288,004.11|
|            0.95| 177,174,633.32|48980|    360,650.00|   30|177,535,283.32|
|0.6620281928050031|  49,413,721.90| 4653|152,191,525.00|11704|201,605,246.90|
+-----------------+----------------+-----+---------------+-----+--------------+
```

From the table, we can see that the lowest total loss for our metrics is based on threshold `0.85`, which represents quite a conservative strategy, which focusing on avoiding bad loans.

We can even define a function that finds the minimal total loss and corresponding threshold:

```
// @Snippet
def findMinLoss(model: DRFModel,
                validHf: H2OFrame,
                defaultThresholds: Array[Double]): (Double, Double,
Double, Double) = {
import _root_.hex.ModelMetrics
import _root_.hex.AUC2.ThresholdCriterion
// Score model
val modelPredHf = model.score(validHf)
val modelMetrics = ModelMetrics.getFromDKV(model, validHf)
val predVActHf: Frame = modelPredHf.add(validHf)
   water.DKV.put(predVActHf)
//
val predVActDf = h2oContext.asDataFrame(predVActHf)(sqlContext)
val min = (DEFAULT_THRESHOLDS :+
ThresholdCriterion.min_per_class_accuracy.max_criterion(modelMetrics.auc_ob
j()))
     .map(threshold =>totalLoss(predVActDf, threshold)).minBy(_._6)
  ( /* Threshold */ min._1, /* Total loss */ min._6, /* Profit loss */
```

```
min._2, /* Loan loss */ min._4)
  }
val minLossModel2 = findMinLoss(loanStatusBaseModel2, validLSBaseModelHf,
DEFAULT_THRESHOLDS)
println(f"Min total loss for model 2: ${minLossModel2._2}%,.2f (threshold =
${minLossModel2._1})")
```

The output is as follows:

```
Min total loss for model 2: 171,918,622.73 (threshold = 0.85)
```

Based on the reported results, we can see that the model minimizes the total loss for threshold ~ 0.85, which is higher than the default threshold identified by the model (F1 = 0.66). However, we still need to realize that this is just a base naive model; we did not perform any tuning and searching of right training parameters. We still have two fields, title and desc, which we can utilize. It's time for model improvements!

The emp_title column transformation

The first column, emp_title, describes the employment title. However, it is not unified- there are multiple versions with the same meaning ("Bank of America" versus "bank of america") or a similar meaning ("AT&T" and "AT&T Mobility"). Our goal is to unify the labels into a basic form, detect similar labels, and replace them by a common title. The theory is the employment title has a direct impact on the ability to pay back the loan.

The basic unification of labels is a simple task-transform labels into lowercase form and drop all non-alphanumeric characters ("&" or "."). For this step, we will use the Spark API for user-defined functions:

```
val unifyTextColumn = (in: String) => {
if (in != null) in.toLowerCase.replaceAll("[^\\w ]|", "") else null
}
val unifyTextColumnUdf = udf(unifyTextColumn)
```

The next step defines a tokenizer, a function that splits a sentence into individual tokens and drops useless and stop words (for example, too short words or conjunctions). In our case, we will make the minimal token length and list of stop words flexible as input parameters:

```
val ALL_NUM_REGEXP = java.util.regex.Pattern.compile("\\d*")
val tokenizeTextColumn = (minLen: Int) => (stopWords: Array[String]) => (w:
String) => {
if (w != null)
    w.split(" ").map(_.trim).filter(_.length >=
```

```
minLen).filter(!ALL_NUM_REGEXP.matcher(_).matches()).filter(!stopWords.cont
ains(_)).toSeq
else
Seq.empty[String]
 }
import org.apache.spark.ml.feature.StopWordsRemover
val tokenizeUdf =
udf(tokenizeTextColumn(3)(StopWordsRemover.loadDefaultStopWords("english"))
)
```

 It is important to mention that Spark API provides a list of stop words already as part of StopWordsRemover transformation. Our definition of tokenizeUdf directly utilizes the provided list of English stop words.

Now, it is time to look at the column in more detail. We will start by selecting the emp_title column from the already created DataFrame, loanStatusBaseModelDf, and apply the two functions defined earlier:

```
val empTitleColumnDf = loanStatusBaseModelDf
   .withColumn("emp_title", unifyTextColumnUdf($"emp_title"))
   .withColumn("emp_title_tokens", tokenizeUdf($"emp_title"))
```

Now, we have a Spark DataFrame with two important columns: the first contains unified emp_title and the second one is represented by a list of tokens. With the help of Spark SQL API, we can easily compute the number of unique values in the emp_title column or the number of unique tokens with a frequency of more than 100 (that is, it means the word was used in more than 100 emp_titles):

```
println("Number of unique values in emp_title column: " +
empTitleColumn.select("emp_title").groupBy("emp_title").count().count())
println("Number of unique tokens with freq > 100 in emp_title column: " +
        empTitleColumn.rdd.flatMap(row => row.getSeq[String](1).map(w =>
(w, 1)))
        .reduceByKey(_ + _).filter(_._2 >100).count)
```

The output is as follows:

```
Number of unique values in emp_title column: 125888
Number of unique tokens with freq > 100 in emp_title column: 717
```

You can see that there are many unique values in the emp_title column. On the other hand, there are only 717 tokens that are repeated over and over. Our goal to *compress* the number of unique values in the column and group similar values together. We can experiment with different methods. For example, encode each emp_title with a representative token or use a more advanced technique based on the Word2Vec algorithm.

 In the preceding code, we combined DataFrame query capabilities with the computation power of raw RDDs. Many queries can be expressed with powerful SQL-based DataFrame APIs; however, if we need to process structured data (such as the sequence of string tokens in the preceding example), often the RDD API is a quick way to go.

Let's look at the second option. The Word2Vec algorithm transforms text features into a vector space where similar words are closed together with respect to cosine distance of corresponding vectors representing the words. That's a nice property; however, we still need to detect "groups of similar words". For this task, we can simply use the KMeans algorithm.

The first step is to create the Word2Vec model. Since we have data in a Spark DataFrame, we will simply use the Spark implementation from the ml package:

```
import org.apache.spark.ml.feature.Word2Vec
val empTitleW2VModel = new Word2Vec()
  .setInputCol("emp_title_tokens")
  .setOutputCol("emp_title_w2vVector")
  .setMinCount(1)
  .fit(empTitleColumn)
```

The algorithm input is defined by a sequence of tokens representing sentences stored in the "tokens" column. The outputCol parameter defines the output of the model if it is used to transform the data:

```
val empTitleColumnWithW2V =   w2vModel.transform(empTitleW2VModel)
empTitleColumnWithW2V.printSchema()
```

The output is as follows:

```
|-- total_bc_limit: integer (nullable = true)
|-- total_il_high_credit_limit: integer (nullable = true)
|-- emp_title_tokens: array (nullable = true)
|    |-- element: string (containsNull = true)
|-- emp_title_w2vVector: vector (nullable = true)
```

From the output of transformation, you can directly see that the DataFrame output contains not only the `emp_title` and `emp_title_tokens` input columns, but also the `emp_title_w2vVector` column, which represents the output of the w2vModel transformation.

 It is important to mention that the Word2Vec algorithm is defined only for words, but the Spark implementation transforms sentences (that is, the sequence of words) into a vector as well by averaging all the word vectors that the sentence represents.

In the next step, we will build a K-means model to partition a vector space representing individual employment titles into a predefined number of clusters. Before doing this, it's important to think about why this would be a good thing to do in the first place. Think about the many different variations of saying "Software Engineer" that you know of: Programmer Analyst, SE, Senor Software Engineer, and so on. Given these variations that all essentially mean the same thing and will be represented by similar vectors, clustering provides us with a means to group similar titles together. However, we need to specify how many K clusters we should detect-this needs more experimentation, but for simplicity, we will try 500 clusters:

```
import org.apache.spark.ml.clustering.KMeans
val K = 500
val empTitleKmeansModel = new KMeans()
  .setFeaturesCol("emp_title_w2vVector")
  .setK(K)
  .setPredictionCol("emp_title_cluster")
  .fit(empTitleColumnWithW2V)
```

The model allows us to transform the input data and explore the clusters. The cluster number is stored in a new column called `emp_title_cluster`.

Specifying the number of clusters is tricky given that we are dealing with the unsupervised world of machine learning. Often, practitioners will use a simple heuristic known as the elbow method(refer the following link: `https://en.wikipedia.org/wiki/Determining_the_number_of_clusters_in_a_data_set`), which basically runs through many K-means models, increasing the number of K-clusters as a function of the heterogeneity (uniqueness) among each of the clusters. Usually, there is a diminishing gain as we increase the number of K-clusters and the trick is to find where the increase becomes marginal to the point where the benefit is no longer "worth" the run time.

Alternatively, there are some information criteria statistics known as **AIC** (**Akaike Information Criteria**) (`https://en.wikipedia.org/wiki/Akaike_information_criterion`) and **BIC** (**Bayesian Information Criteria**) (`https://en.wikipedia.org/wiki/Bayesian_information_criterion`) that those of you who are interested should look into for further insight. Note that at of the time of writing this book, Spark has yet to implement these information criteria, and hence, we will not cover this in more detail.

Take a look at the following code snippet:

```
val clustered = empTitleKmeansModel.transform(empTitleColumnWithW2V)
clustered.printSchema()
```

The output is as follows:

```
|-- total_bc_limit: integer (nullable = true)
|-- total_il_high_credit_limit: integer (nullable = true)
|-- emp_title_tokens: array (nullable = true)
|    |-- element: string (containsNull = true)
|-- emp_title_w2vVector: vector (nullable = true)
|-- emp_title_cluster: integer (nullable = true)
```

Additionally, we can explore words associated with a random cluster:

```
println(
s"""Words in cluster '133':
    |${clustered.select("emp_title").where("emp_title_cluster =
133").take(10).mkString(", ")}
    |""".stripMargin)
```

The output is as follows:

```
Words in cluster '133':
[lead business analyst], [data analyst], [sr  benefits analyst], [senior policy analyst], [data analyst],
[reimbursement analyst], [sr purchasing analyst], [sr  business analyst ], [computer analyst], [meas    rep
orting analyst]
```

Look at the preceding cluster and ask yourself, "Do these titles seem like a logical cluster?" Perhaps more training may be required, or perhaps we need to consider further feature transformations, such as running an n-grammer, which can identify sequences of words that occur with a high degree of frequency. Interested parties can check out the n-grammer section in Spark here.

Furthermore, the `emp_title_cluster` column defines a new feature that we will use to replace the original `emp_title` column. We also need to remember all the steps and models we used in the process of the column preparation, since we will need to reproduce them to enrich the new data. For this purpose, the Spark pipeline is defined:

```
import org.apache.spark.ml.Pipeline
import org.apache.spark.sql.types._

val empTitleTransformationPipeline = new Pipeline()
    .setStages(Array(
new UDFTransformer("unifier", unifyTextColumn, StringType, StringType)
        .setInputCol("emp_title").setOutputCol("emp_title_unified"),
new UDFTransformer("tokenizer",
tokenizeTextColumn(3)(StopWordsRemover.loadDefaultStopWords("english")),
                    StringType, ArrayType(StringType, true))
        .setInputCol("emp_title_unified").setOutputCol("emp_title_tokens"),
    empTitleW2VModel,
    empTitleKmeansModel,
new ColRemover().setKeep(false).setColumns(Array("emp_title",
"emp_title_unified", "emp_title_tokens", "emp_title_w2vVector"))
    ))
```

The first two pipeline steps represent the application of user-defined functions. We used the same trick that was used in Chapter 4, *Predicting Movie Reviews Using NLP and Spark Streaming*, to wrap an UDF into a Spark pipeline transformer with help of the defined `UDFTransformer` class. The remaining steps represent models that we built.

The defined UDFTransformer class is a nice way to wrap UDF into Spark pipeline transformer, but for Spark, it is a black box and it cannot perform all the powerful transformations. However, it could be replaced by an existing concept of the Spark SQLTransformer, which can be understood by the Spark optimizer; on the other hand, its usage is not so straightforward.

The pipeline still needs to be fit; however, in our case, since we used only Spark transformers, the fit operation bundles all the defined stages into the pipeline model:

```
val empTitleTransformer =
empTitleTransformationPipeline.fit(loanStatusBaseModelDf)
```

Now, it is time to evaluate the impact of the new feature on the model quality. We will repeat the same steps we did earlier during the evaluation of the quality of the base model:

- Prepare training and validation parts and enrich them with a new feature, emp_title_cluster.
- Build a model.
- Compute total the money loss and find the minimal loss.

For the first step, we will reuse the prepared train and validation parts; however, we need to transform them with the prepared pipeline and drop the "raw" column, desc:

```
val trainLSBaseModel3Df =
empTitleTransformer.transform(loanStatusDfSplits(0))
val validLSBaseModel3Df =
empTitleTransformer.transform(loanStatusDfSplits(1))
val trainLSBaseModel3Hf = toHf(trainLSBaseModel3Df.drop("desc"),
"trainLSBaseModel3Hf")(h2oContext)
val validLSBaseModel3Hf = toHf(validLSBaseModel3Df.drop("desc"),
"validLSBaseModel3Hf")(h2oContext)
```

When we have the data ready, we can repeat the model training with the same parameters we used for the base model training, except that we use the prepared input training part:

```
loanStatusBaseModelParams._train = trainLSBaseModel3Hf._key
val loanStatusBaseModel3 = new DRF(loanStatusBaseModelParams,
water.Key.make[DRFModel]("loanStatusBaseModel3"))
    .trainModel()
    .get()
```

Finally, we can evaluate the model on the validation data and compute our evaluation metrics based on the total money loss:

```
val minLossModel3 = findMinLoss(loanStatusBaseModel3, validLSBaseModel3Hf,
DEFAULT_THRESHOLDS)
println(f"Min total loss for model 3: ${minLossModel3._2}%,.2f (threshold =
${minLossModel3._1})")
```

The output is shown here:

```
Min total loss for model 3: 172,569,355.39 (threshold = 0.85)
```

We can see that employing an NLP technique to detect a similar job title slightly improves the quality of the model, resulting in decreasing the total dollar loss computed on the unseen data. However, the question is whether we can improve our model even more based on the desc column, which could include useful information.

The desc column transformation

The next column we will explore is desc. Our motivation is still to mine any possible information from it and improve model's quality. The desc column contains purely textual descriptions for why the lender wishes to take out a loan. In this case, we are not going to treat them as categorical values since most of them are unique. However, we will apply NLP techniques to extract important information. In contrast to the emp_title column, we will not use the Word2Vec algorithm, but we will try to find words that are distinguishing bad loans from good loans.

For this goal, we will simply decompose descriptions into individual words (that is, tokenization) and assign weights to each used word with the help of tf-idf and explore which words are most likely to represent good loans or bad loans. Instead of tf-idf, we could help just word counts, but tf-idf values are a better separation between informative words (such as "credit") and common words (such as "loan").

Let's start with the same procedure we performed in the case of the emp_title column-defining transformations that transcribe the desc column into a list of unified tokens:

```
import org.apache.spark.sql.types._
val descColUnifier = new UDFTransformer("unifier", unifyTextColumn,
StringType, StringType)
    .setInputCol("desc")
.setOutputCol("desc_unified")

val descColTokenizer = new UDFTransformer("tokenizer",
```

```
tokenizeTextColumn(3)(StopWordsRemover.loadDefaultStopWords("english")),
                                    StringType,
ArrayType(StringType, true))
.setInputCol("desc_unified")
.setOutputCol("desc_tokens")
```

The transformation prepares a `desc_tokens` column that contains a list of words for each input `desc` value. Now, we need to translate string tokens into numeric form to build the tf-idf model. In this context, we will use `CountVectorizer`, which extracts the vocabulary of used words and generates a numeric vector for each row. A position in a numeric vector corresponds to a single word in the vocabulary and the value represents the number of occurrences. Un which g tokens into a numeric vector, since we would like to keep the relation between a number in the vector and token representing it. In contrast to Spark HashingTF, `CountVectorizer` preserves bijection between a word and the number of its occurrences in a generated vector. We will reuse this capability later:

```
import org.apache.spark.ml.feature.CountVectorizer
val descCountVectorizer = new CountVectorizer()
  .setInputCol("desc_tokens")
  .setOutputCol("desc_vector")
  .setMinDF(1)
  .setMinTF(1)
```

Define the IDF model:

```
import org.apache.spark.ml.feature.IDF
val descIdf = new IDF()
  .setInputCol("desc_vector")
  .setOutputCol("desc_idf_vector")
  .setMinDocFreq(1)
```

When we put all the defined transformations into a single pipeline, we can directly train it on input data:

```
import org.apache.spark.ml.Pipeline
val descFreqPipeModel = new Pipeline()
  .setStages(
Array(descColUnifier,
        descColTokenizer,
        descCountVectorizer,
        descIdf)
  ).fit(loanStatusBaseModelDf)
```

Now, we have a pipeline model that can transform a numeric vector for each input `desc` value. Furthermore, we can inspect the pipeline model's internals and extract vocabulary from the computed `CountVectorizerModel` and individual word weights from `IDFModel`:

```scala
val descFreqDf = descFreqPipeModel.transform(loanStatusBaseModelDf)
import org.apache.spark.ml.feature.IDFModel
import org.apache.spark.ml.feature.CountVectorizerModel
val descCountVectorizerModel =
descFreqPipeModel.stages(2).asInstanceOf[CountVectorizerModel]
val descIdfModel = descFreqPipeModel.stages(3).asInstanceOf[IDFModel]
val descIdfScores = descIdfModel.idf.toArray
val descVocabulary = descCountVectorizerModel.vocabulary
println(
s"""
    ~Size of 'desc' column vocabulary: ${descVocabulary.length}
    ~Top ten highest scores:
    ~${table(descVocabulary.zip(descIdfScores).sortBy(-_._2).take(10))}
""".stripMargin('~'))
```

The output is as follows:

```
Size of 'desc' column vocabulary: 30243
Top ten highest scores:

+------------------+------------------+
|          moviebox|11.655799949660315|
|           liveing|11.655799949660315|
|          ablation|11.655799949660315|
|        startupsnax|11.655799949660315|
|           paladin|11.655799949660315|
|collegeclassifieds|11.655799949660315|
|             corix|11.655799949660315|
|             xxxxx|11.655799949660315|
|         databases|11.655799949660315|
|           00int19|11.655799949660315|
+------------------+------------------+
```

At this point, we know individual word weights; however, we still need to compute which words are used by "good loans" and "bad loans". For this purpose, we will utilize information about word frequencies computed by the prepared pipeline model and stored in the `desc_vector` column (in fact, this is an output of `CountVectorizer`). We will sum all these vectors separately for good and then for bad loans:

```
import org.apache.spark.ml.linalg.{Vector, Vectors}
val rowAdder = (toVector: Row => Vector) => (r1: Row, r2: Row) => {
Row(Vectors.dense((toVector(r1).toArray,
toVector(r2).toArray).zipped.map((a, b) => a + b)))
  }

val descTargetGoodLoan = descFreqDf
    .where("loan_status == 'good loan'")
    .select("desc_vector")
    .reduce(rowAdder((row:Row) =>
row.getAs[Vector](0))).getAs[Vector](0).toArray

val descTargetBadLoan = descFreqDf
    .where("loan_status == 'bad loan'")
    .select("desc_vector")
    .reduce(rowAdder((row:Row) =>
row.getAs[Vector](0))).getAs[Vector](0).toArray
```

Having computed values, we can easily find words that are used only by good/bad loans and explore their computed IDF weights:

```
val descTargetsWords = descTargetGoodLoan.zip(descTargetBadLoan)
    .zip(descVocabulary.zip(descIdfScores)).map(t => (t._1._1, t._1._2,
t._2._1, t._2._2))
println(
s"""
        ~Words used only in description of good loans:
        ~${table(descTargetsWords.filter(t => t._1 >0 && t._2 == 0).sortBy(-
_._1).take(10))}
        ~
        ~Words used only in description of bad loans:
        ~${table(descTargetsWords.filter(t => t._1 == 0 && t._2 >0).sortBy(-
_._1).take(10))}
""".stripMargin('~'))
```

The output is as follows:

```
Words used only in description of good loans:

+----+---+---------------+------------------+
|43.0|0.0|          rifle|8.660067676106323 |
|25.0|0.0|    spreadsheet|9.170893299872313 |
|23.0|0.0|  simultaneously| 9.21345291429111 |
|23.0|0.0|         daniel|9.170893299872313 |
|22.0|0.0|        spender|9.257904676861944 |
|21.0|0.0|        affords|9.304424692496836 |
|20.0|0.0|         boards|9.404508151053818 |
|20.0|0.0|       mattress|9.709889800605001 |
|19.0|0.0|        adopted|9.404508151053818 |
|18.0|0.0|            sod|9.458575373234095 |
+----+---+---------------+------------------+


Words used only in description of bad loans:

+---+---+------------------+-----------------+
|0.0|9.0|           ablation|11.655799949660315|
|0.0|8.0|             tavern| 10.96265276910037|
|0.0|7.0|  collegeclassifieds|11.655799949660315|
|0.0|6.0|                cqf|11.655799949660315|
|0.0|6.0|          vinyasamt|11.655799949660315|
|0.0|6.0|             aerial| 11.25033484155215|
|0.0|6.0|           atricure|11.655799949660315|
|0.0|6.0|          paintball|11.655799949660315|
|0.0|6.0|         inventories|10.557187660992204|
|0.0|5.0|             nikoli|11.655799949660315|
+---+---+------------------+-----------------+
```

The produced information does not seem helpful, since we got only very rare words that allow us detect only a limited number of highly specific loan descriptions. However, we would like to be more generic and find more common words that are used by both loan types, but will still allow us to distinguish between bad and good loans.

Therefore, we need to design a word score that will target words with high-frequency usage in good (or bad) loans but penalize rare words. For example, we can define it as follows:

```
def descWordScore = (freqGoodLoan: Double, freqBadLoan: Double,
wordIdfScore: Double) =>
    Math.abs(freqGoodLoan - freqBadLoan) * wordIdfScore * wordIdfScore
```

If we apply the word score method on each word in the vocabulary, we will get a sorted list of words based on the descending score:

```
val numOfGoodLoans = loanStatusBaseModelDf.where("loan_status == 'good
loan'").count()
val numOfBadLoans = loanStatusBaseModelDf.where("loan_status == 'bad
loan'").count()

val descDiscriminatingWords = descTargetsWords.filter(t => t._1 >0 && t._2
>0).map(t => {
val freqGoodLoan = t._1 / numOfGoodLoans
val freqBadLoan = t._2 / numOfBadLoans
val word = t._3
val idfScore = t._4
        (word, freqGoodLoan*100, freqBadLoan*100, idfScore,
descWordScore(freqGoodLoan, freqBadLoan, idfScore))
    })
println(
table(Seq("Word", "Freq Good Loan", "Freq Bad Loan", "Idf Score", "Score"),
    descDiscriminatingWords.sortBy(-_._5).take(100),
Map(1 ->"%.2f", 2 ->"%.2f")))
```

The output is as follows:

Word	Freq Good Loan	Freq Bad Loan	Idf Score	Score
rate	8.73	5.31	2.7381541919594565	0.2567584205600344
interest	16.64	11.15	2.1241372376883954	0.247900916992075 9
years	11.19	7.53	2.5629489064765987	0.2403971951168683 3
job	6.49	4.20	3.0203793768794271	0.20830086689123261
loan	33.66	25.55	1.5756526716235382	0.20137229509924753
lending	3.08	1.86	3.8027778305670505	0.1768315182063665
card	16.97	12.87	2.0674341853347491	0.1749266688124269
paying	7.25	5.18	2.8787841826713750	0.17211749717235683
stable	3.49	2.13	3.5535163251802406	0.17171241306738122
never	3.69	2.35	3.5313530939444666	0.16742805858829812
apr	1.60	0.80	4.5221050320619660	0.16473217688951075
club	2.85	1.75	3.8690405235900385	0.16359800525597654
lower	5.45	3.77	3.106042767370814	0.1615294368668545
year	3.85	2.58	3.5673916716738576	0.16148734315737961
paid	4.76	3.29	3.311176023595353	0.16110217845204663
rates	3.52	2.31	3.5620321917292337	0.15404032854519037
balance	2.34	1.44	4.115443989986265	0.15173652504398522
time	8.03	6.20	2.8295057184189956	0.1471401157973573

Based on the produced list, we can identify interesting words. We can take 10 or 100 of them. However, we still need to figure out what to do with them. The solution is easy; for each word, we will generate a new binary feature-1 if a word is present in the `desc` value; otherwise, 0:

```
val descWordEncoder = (denominatingWords: Array[String]) => (desc: String)
=> {
if (desc != null) {
val unifiedDesc = unifyTextColumn(desc)
      Vectors.dense(denominatingWords.map(w =>if (unifiedDesc.contains(w))
1.0 else 0.0))
    } else null
}
```

We can test our idea on the prepared training and validation sample and measure the quality of the model. Again, the first step is to prepare the augmented data with a new feature. In this case, a new feature is a vector that contains binary features generated by descWordEncoder:

```
val trainLSBaseModel4Df =
trainLSBaseModel3Df.withColumn("desc_denominating_words",
descWordEncoderUdf($"desc")).drop("desc")
val validLSBaseModel4Df =
validLSBaseModel3Df.withColumn("desc_denominating_words",
descWordEncoderUdf($"desc")).drop("desc")
val trainLSBaseModel4Hf = toHf(trainLSBaseModel4Df, "trainLSBaseModel4Hf")
val validLSBaseModel4Hf = toHf(validLSBaseModel4Df, "validLSBaseModel4Hf")
 loanStatusBaseModelParams._train = trainLSBaseModel4Hf._key
val loanStatusBaseModel4 = new DRF(loanStatusBaseModelParams,
water.Key.make[DRFModel]("loanStatusBaseModel4"))
   .trainModel()
   .get()
```

Now, we just need to compute the model's quality:

```
val minLossModel4 = findMinLoss(loanStatusBaseModel4, validLSBaseModel4Hf,
DEFAULT_THRESHOLDS)
println(f"Min total loss for model 4: ${minLossModel4._2}%,.2f (threshold =
${minLossModel4._1})")
```

The output is as follows:

```
Min total loss for model 4: 171,637,932.10 (threshold = 0.9)
```

We can see that the new feature helps and improves the precision of our model. On the other hand, it also opens a lot of space for experimentation-we can select different words, or even use IDF weights instead of binary values if the word is part of the desc column.

To summarize our experiments, we will compare the computed results for the three models we produced: (1) the base model, (2) the model trained on the data augmented by the emp_title feature, and (3) the model trained on the data enriched by the desc feature:

```
println(
s"""
    ~Results:
    ~${table(Seq("Threshold", "Total loss", "Profit loss", "Loan loss"),
Seq(minLossModel2, minLossModel3, minLossModel4),
Map(1 ->"%,.2f", 2 ->"%,.2f", 3 ->"%,.2f"))}
""".stripMargin('~'))
```

The output is as follows:

```
+---------+-------------+-------------+------------+
|Threshold|   Total loss|  Profit loss|   Loan loss|
+---------+-------------+-------------+------------+
|     0.85|171,918,622.73|126,258,672.73|45,659,950.00|
|     0.85|172,569,355.39|123,947,980.39|48,621,375.00|
|      0.9|171,637,932.10|161,017,157.10|10,620,775.00|
+---------+-------------+-------------+------------+
```

Our small experiments demonstrated the powerful concept of feature generation. Each newly generated feature improved the quality of the base model with respect to our model-evaluation criterion.

At this point, we can finish with exploration and training of the first model to detect good/bad loans. We will use the last model we prepared since it gives us the best quality. There are still many ways to explore data and improve our model quality; however, now, it is time to build our second model.

Interest RateModel

The second model predicts the interest rate of accepted loans. In this case, we will use only the part of the training data that corresponds to good loans, since they have assigned a proper interest rate. However, we need to understand that the remaining bad loans could carry useful information related to the interest rate prediction.

As in the rest of the cases, we will start with the preparation of training data. We will use initial data, filter out bad loans, and drop string columns:

```
val intRateDfSplits = loanStatusDfSplits.map(df => {
  df
    .where("loan_status == 'good loan'")
    .drop("emp_title", "desc", "loan_status")
    .withColumn("int_rate", toNumericRateUdf(col("int_rate")))
})
val trainIRHf = toHf(intRateDfSplits(0), "trainIRHf")(h2oContext)
val validIRHf = toHf(intRateDfSplits(1), "validIRHf")(h2oContext)
```

In the next step, we will use the capabilities of H2O random hyperspace search to find the best GBM model in a defined hyperspace of parameters. We will also constrain the search by additional stopping criteria based on the requested model precision and overall search time.

The first step is to define common GBM model builder parameters, such as training, validation datasets, and response column:

```
import _root_.hex.tree.gbm.GBMModel.GBMParameters
val intRateModelParam = let(new GBMParameters()) { p =>
  p._train = trainIRHf._key
p._valid = validIRHf._key
p._response_column = "int_rate"
p._score_tree_interval  = 20
}
```

The next step involves definition of hyperspace of parameters to explore. We can encode any interesting values, but keep in mind that the search could use any combination of parameters, even those that are useless:

```
import _root_.hex.grid.{GridSearch}
import water.Key
import scala.collection.JavaConversions._
val intRateHyperSpace: java.util.Map[String, Array[Object]] = Map[String,
Array[AnyRef]](
"_ntrees" -> (1 to 10).map(v => Int.box(100*v)).toArray,
"_max_depth" -> (2 to 7).map(Int.box).toArray,
"_learn_rate" ->Array(0.1, 0.01).map(Double.box),
"_col_sample_rate" ->Array(0.3, 0.7, 1.0).map(Double.box),
"_learn_rate_annealing" ->Array(0.8, 0.9, 0.95, 1.0).map(Double.box)
  )
```

Now, we will define how to traverse the defined hyperspace of parameters. H2O provides two strategies: a simple cartesian search that step-by-step builds the model for each parameter's combination or a random search that randomly picks the parameters from the defined hyperspace. Surprisingly, the random search has quite a good performance, especially if it is used to explore a huge parameter space:

```
import
_root_.hex.grid.HyperSpaceSearchCriteria.RandomDiscreteValueSearchCriteria
val intRateHyperSpaceCriteria = let(new RandomDiscreteValueSearchCriteria)
{ c =>
    c.set_stopping_metric(StoppingMetric.RMSE)
    c.set_stopping_tolerance(0.1)
    c.set_stopping_rounds(1)
    c.set_max_runtime_secs(4 * 60 /* seconds */)
}
```

In this case, we will also limit the search by two stopping conditions: the model performance based on RMSE and the maximum runtime of the whole grid search. At this point, we have defined all the necessary inputs, and it is time to launch the hyper search:

```
val intRateGrid = GridSearch.startGridSearch(Key.make("intRateGridModel"),
                                            intRateModelParam,
                                            intRateHyperSpace,
new GridSearch.SimpleParametersBuilderFactory[GBMParameters],
intRateHyperSpaceCriteria).get()
```

The result of the search is a set of models called `grid`. Let's find one with the lowest RMSE:

```
val intRateModel =
intRateGrid.getModels.minBy(_._output._validation_metrics.rmse())
println(intRateModel._output._validation_metrics)
```

The output is as follows:

```
Model Metrics Type: Regression
Description: N/A
model id: intRateGridModel_model_7
frame id: validIRHf
MSE: 7.4822593
RMSE: 2.7353718
mean residual deviance: 7.4822593
mean absolute error: 2.2029567
root mean squared log error: 0.20714988
```

Here, we can define our evaluation criteria and select the right model not only based on selected model metrics, but also consider the term and difference between predicted and actual value, and optimize the profit. However, instead of that, we will trust our search strategy that it found the best possible model and directly jump into deploying our solution.

Using models for scoring

In the previous sections, we explored different data processing steps, and built and evaluated several models to predict the loan status and interest rates for the accepted loans. Now, it is time to use all built artifacts and compose them together to score new loans.

There are multiple steps that we need to consider:

1. Data cleanup
2. The `emp_title` column preparation pipeline
3. The `desc` column transformation into a vector representing significant words
4. The binomial model to predict loan acceptance status
5. The regression model to predict loan interest rate

To reuse these steps, we need to connect them into a single function that accepts input data and produces predictions involving loan acceptance status and interest rate.

The scoring functions is easy-it replays all the steps that we did in the previous chapters:

```scala
import _root_.hex.tree.drf.DRFModel
def scoreLoan(df: DataFrame,
                empTitleTransformer: PipelineModel,
                loanStatusModel: DRFModel,
                goodLoanProbThreshold: Double,
                intRateModel: GBMModel)(h2oContext: H2OContext):
DataFrame = {
val inputDf = empTitleTransformer.transform(basicDataCleanup(df))
    .withColumn("desc_denominating_words",
descWordEncoderUdf(col("desc")))
    .drop("desc")
val inputHf = toHf(inputDf, "input_df_" + df.hashCode())(h2oContext)
// Predict loan status and int rate
val loanStatusPrediction = loanStatusModel.score(inputHf)
val intRatePrediction = intRateModel.score(inputHf)
val probGoodLoanColName = "good loan"
val inputAndPredictionsHf =
loanStatusPrediction.add(intRatePrediction).add(inputHf)
    inputAndPredictionsHf.update()
// Prepare field loan_status based on threshold
```

```
val loanStatus = (threshold: Double) => (predGoodLoanProb: Double) =>if
(predGoodLoanProb < threshold) "bad loan" else "good loan"
val loanStatusUdf = udf(loanStatus(goodLoanProbThreshold))
h2oContext.asDataFrame(inputAndPredictionsHf)(df.sqlContext).withColumn("lo
an_status", loanStatusUdf(col(probGoodLoanColName)))
  }
```

We use all definitions that we prepared before-`basicDataCleanup` method,
`empTitleTransformer`, `loanStatusModel`, `intRateModel`-and apply them in the
corresponding order.

 Note that in the definition of the `scoreLoan` functions, we do not need to
remove any columns. All the defined Spark pipelines and models use only
features they were defined on and keep the rest untouched.

The method uses all the generated artifacts. For example, we can score the input data in the
following way:

```
val prediction = scoreLoan(loanStatusDfSplits(0),
                           empTitleTransformer,
                           loanStatusBaseModel4,
                           minLossModel4._4,
                           intRateModel)(h2oContext)
prediction.show(10)
```

The output is as follows:

predict	bad loan	good loan	predict0	loan_amnt	term	int_rate	installment	emp_length
good loan	0.09943606972988155	0.90056393027011184	9.60615000208223	1000	36 months	6.030000209808835	30.44	2 years
good loan	0.07055716243979132	0.92944283756020087	9.512018911166848	1000	36 months	7.510000228881836	31.12	6 years
good loan	0.15596976410490054	0.8440302358950994	10.946047494508555	1000	36 months	7.900000095367432	31.3	10+ years
good loan	0.09389684021726647	0.9006103159782735	10.528133837653808	1000	36 months	7.900000095367432	31.3	3 years
good loan	0.05944657211320983	0.9405534278867901	9.024843191106648	1000	36 months	8.899999618530273	31.76	5 years
good loan	0.10989649036497645	0.8901035096350235	9.684546958706619	1000	36 months	8.899999618530273	31.76	n/a
good loan	0.12613249339911026	0.8738675066008896	11.949588630597061	1000	36 months	9.909999847412111	32.230000000000004	10+ years
good loan	0.12296800006807436	0.8770319993319257	12.49360951737395271	1000	36 months	9.909999847412111	32.230000000000004	10+ years
bad loan	0.42791793026795661	0.5720826069732043	13.279324036059698	1000	36 months	10.649999618530273	32.58	< 1 year

However, to score new loans independently from our training code, we still need to export
trained models and pipelines in some reusable form. For Spark models and pipelines, we
can directly use Spark serialization. For example, the defined `empTitleTransormer` can be
exported in this way:

```
val MODELS_DIR = s"${sys.env.get("MODELSDIR").getOrElse("models")}"
val destDir = new File(MODELS_DIR)
  empTitleTransformer.write.overwrite.save(new File(destDir,
```

```
"empTitleTransformer").getAbsolutePath)
```

 We also defined the transformation for the `desc` column as a `udf` function, `descWordEncoderUdf`. However, we do not need to export it, since we defined it as part of our shared library.

For H2O models, the situation is more complicated since there are several ways of model export: binary, POJO, and MOJO. The binary export is similar to the Spark export; however, to reuse the exported binary model, it is necessary to have a running instance of the H2O cluster. This limitation is removed by the other methods. The POJO exports the model as Java code, which can be compiled and run independently from the H2O cluster. Finally, the MOJO export model is in a binary form, which can be interpreted and used without running the H2O cluster. In this chapter, we will use the MOJO export, since it is straightforward and also the recommended method for model reuse:

```
loanStatusBaseModel4.getMojo.writeTo(new FileOutputStream(new File(destDir,
"loanStatusModel.mojo")))
  intRateModel.getMojo.writeTo(new FileOutputStream(new File(destDir,
"intRateModel.mojo")))
```

We can also export the Spark schema that defines the input data. This will be useful for the definition of a parser of the new data:

```
def saveSchema(schema: StructType, destFile: File, saveWithMetadata:
Boolean = false) = {
import java.nio.file.{Files, Paths, StandardOpenOption}

import org.apache.spark.sql.types._
val processedSchema = StructType(schema.map {
case StructField(name, dtype, nullable, metadata) =>StructField(name,
dtype, nullable, if (saveWithMetadata) metadata else Metadata.empty)
case rec => rec
    })

   Files.write(Paths.get(destFile.toURI),
processedSchema.json.getBytes(java.nio.charset.StandardCharsets.UTF_8),
             StandardOpenOption.TRUNCATE_EXISTING,
StandardOpenOption.CREATE)
 }

saveSchema(loanDataDf.schema, new File(destDir, "inputSchema.json"))
```

Note that the `saveSchema` method processes a given schema and removes all metadata. This is not common practice. However, in this case, we will remove them to save space.

It is also important to mention that the data-creation process from the H2O frame implicitly attaches plenty of useful statistical information to the resulting Spark DataFrame.

Model deployment

The model deployment is the most important part of model life cycle. At this stage, the model is fed by real-life data and produce results that can support decision making (for example, accepting or rejecting a loan).

In this chapter, we will build a simple application combining the Spark streaming the models we exported earlier and shared code library, which we defined while writing the model-training application.

The latest Spark 2.1 introduces structural streaming, which is built upon the Spark SQL and allows us to utilize the SQL interface transparently with the streaming data. Furthermore, it brings a strong feature in the form of "exactly-once" semantics, which means that events are not dropped or delivered multiple times. The streaming Spark application has the same structure as a "regular" Spark application:

```
object Chapter8StreamApp extends App {

val spark = SparkSession.builder()
      .master("local[*]")
      .appName("Chapter8StreamApp")
      .getOrCreate()


script(spark,
        sys.env.get("MODELSDIR").getOrElse("models"),
        sys.env.get("APPDATADIR").getOrElse("appdata"))

def script(ssc: SparkSession, modelDir: String, dataDir: String): Unit = {
// ...
val inputDataStream = spark.readStream/* (1) create stream */

val outputDataStream = /* (2) transform inputDataStream */
```

```
    /* (3) export stream */
    outputDataStream.writeStream.format("console").start().awaitTermination()
      }
   }
```

There are three important parts: (1) The creation of input stream, (2) The transformation of the created stream, and (3) The writing resulted stream.

Stream creation

There are several ways to create a stream, described in the Spark documentation (https://spark.apache.org/docs/2.1.1/structured-streaming-programming-guide.html), including socket-based, Kafka, or file-based streams. In this chapter, we will use file-based streams, streams that are pointed to a directory and deliver all the new files that appear in the directory.

Moreover, our application will read CSV files; thus, we will connect the stream input with the Spark CSV parser. We also need to configure the parser with the input data schema, which we exported from the mode-training application. Let's load the schema first:

```
def loadSchema(srcFile: File): StructType = {
import org.apache.spark.sql.types.DataType
StructType(
DataType.fromJson(scala.io.Source.fromFile(srcFile).mkString).asInstanceOf[
StructType].map {
case StructField(name, dtype, nullable, metadata) =>StructField(name,
dtype, true, metadata)
case rec => rec
    }
  )
 }

val inputSchema = Chapter8Library.loadSchema(new File(modelDir,
"inputSchema.json"))
```

The loadSchema method modifies the loaded schema by marking all the loaded fields as nullable. This is a necessary step to allow input data to contain missing values in any column, not only in columns that contained missing values during model training.

In the next step, we will directly configure a CSV parser and the input stream to read CSV files from a given data folder:

```
val inputDataStream = spark.readStream
  .schema(inputSchema)
  .option("timestampFormat", "MMM-yyy")
```

```
.option("nullValue", null)
.CSV(s"${dataDir}/*.CSV")
```

The CSV parser needs a minor configuration to set up the format for timestamp features and representation of missing values. At this point, we can even explore the structure of the stream:

```
inputDataStream.schema.printTreeString()
```

The output is as follows:

```
root
 |-- id: integer (nullable = true)
 |-- member_id: integer (nullable = true)
 |-- loan_amnt: integer (nullable = true)
 |-- funded_amnt: integer (nullable = true)
 |-- funded_amnt_inv: double (nullable = true)
 |-- term: string (nullable = true)
 |-- int_rate: string (nullable = true)
 |-- installment: double (nullable = true)
 |-- grade: string (nullable = true)
 |-- sub_grade: string (nullable = true)
 |-- emp_title: string (nullable = true)
 |-- emp_length: string (nullable = true)
 |-- home_ownership: string (nullable = true)
 |-- annual_inc: double (nullable = true)
 |-- verification_status: string (nullable = true)
 |-- issue_d: timestamp (nullable = true)
 |-- loan_status: string (nullable = true)
 |-- pymnt_plan: string (nullable = true)
 |-- url: string (nullable = true)
 |-- desc: string (nullable = true)
 |-- purpose: string (nullable = true)
 |-- title: string (nullable = true)
```

Stream transformation

The input stream publishes a similar interface as a Spark DataSet; thus, it can be transformed via a regular SQL interface or machine learning transformers. In our case, we will reuse all the trained models and transformation that were saved in the previous sections.

First, we will load `empTitleTransformer`-it is a regular Spark pipeline transformer that can be loaded with help of the Spark `PipelineModel` class:

```
val empTitleTransformer =
PipelineModel.load(s"${modelDir}/empTitleTransformer")
```

The `loanStatus` and `intRate` models were saved in the H2O MOJO format. To load them, it is necessary to use the `MojoModel` class:

```
val loanStatusModel = MojoModel.load(new
File(s"${modelDir}/loanStatusModel.mojo").getAbsolutePath)
val intRateModel = MojoModel.load(new
File(s"${modelDir}/intRateModel.mojo").getAbsolutePath)
```

At this point, we have all the necessary artifacts ready; however, we cannot use H2O MOJO models directly to transform Spark streams. However, we can wrap them into a Spark transformer. We have already defined a transformer called UDFTransfomer in Chapter 4, *Predicting Movie Reviews Using NLP and Spark Streaming* so we will follow a similar pattern:

```
class MojoTransformer(override val uid: String,
                      mojoModel: MojoModel) extends Transformer {

case class BinomialPrediction(p0: Double, p1: Double)
case class RegressionPrediction(value: Double)

implicit def toBinomialPrediction(bmp: AbstractPrediction) =
BinomialPrediction(bmp.asInstanceOf[BinomialModelPrediction].classProbabili
ties(0),
bmp.asInstanceOf[BinomialModelPrediction].classProbabilities(1))
implicit def toRegressionPrediction(rmp: AbstractPrediction) =
RegressionPrediction(rmp.asInstanceOf[RegressionModelPrediction].value)

val modelUdf = {
val epmw = new EasyPredictModelWrapper(mojoModel)
    mojoModel._category match {
case ModelCategory.Binomial =>udf[BinomialPrediction, Row] { r: Row =>
epmw.predict(rowToRowData(r)) }
case ModelCategory.Regression =>udf[RegressionPrediction, Row] { r: Row =>
epmw.predict(rowToRowData(r)) }
    }
  }

val predictStruct = mojoModel._category match {
case ModelCategory.Binomial =>StructField("p0",
DoubleType)::StructField("p1", DoubleType)::Nil
case ModelCategory.Regression =>StructField("pred", DoubleType)::Nil
}
```

```scala
val outputCol = s"${uid}Prediction"

override def transform(dataset: Dataset[_]): DataFrame = {
val inputSchema = dataset.schema
val args = inputSchema.fields.map(f => dataset(f.name))
    dataset.select(col("*"), modelUdf(struct(args: _*)).as(outputCol))
  }

private def rowToRowData(row: Row): RowData = new RowData {
    row.schema.fields.foreach(f => {
      row.getAs[AnyRef](f.name) match {
case v: Number => put(f.name, v.doubleValue().asInstanceOf[Object])
case v: java.sql.Timestamp => put(f.name,
v.getTime.toDouble.asInstanceOf[Object])
case null =>// nop
case v => put(f.name, v)
      }
    })
  }

override def copy(extra: ParamMap): Transformer =  defaultCopy(extra)

override def transformSchema(schema: StructType): StructType =  {
val outputFields = schema.fields :+ StructField(outputCol,
StructType(predictStruct), false)
    StructType(outputFields)
  }
}
```

The defined `MojoTransformer` supports binomial and regression MOJO models. It accepts a Spark dataset and enriches it by new columns: two columns holding true/false probabilities for binomial models and a single column representing the predicted value of the regression model. This is reflected in `transform` method, which is using the MOJO wrapper `modelUdf` to transform the input dataset:

dataset.select(*col*("*"), *modelUdf*(*struct*(args: _*)).as(*outputCol*))

The `modelUdf` model implements the transformation from the data represented as Spark Row into a format accepted by MOJO, the call of MOJO, and the transformation of the MOJO prediction into a Spark Row format.

The defined `MojoTransformer` allows us to wrap the loaded MOJO models into the Spark transformer API:

```
val loanStatusTransformer = new MojoTransformer("loanStatus",
loanStatusModel)
val intRateTransformer = new MojoTransformer("intRate", intRateModel)
```

At this point, we have all the necessary building blocks ready, and we can apply them on the input stream:

```
val outputDataStream =
    intRateTransformer.transform(
      loanStatusTransformer.transform(
        empTitleTransformer.transform(
          Chapter8Library.basicDataCleanup(inputDataStream))
          .withColumn("desc_denominating_words",
descWordEncoderUdf(col("desc")))))
```

The code first calls the shared library function `basicDataCleanup` and then transform the `desc` column with another shared library function, `descWordEncoderUdf`: both cases are implemented on top of Spark DataSet SQL interfaces. The remaining steps will apply defined transformers. Again, we can explore the structure of the transformed stream and verify that it contains fields introduced by our transformations:

```
outputDataStream.schema.printTreeString()
```

The output is as follows:

```
|-- emp_title_cluster: integer (nullable = true)
|-- desc_denominating_words: vector (nullable = true)
|-- loanStatusPrediction: struct (nullable = true)
|    |-- p0: double (nullable = false)
|    |-- p1: double (nullable = false)
|-- intRatePrediction: struct (nullable = true)
|    |-- value: double (nullable = false)
```

We can see that there are several new fields in the schema: representation of the empTitle cluster, the vector of denominating words, and model predictions. Probabilities are from the loab status model and the real value from the interest rate model.

Stream output

Spark provides the so-called "Output Sinks" for streams. The sink defines how and where the stream is written; for example, as a parquet file or as a in-memory table. However, for our application, we will simply show the stream output in the console:

```
outputDataStream.writeStream.format("console").start().awaitTermination()
```

The preceding code directly starts the stream processing and waits until the termination of the application. The application simply process every new file in a given folder (in our case, given by the environment variable, `APPDATADIR`). For example, given a file with five loan applications, the stream produces a table with five scored events:

```
--------------------------------------------
Batch: 0
--------------------------------------------

+--------+---------+---------+------------+--------------+----------+--------+-----------+-----+---------+
|      id|member_id|loan_amnt|funded_amnt|funded_amnt_inv|      term|int_rate|installment|grade|sub_grade|
+--------+---------+---------+------------+--------------+----------+--------+-----------+-----+---------+
|10753358|  1311748|     3000|        3000|        3000.0| 60 months|   12.69|      67.79|    B|       B5|
|10752691|  1311441|     5000|        5000|        5000.0| 36 months|     7.9|     156.46|    A|       A4|
|10696391|  1304742|     7000|        7000|        7000.0| 60 months|   15.96|     170.08|    C|       C5|
|10720531|  1288686|     3000|        3000|        3000.0| 36 months|   18.64|     109.43|    E|       E1|
|10717951|  1306957|     5600|        5600|        5600.0| 60 months|   21.28|     152.39|    F|       F2|
+--------+---------+---------+------------+--------------+----------+--------+-----------+-----+---------+
```

The important part of the event is represented by the last columns, which contain predicted values:

```
+----------------+-----------------------+----------------------+----------------------+
|emp_title_cluster|desc_denominating_words|     loanStatusPrediction|       intRatePrediction|
+----------------+-----------------------+----------------------+----------------------+
|             451|   [0.0,1.0,0.0,1.0,...|[0.13233598490213...|[14.033310199150307]|
|             303|                   null|[0.11356223411821...|[10.206674059439298]|
|             420|   [1.0,1.0,0.0,0.0,...|[0.18897814052707...|[15.447762748422647]|
|              88|   [0.0,0.0,0.0,0.0,...|[0.17876877695816...|[12.885693488434374]|
|              46|   [0.0,0.0,1.0,0.0,...|[0.48679298373377...|[13.157484044429218]|
+----------------+-----------------------+----------------------+----------------------+
```

If we write another file with a single loan application into the folder, the application will show another scored batch:

```
------------------------------------------------
Batch: 1
------------------------------------------------
+--------+----------+----------+-----------+---------------+----------+----------+-----------+------+
|      id|member_id|loan_amnt|funded_amnt|funded_amnt_inv|      term|int_rate|installment|grade|:
+--------+----------+----------+-----------+---------------+----------+----------+-----------+------+
|10775011| 1296599|     5000|       5000|         4975.0| 36 months|    10.65|     162.87|    B|
+--------+----------+----------+-----------+---------------+----------+----------+-----------+------+
```

In this way, we can deploy trained models and corresponding data-processing operations and let them score actual events. Of course, we just demonstrated a simple use case; a real-life scenario would be much more complex involving a proper model validation, A/B testing with the currently used models, and the storing and versioning of the models.

Summary

This chapter summarizes everything you learned throughout the book with end-to-end examples. We analyzed the data, transformed it, performed several experiments to figure out how to set up the model-training pipeline, and built models. The chapter also stresses on the need for well-designed code, which can be shared across several projects. In our example, we created a shared library that was used at the time of training as well as being utilized during the scoring time. This was demonstrated on the critical operation called "model deployment" when trained models and related artifacts are used to score unseen data.

This chapter also brings us to the end of the book. Our goal was to show that solving machine learning challenges with Spark is mainly about experimentation with data, parameters, models, debugging data / model-related issues, writing code that can be tested and reused, and having fun by getting surprising data insights and observations.

Index

holdout method 40

I

International Movie Database (IMDb) 118

J

Java Virtual Machine (JVM) 16

L

labeled point vector 38
labeled vector
  data caching 38
Large Hadron Collider (LHC) 25
Latent Dirichlet Allocation (LDA) 118
Latent Semantic Analysis (LSA) 118
lazy evaluation 30
Leave-One-Out (LOO) 42
Lending Club loan prediction
  data analysis 272
Lending Club
  about 267
  data 270
  data dictionary 271
  data load 272
  environment, preparing 271
  goal 268, 269
  motivation 267, 268
libraries, Spark
  Core 17
  Graphx 17
  MLlib (Machine Learning Library) 17
  SQL 17
  streaming 18
loan status model
  about 282, 283
  base model 283, 284, 286
  base model performance 287, 288, 289, 291
  desc column transformation 299, 302, 303, 305,
    306
  emp_title column transformation 292, 294, 295,
    297, 299
loss functions
  log-loss 56
  squared-error 56

M

machine learning workflow, modeling goal
  data unification 89
  data, exploring 76, 77, 78, 79
  Spark shell, starting 75
Maven
  reference 28
model deployment
  about 312
  stream creation 313
  stream output 318
  stream transformation 314, 317
model training
  about 132
  Spark decision tree model 133
  Spark Naive Bayes model 134
  Spark random forest model 136
  super-learner model 138
modeling goal
  about 74
  challenges 74
  machine learning workflow 75
multi-class classification 71

N

Natural Language Processing (NLP)
  about 115, 117
  information extraction (IE) 117
  information retrieval (IR) 117
  machine translation (MT) 117
  speech recognition (SR) 117
  text summarization 118

O

Overview view, Gephi
  about 244
  Appearance tab 246
  Graph tab 244
  Layout tab 246
  Preview settings 245
  Statistics tab 246

www.ingramcontent.com/pod-product-compliance
Lightning Source LLC
Chambersburg PA
CBHW080621060326
40690CB00021B/4768